LAW AND LAND

A publication of the Joint Center for Urban Studies of the Massachusetts Institute of Technology and Harvard University

LAW AND LAND

Anglo-American Planning Practice

Edited by Charles M. Haar

HARVARD UNIVERSITY PRESS
and the M.I.T. PRESS
Cambridge, Massachusetts
1 9 6 4

141300

Distributed in Great Britain by Oxford University Press, London

The preparation of these papers was made possible through the assistance of the Rockefeller Foundation and the Brookings Institution. The Joint Center for Urban Studies and the authors are grateful for their generosity.

Library of Congress Catalog Card Number 64-11129

Printed in the United States of America

Distributed by Harvard University Press, Cambridge 38, Massachusetts

CONTENTS

INTRODUCTION

CHARLES M. HAAR
PROFESSOR OF LAW, HARVARD UNIVERSITY

VOLTAIRE'S FINAL ADVICE in *Candide* — cultivate your own garden — is becoming even a metaphorical impossibility under twentieth century conditions. Steadily increasing demands on a fixed quantity of land bring into sharp focus issues of adequate housing, optimal uses of land, and effective relations among the city, suburban, and rural areas. Increasingly, the world over, there is a call for creativity in coping with the problems of the metropolis. To adjust community and private interest in the urban environment, all sides agree, requires fresh and bold legal thinking.

The experience of the Western world with land-use planning and controls therefore is being reappraised, not only so that Western legal structure will be able to meet the rising needs and aspirations of its own society, but also so that it may serve as an example for the developing countries. The great common-law systems of Great Britain and the United States represent an avowed democratic fusion of public and private values. How successful has this mixture proven? Can either system provide fruitful insights for the other? Is there a common pattern of experience which can benefit other societies? An examination of city planning in the context of the legal systems of both countries may show whether the institutions of law and property can be molded into a more rational and effective means for organizing the use of land.

Out of the belief that each system has much to learn from the experience of the other, it was proposed that a comparative study be made of the legal control of land use in England and the United States. The September 1960 meeting of the American Bar Association in Washington, D.C., with British barristers and solicitors present as special guests, offered an excellent opportunity to bring together the legal experience of both countries; thus, at the Brookings Institution a seminar in comparative planning law was organized. Essentially its purpose was to contrast, criticize, and evaluate the approaches taken by the two nations toward land-use and resource-allocation planning. The seminar aimed at greater understanding of the common problems of controlling land use from the standpoint of property rights, democratic goals, and the creation of new legal instrumentalities and organizations capable of channeling changing social energies. It also sought to attain a better understanding of the legal philosophy underlying the concept of property in both countries in their respective stages of development. The papers from the seminar, amplified and revised through the discussions, with a general appraisal of each of the four topics covered, are collected in this volume.

Land Planning and Land Ownership. This section deals with the theory and framework of planning. The papers by W. O. Hart and Allison Dunham raise the fundamental question of justifying the intervention of law in the free market of land transactions. In an area so close to the nerve of a mixed society — the concept of property — statutes governing land use reflect the evolving assumptions, goals, and aspirations of the community concerning the unique resource of land. What is the current meaning of "property rights" in view of the transformation of the "fee simple absolute" in both societies? What are the legitimate objectives of physical planning on the continuous spectrum that runs from no interference, chopping off the offensive or dangerous, permitting a wide range of choice, to securing the "best" in the "best places"? To what extent is the control incident to planning an infringement of the liberty of the individual, particularly in relation to property? Are the wishes of the consumers — and if so, of which classes and of what generations in time — the be-all and end-all of resource allocation?

Questions recurring time and again throughout the papers make their appearance at the outset — such as the extent to which rules can be set down beforehand, as opposed to relatively *ad hoc* decisions tailored to individual cases though guided by some sort of policy formulation; and the extent to which planners either can or should attempt to control the shape of things to come.

The Making and Effect of the Land Plan. The second section takes up the formulation of plans. The papers by Desmond Heap and James B. Milner evaluate the typical American master plan and the British development plan established by the Town and Country Planning Act of 1947. The authors raise interesting and troubling questions as to the agency to be entrusted with making the plan, the relation of the plan to implementary ordinances, the degree of guidance to be given to courts, administrators, and private developers, and the extent of public participation in preparing the plan. On the basis of the alternatives chosen the extent of private sovereignty accorded by the state can be perceived.

The Individual and the Machinery of Planning. This section focuses on the individual's relation to the machinery of planning. The extent to which law rests on public sentiment; legislative sensitivity and adaptability to changes in attitudes over time; the role of law in shaping opinions — all are important considerations in determining how far law should enter into any particular activity. There is no doubt that if planning is to be successful it must gain acceptance among the persons whose lives and property are to be affected. This means, of course, that there must be some procedure by which the individual can seek correction of erroneous official action. The British system, which stresses administrative as opposed to judicial review, is evaluated by F. H. B. Layfield. American procedure, with its greater reliance on judicial review, is discussed by Lawrence A. Sullivan, who also compares the merits and defects of the two systems.

The goal of public acceptance suggests that there is a need for greater understanding through increased public participation in the planning process. A troublesome point is the extent to which the planning arm of government — probably more sensitive to public opinion than the ministerial departments — should control the action of the departments. Safeguards against abuse of power are a peculiar concern of the lawyer, and both Sullivan and Layfield discuss the means of preventing unfair use of planning powers. Should interstitial safeguards be left to a court or to some outside executive agency? Should review be confined to the narrow issues raised in the adversary process, or should it extend to a thorough cross-examination of planning policy? By raising, in the context of land planning, the problem of balancing the demands of exact and individualized justice against the attractions of broad, general rules that are easily applied and reviewed, these papers reach to the fundamentals not only of administrative decision and court review, but also of the legal system as a whole.

Exacting compliance with land-use controls is a thorny problem unsolved as yet by either country. Uncovering violations of regulations and assuring compliance with enforcement orders are perhaps the most difficult problems of planning administration. In 1960 the English amended their 1947 act to gain greater compliance but have achieved only varied results. J. G. Barr treats the complexities of dealing with the apparently infinite number of techniques for avoiding planning controls.

Regulation and Taking of Property under Planning Laws. In this final section, David W. Craig, David R. Levin, and R. E. Megarry present papers on the financial underpinning of land-use planning. The problem here is divided into two parts. The first, and perhaps the more difficult, is compensation. How should a government determine whether to compensate a person adversely affected by its action? This question is not answered by the applicable provisions of the United States Constitution, for although compensation in the event of a "taking" is required, the Constitution does not specify the limitations on land use which amount to a "taking." Mr. Craig's paper is an attempt to prick out the line between the police and eminent domain powers as developed by the various state courts. The English Parliament does not have to grapple with the problem in a constitutional context, but this may not simplify the decision of whether to compensate, which must, of course, still be made in a political context.

The other half of the discussion of compensation focuses on the reverse side of the coin: how might a government admeasure and recapture those benefits which accrue to some individuals and not to others, without rational or equitable basis, as a by-product of particular planning controls? These may be tangible, as in improving property, or intangible, as in permitting some property use not permitted to one's neighbors. Many planning principles have acute economic consequences: a cluster of pressures, temptations, rewards, and burdens arises in any system which decides that A can, B cannot, and C cannot for some time, but perhaps can after a bit.

One of the seminar's functions was to delineate the similarities and differences between the British and American systems. When all the papers had been submitted, it became clear (with some surprise) that a considerable area of similarity exists. True, as with all comparative law studies, there are dangers in glossing over differences and being trapped into thinking that use of the same terms — or as Whitehead put it, use of a common language — means a similarity in approach. Yet there is an emergence of truly common principles, not only in respect to the two nations, but within the United States as well: despite the fifty state laboratories, there is a more or less standardized product of American planning and zoning.

That the legal resemblances are many seems even more remarkable in view of the divergencies of physical conditions and experiences of Great Britain and the United States. The land areas are not physically comparable, and the conditions affecting use differ in many respects. Great Britain has always had a fairly homogeneous population, and only very recently has had to confront the problem of providing equal access to, and quality of, housing for racial and religious minority groups. The United States did not suffer the destruction of a large percentage of its business and residential properties in wartime bombings; and thus it has not had the same impetus for a physical rebirth to redeem the devastation of battle. Institutionally, there is the striking difference between a unitary form of government, with parliamentary supremacy, and a federal system, composed of fifty semisovereign jurisdictions subject to the ultimate check of an independent judiciary. Finally, the United States has never experienced anything of the magnitude of the Labour Party's 1947 program: the invention of "development values," the nationalization of these values by paying a global sum, and the subsequent reselling of rights to develop are perhaps the most sweeping instrumentalities yet fashioned for coping with the costs and the gains created by planning controls.

But in examining apparently divergent factors influencing legislation, greater subtlety must be exercised. The significance of the vast physical expanse of the United States is overshadowed by the great percentage of population and industry crowding into a few swollen metropolitan areas. Although the problem of racial discrimination through exclusionary zoning ordinances is less intense in England, there turns out to be a rural-town conflict, the people being divided sharply along class — and sometimes party — lines, with the Conservatives fearing the migration of surplus Labour voters to marginal Conservative constituencies. The United States Housing and Home Finance Agency, especially in its insistence on master planning and implementary ordinances as prerequisites to federal urban renewal assistance, is exerting a great — and potentially decisive — unifying influence on the planning activities of state and local authorities. With the rise of mortgages insured by the Federal Housing Administration — and availability of capital as the determinant for land developers — national regulation of land-use investors pervades local controls and has a centralizing influence comparable to that of the British Ministry of Housing and Local Government. The United States, working from its own notions of the welfare state, has also developed ingenious permutations of public and private financing — witness the governmental guarantee of housing mortgage systems created by the FHA, often coupled with the backing of secondary market purchases by the Federal National Mortgage Association; or the establishment of various conservation and forestry districts with taxing and land-assembly powers.

Also, there are striking historical parallels between the two countries. Both undertook their initial tentative steps at legislative control of land use in the first quarter of the twentieth century. Although Britain's first Town and Country Planning Act (1909) antedates American legislation, it typifies contemporary thinking in the United States as expressed at the National City Planning Conferences and other early discussions on the legal stratagems of zoning. The first English legislation in town planning with any bite — the 1932 act — came into being at about the time in the United States when much state enabling legislation was passed, modeled upon the Standard Zoning Enabling Act and the Standard Planning Enabling Act, drafted by the advisory committees to the then Secretary of Commerce, Herbert Hoover, in 1926 and 1928.

There can be little doubt of the unifying role played by the concepts common to the real property law of both nations. The estates in land, the notion of relativity of title, the systems of conveyancing — all run in parallel grooves. The unique quality (and strength) of both common-law systems has been the quality of abstraction which has permitted them to evolve over time to meet the changing needs of society. The weaving of these abstract entities constitutes the development of property law; they can be moved as mathematical units in the lawyer's calculus and mixed into novel constructions. The planning of a new town in England or of a western watershed in the United States, of course, presents different issues from those of planning for an already developed urban center. But they all can be fitted into the familiar legal framework of rights, powers, liabilities, and duties. In some instances, therefore, it is helpful to put the differentiating detail to one side and to focus on the common characteristic of, say, a fee simple estate in land.

Nevertheless, the similarities are the more surprising because the two countries have traditionally approached the problem of land-use controls from polar positions. The American approach is first to legislate the specifics, not just a vague guideline, and then to act accordingly. The British approach has been more an *ad hoc* solution, formulated for individual problems as they emerge in the exercise of broad powers conferred in advance. This difference may still exist in the respective philosophies or ideals. Whether it has any longer more than a remote bearing upon the daily operation of controls is another question. The positions of the two countries are no longer so far apart as they had been. Multiple forces are producing a more flexible planning machinery in this country, most notably in urban renewal, subdivision regulations, and "floating" zones. The sentiment of the British is that, for better or worse, their system of conferring a wide measure of discretion has not evolved guides enabling the individual to predict his rights with any great degree of accuracy. This may be challenged by pointing out that major departures from the development plan can only be made with prior approval of the Minister; the effect could be that the plan is given a status approaching that of a rule of law.

It is easy to exaggerate the rapport; present differences in outlook as well as aspiration do exist. The conflicting attitudes toward excess condemnation illustrate the gap. That expedient, barred in the United States for ethical or political reasons, is in Britain a simple monetary problem. This may be purely accidental, or it may reflect much deeper differences in attitude as to the proper function of government.

Similarly, the rule-versus-policy divergence, however defined, does exist, and several explanations for it should be weighed. It may result from differences in what has been called national genius: the American may be temperamentally ill-adapted to endure the uncertainty endemic in flexibility, whereas the British may be undisturbed by it. There may be a difference in the relative prestige of administrators and judges; some basis exists for asserting that the English administrators are, in the main, held in higher repute than their American counterparts.

The greatest benefit of the comparative approach is that each side has something to learn and something to teach. Any solution to problems of the planning system will succeed only to the extent that it meets with public acceptance. Much of the English system of achieving such acceptance should be reinterpreted in terms of American needs. For example, although public hearings on the adoption or major amendment of a plan are held in most United States jurisdictions, hearings in England and Wales are much better attended. In Britain the development plan makes the best-seller list, while in the United States it ranks among the more obscure literature.

Britain has much that is timely to say to the United States about a unified system of planning. Although regionalism is a problem there also, it is a much less serious one than here, and in many respects British planning is genuinely national. Planning appeals, wherever originating, are channeled up to the Minister, who is the highest level of administrative authority. Surveys and development plans are compulsory and are reviewed by the Ministry. Just beneath the administrative pinnacle, however, the English system is fragmented into eight geographic areas, and this has tended to create undesirable differences in results on similar facts. Here — and it is no less valuable — is a negative lesson.

The successful handling of advertisement controls and mineral undertakings may serve as models for future American action. From the British development-rights scheme the United States has imported the condemnation of scenic, conservation, and other easements; still more extensive use of this fractioning of legal incidents of ownership may be anticipated in future renewal programs. The techniques and membership of the Lands Tribunal seem important prototypes for a more efficient and fairer system of land takings and assessments in the various states.

Among the lessons taught by the American system, perhaps the most valuable one is that incentives often produce better results than legislative edicts. In the United States the triumvirate of federal government, state government, and private enterprise has shown enough effectiveness in urban redevelopment and renewal to raise hopes for the future. Britain may well ponder this alternative to inaction due not to lack of authority but to the inability to finance its exercise. The American lawyer's preference for expressing policy through prospective regulations might also be considered by architects of the British system. Finally, some of the attributes of judicial decision — such as articulation of factors and use of precedents — could be incorporated into the British system of ministerial review.

Besides the lessons to be learned from a foreign system, the comparative approach reveals new perspectives on one's own system. The British generally seem to consider their arrangement as one founded on quite broad policy considerations. They assume that public interests are predominant, and that their land-use laws exist to promote the common good rather than what they regard as the narrower aim in the United States of protecting private property. More careful scrutiny reveals, however, that this breadth of policy does not extend to economic aspects, on which there is concededly little being done, despite the theoretical control over industry found in section 14(4) of the Planning Act of 1947. Nor does British planning law appear to accomplish, or even attempt to accomplish, a redistribution of wealth. Even the unquestionable control over aesthetics, on close examination, turns out to be weaker than one might have originally supposed.

One comes to a realization that the representatives of the two bars do not see themselves in quite the same light as they appear to their opposite numbers. Some Americans are self-critical for insufficiently evaluating the planning laws with which they work, for being overzealous in servicing private clients, and for making the judiciary the repository of ethical standards — especially when contrasted with the British, who are thought (by Americans) to be more given to viewing their laws in terms of good or bad, better or worse. The British, on the other hand, seem more nearly content with their planning machinery. The explanation may lie in the differing political structures of the two nations. Britain, having a national form of government, knows but one sovereign lawmaker. Although Her Majesty's Loyal Opposition may vigilantly criticize what is and propagandize for what should be, at any one time there is but one body of statute law. There is a tendency to say that if there has been a failure of planning, it is not due to a defect in the law, because Parliament has clothed the planning authorities with sufficient powers. In the United States, the existence of a different rule in a sister state, available as persuasive though not "controlling" authority, is probably conducive to a habitually comparative frame of mind. There may also be a difference in attitude toward the profession and the extent of the lawyer's province — specifically whether he is an inventor or translator of policy. Depending upon the outlook, different grades will be given to a planning regulation.

A few caveats are in order. There is no over-all answer to the problem of compensation — which remains still to be resolved in both nations. Excess condemnation has its advocates, but it goes only as far as value increments arising from public improvements; it leaves unanswered the companion question — how to finance the staggering, albeit temporary, outlay needed for such improvements. And it is no answer at all to the question of how to precipitate out the windfall profits of planning permission; through the purely fortuitous circumstance of an intangible line drawn by a planner, owners on one side of the urban fence can reap an unearned increment denied to their fellows on the other side. This quicksand of inequity might drag down the entire structure of planning control so laboriously erected.

Problems of enforcement and nonconforming uses have also withstood attempts at solution. To a certain extent, as in the case of compensation, insufficient finances are the obstacle, but by no means the only one, nor necessarily the most important. The concepts of liberty and dignity prohibit the practice of having inspectors constantly investigating to detect infractions of density regulations. Equally abhorrent, assuming it could be achieved, would be a situation in which each man spied on his neighbor to discover and report violations of the law. There is also the problem of securing to the individual the opportunity to contest the decision of the planning officials without frustrating the planning machinery by subjecting it to excessive judicial intervention.

The nonconforming use is more amenable to the cure of gold, but here also money is not a complete answer. Suppose a certain area is zoned today as residential. In one way or another, the ideal of the planner is superimposed on reality. Then new planners come in, or the old are won over to new concepts. The ideal for that same area accordingly changes from pure residential to a controlled mixture of residential, commercial, and industrial elements. Even under the most scrupulously honest and fair-minded administration the original owners may feel they have been dealt with most unfairly. Moreover, discrimination and corruption in this situation are constant temptations, and are intensified as planning officials are given greater discretion.

In a few instances the space limitations on the papers have prevented even agreement on the issues, much less their resolution. Most notable among these is the relation of planning permission to the plan. Is one more significant than the other? Should one precede the other? Or is it meaningless to talk in such terms? While this aspect of the subject is of considerable interest to all, there is some doubt as to whether the positions of the two national groups has been made clear.

The rule-versus-policy conflict is similarly suspect. Here the fuzziness seems to center about the word "policy." Several of the visitors assert that the difference between Britain's planning system and that of the United States is that they regard planning as policy whereas Americans would reduce it to rules. Apparently the term "policy" does not have the same connotation for all. Most of the Americans seem to view it as a guiding principle, a statement of a standard, equally articulated with "rules," though less specific. Some of the British, on the other hand, apply "policy" in a quite different sense — as an inarticulable, perhaps intuitive, or at times mystical, sense of values.

Anyone who has worked intensively on a particular subject will agree on the usefulness of circumscribing the areas of confusion, which is the first step toward clarification; of defining the problems, which is a step toward their solution; and of exploring possible solutions, which is the next step, even if all are rejected. At times the land planning picture emerging from these papers looks like a large department store where the police have moved in on the ground floor and are conducting some sort of operation; on the next floor, the bona fide manager of the store appears to have some small islands which he controls; here and there, punctuating the whole machinery, are a series of street gangs who carry on operations which nobody quite understands, while there are other people including customers whom nobody can identify roaming around the floor; the elevator operators are all on strike.

A further conclusion can be drawn, however: such seminars serve a useful purpose, and further ones could profitably be held. A future land-use seminar might be composed of planners. Some of the most important questions, suggested but unanswered by the assembled lawyers, involve the technical aspects of land control. Why have four decades of experience with land-use controls, the last of which saw those controls strengthened and intensified in several respects, failed to produce a comprehensive, coherent set of standards? Why have planners failed to clearly differentiate their requirements according to the differing features of an area — for example, in the rural countryside or the metropolitan center? Why have planners lagged behind private enterprise in recognizing and interpreting the need for changes? Are there any usable guides for controlling aesthetics? What economic models and techniques can be devised for handling the compensation-betterment issue? These are questions which the lawyer cannot answer. Perhaps the planner can.

Another future seminar might profitably be composed of lawyers expert in the planning field and lawyers specializing in administrative law. One question touched on by the present group is whether any justification exists for singling out land from other scarce goods for special governmental control. The majority view is that special treatment is warranted because land has a unique inelasticity of supply. Even the small dissenting minority concede that some control is necessitated by the interrelatedness of land uses. But problems such as the scope of judicial review, the formulation of administrative standards, and the mode of administrative procedure (quasi-legislative or quasi-judicial) are more or less common to all regulatory agencies. Is there a wide divergence in the different areas of state intervention between the law as promulgated in the books and the law as it operates in practice and by negotiation? Not all regulatory programs are in the same stage of development. Some are older, and in others greater efforts have been made to achieve a satisfactory equilibrium among competing interests. A comparative study might suggest techniques and procedures which could be adopted by regulatory agencies exercising land-use controls.

What are the new legal mechanisms and institutions for harnessing the energies of individuals and of society in attaining community ends for land resources? Total solutions are not possible. In the dreams of some reformers the message has too often presented itself in terms of ideals and goals having little relation to the political realities, and lacking a full understanding of the limits and possibilities of human nature and history. Many other groups view any change in the environment with suspicion and hostility. The important function of planning legislation is to redefine thinking and to provide outlets for action by private initiative, within the general framework of community ends, and to encourage diversity and experiment in the form, goals, and types of activity government can participate in most effectively. Drafting legislation of this kind calls for the best efforts of the creative imagination to see the extent to which the ideals of planning and of private property can be harmonized.

Throughout the proceedings of the seminar there was a sense of challenge: while the scale of activities and concentration of resources involved in planning may entail great dangers, a new creativity can evolve. New forms of cities, regional arrangements for residential and industrial development, new technologies of building — these have been made possible by science and practicable through the legal means for harnessing and shaping social energies. Blight in the human environment can be removed. Laws can be reshaped to correspond with the broad forces at work in society. But the law must proceed from knowledge and within proven channels; the symbols of order await the appearance of the legal scientist, if we but have the will.

In this book the contributors, from their own sometimes clearly divergent positions, have addressed themselves to a better understanding of the two legal systems. It is to be hoped that these papers will stimulate fresh thinking and the growth of legal doctrines in a field where it is of paramount importance that the law be an effective instrument of public control.

Land Planning
and Land Ownership

CONTROL OF THE USE OF LAND IN ENGLISH LAW

W. O. HART, C.M.G.
CLERK OF THE LONDON COUNTY COUNCIL

LIMITS EXIST — and always must have existed — on the use to which
land may be put for the protection of neighboring owners and occupiers.
Even in its more drastic forms of prescribing to what use individual parcels
of land shall be put and, indeed, the layout of those parcels themselves,
the control of the use of land is not a new conception, although it may
appear an interference with traditional rights of property, if not of individual liberty. In the past there have been vast systems of land-use control
based on the economic and social needs of the community and designed
to secure the exploitation and development of the land to the best advantage of the society which lived on it.

The open field system established by the Saxon settlers in England and
extended by their descendants, for example, reflected a rigidly controlled
pattern of land use: arable fields, divided into furlongs, subdivided into
separate strips, scattered groups of which formed individual holdings,
all cultivated in accordance with a traditional rotation of crops and all
subject to common grazing at certain seasons of the year, with similar
rights in the meadows and common rights in the waste. But the economic
and social wants of the community changed as new forms of agricultural
exploitation developed, and to meet this the pattern of land use itself
gradually changed. At first in many places this change took place by some
form of private agreement. There were exchanges of scattered strips to
form compact holdings, enclosure of waste, or even the ouster of separate
owners to permit consolidation into large single ownerships. At a later
stage the process was accelerated by resort to legislation — at first by private and local acts of Parliament. The open field pattern was altered to
one of separate closes by commissioners empowered to inquire into existing rights and to survey and allot lands and ways in exchange for the
rights their work was intended to supersede. All these changes resulted

in a marked alteration in the layout and permanent appearance of the land. G. K. Chesterton spoke of the rolling English drunkard as having made the rolling English road; but that is a piece of purely poetical fantasy. Apart altogether from the great Roman roads, which still run straight across modern England, the parish highways were planned routes for moving the Saxon eight-ox plow to the furlongs in the common fields, or they were the roads laid out by the enclosure commissioners for the convenient movement of horse-drawn agricultural implements through the newly enclosed country side. Indeed, the majority of the main roads of today are the turnpikes planned and built under eighteenth century acts of Parliament to accommodate the stage coach.

In each of the legal systems of land-use control, ownership played a leading part. The economic needs of a predominantly agricultural society demanded a certain form of layout and this in turn dictated the corresponding pattern of ownership. Ownership in the open fields was based upon individual holdings of groups of strips scattered through the furlongs. Ownership in the system which succeeded it was based on the separate closes. A state of equilibrium is reached when the layout needed for the most beneficial exploitation of land has come to be supported by the pattern of ownership. In this respect both systems differed from the present, where control rests upon statutory powers conferred on public authorities who do not themselves own the land.

The process of change from one system to the next, of course, occurred gradually over a period of centuries, allowing time for the pattern of ownership to change to conform to the demands of the new layout and thus restore the equilibrium. Our present difficulties in controlling land use arise largely because the pace of economic and social change has greatly quickened and left no time for the corresponding changes in the ownership pattern. The vast and rapid development in industry which began in the latter part of the eighteenth century and was accompanied by a progressively great increase in population brought an equally vast and rapid development of towns. This was the physical manifestation of the new layout demanded by a largely industrial and urban economy. There was not, however, enough time for this new layout to alter the pattern of ownership to meet its requirements. Instead a pattern of ownership based on an earlier agricultural system of land use dictated and often distorted the layout. Occasionally, by the accident of past happenings, large estates in one ownership felt the pressure of urban development, often providing scope for obtaining a satisfactory layout. But too often this was not so.

In the city of Nottingham, for example, the rapid increase of industry and population could not be spread over the land adjoining the older town because it was nearly surrounded by still unenclosed open fields. This resulted in gross overcrowding and a legacy of slums. It was not until 1845 that the surrounding lands were enclosed and the pressure of population somewhat relieved. Yet even then the street and housing pattern of the extended town was forced into and still perpetuates the lines of the commissioners' closes and accommodation roads.

Just as the ruins of earlier erections make difficult redevelopment of a building site, so these remnants of an earlier system of land use, solidified into a pattern of ownership, complicated the new system of development. The nineteenth century by-laws controlling building standards were insufficient to overcome the difficulty and tended merely to produce uniformity without convenience or amenity. For example, it was not possible until 1907 to insist that a new street be so laid out as to form a convenient means of communication with other streets.[1] As a result, the extensive urban development of the nineteenth century generally created poor living conditions, was often inefficient in its means of communication, and was frequently lacking in amenity. By contrast, very different conditions resulted where a large estate in single ownership had been developed in accordance with a comprehensive plan and where, if the development had been carried out under building leases, the doctrine of *Spencer's Case*[2] made it possible to retain a tight control over the continued use of the land and buildings comprised in it. Moreover, this leasehold control of a big estate was more likely to encourage the preservation of elements of natural beauty, if only for their economic value to the developed portion.

PLANNING LEGISLATION

Recognition of the unsatisfactory layout and development which had too frequently occurred and of the marked contrast which ownership control on a large scale often showed to be possible led to the first English town planning legislation. The Housing, Town Planning, &c., Act of 1909 conferred on local authorities limited powers which could be re-

[1] Public Health Acts Amendment Act, 1907, 7 Edw. 7, c. 53, § 17.
[2] 5 Co. Rep. 16a, 77 Eng. Rep. 72 (K.B. 1583).

garded as modest extensions of the principle already accepted in the by-laws. Subject to various safeguards, these applied only to land which was in course of development or which appeared likely to be used for building. Through a town-planning scheme prepared by the local authority, relatively simple objectives could be pursued, such as prevention of an inconvenient mixture of uses, earmarking of sites for public requirements, inclusion of roads, and orderly programming of development. From this beginning there was a gradual extension until the Town and Country Planning Act of 1932, under which planning powers could be applied to all land, urban and rural, developed and undeveloped. The machinery of the acts, however, was still based on preparation of a planning scheme, and too often the schemes were largely academic in character. The control was negative, on the assumption that initiative would come from private developers, and, moreover, it was weak. Compensation was payable where property was adversely affected, but the mechanism for recovering betterment from owners whose property was enhanced in value was defective. In consequence the few schemes which came into operation were hesitant, if not timid, in the restrictions they sought to impose.

The period of the Second World War saw acceptance of a much wider conception of planning and much thought on how these new functions could be carried out. Depression and unemployment in the older industrial areas before the outbreak of war, coupled with a shift of industry southward, led to the creation in 1938 of a Royal Commission to Consider the Distribution of the Industrial Population. This Barlow Commission reported in 1940.[3] In the twenty years between the two World Wars the population of Greater London had increased by one and a quarter million, of whom one million were immigrants from other parts of the country. This movement had been accompanied by a substantial influx in the same area of new industry, now able to operate away from the traditional manufacturing areas adjacent to the coal fields because of new means of transmitting electrical energy. The Barlow Commission pointed to the connection between population and industrial employment and recommended that the location of industry be controlled nationally to effect the decentralization of population needed to correct the manifest disadvantages of overly large urban areas. On this view planning was to take place on a regional if not a national scale.

The war interrupted the preparation of planning schemes and thus threatened to undo much of the work already undertaken. To meet this

[3] Report by the Royal Commission on Industrial Population, CMD. No. 6153 (1940).

the Town and Country Planning Act of 1943 extended planning control to the whole country. The war also produced a demand that older areas, struck by enemy bombing, be replaced by much better development, and a series of regional plans were commissioned as bases for postwar action. The County of London and Greater London plans accepted the Barlow Commission's policy of decentralization, while generally Parliament furthered the same object by passing, in 1945, the first of a series of distribution of industry acts by which the location of industrial employment is sought to be controlled and influenced. Meanwhile, in the Town and Country Planning Act of 1944, Parliament provided for the designation and compulsory acquisition of areas of extensive war damage or obsolete development so that they might be comprehensively redeveloped, thus reverting to the traditional principle that layout ought to determine ownership, and not ownership dictate layout.[4]

Further objectives which have come into prominence since the war are the cure of urban congestion and traffic problems, now accentuated by the office as a source of employment, which in central city areas is becoming more important in this respect than manufacturing industry. In these new conditions the Barlow policy of decentralization appears to many to require a corresponding control of the location of offices. And as the immediate postwar concentration on war damage and housing tends to recede in time and importance, the problem of urban renewal to meet the decay of the older parts of cities is becoming insistent in requiring comprehensive planning of the consequent redevelopment. Finally, the growing mobility of the population is making preservation of the countryside an urgent demand. The objectives of planning have thus grown from a narrow desire to secure convenience and amenity in the layout and development of building land to wide aims of national policy, such as the distribution of industry and population.

The achievement of these aims required strong control over the use of land, not only negative, approving or disapproving privately initiated proposals, but also positive, effectuating publicly desired proposals. This was perhaps the easier to bring about because in England a sovereign Parliament has been the instrument by which planning legislation has been enacted. No question of constitutional competence can delay or limit

---

[4] If, however, outside these areas of "blitz" and "blight" effective planning was to match the new conception of broader public control over the use of land, the practical limitations imposed by the need to pay compensation had to be overcome. This problem was studied by a committee which reported in 1942. Expert Committee on Compensation and Betterment, Final Report, CMD. No. 6386 (1942).

the scope of the legislation. Neither in the range of the powers it confers nor in the choice of the organs it employs is this legislation confined within predetermined limits. The absence of a written constitution gives the widest scope for legislation, which by long tradition has been used to override individual rights of ownership in the use of land. By act of Parliament the open fields were enclosed, the turnpikes, the canals, and railways were built, and the necessary lands compulsorily purchased. Even the rebuilding of the City of London after the Great Fire of 1666 was controlled by an act of Parliament,[5] which prescribed the type of house which should be erected in the various parts and provided for compulsory purchase of lands needed for public improvements.

Some postwar objectives were already the subject of legislation. For example, the Housing Acts, providing for slum clearance and rebuilding, play an important part in urban renewal. But still wider powers were needed. Within a limited field the Planning Act of 1944 had already taken the logical step of effecting direct control through actual public ownership. But nationalizing the land, however logical and legally tidy, would have raised immense political issues and presented a formidable financial operation. In consequence, planning legislation has in general proceeded along its earlier lines. It has, moreover, always shown great moderation, if not tenderness, for the rights with which it interferes. Compulsory acquisition as well as enforced restrictions on ownership have always carried a statutory obligation to pay fair compensation. It was to remain a free-enterprise world even if planning legislation made it subject to public control.

Powers were needed to deal in general with four sets of conditions. First, power to control change of land use was needed. This would be largely a negative power, to grant or refuse approval to proposed changes. Second, there had to be the more positive power to compel termination or modification of existing uses so as to enforce conformance to the plan. Third, power was needed to acquire, compulsorily if essential, sites for public buildings and works and, until they were needed, to refuse approval to other changes which might make more difficult or expensive their ultimate acquisition. Finally, where a multiplicity of wants made it too difficult to define a complex of specific powers sufficient to ensure the desired result, resort was necessary to wholesale purchase of the area affected and its development under the control which real ownership by a public authority could give. Special corporations, for example, have been

---

[5] 19 Car. 2, c. 3 (1667).

established to acquire the site and undertake the involved task of developing new towns.[6] In short, these groups of powers can be reduced to two: power to acquire land compulsorily and thus control its use by virtue of ownership, and power to control the use of land without ownership.

So far as the Town and Country Planning acts are the source of these two sets of powers they are both reflected in the development plan which each local authority must prepare for the Minister's approval and review quinquennially. The plan designates for compulsory purchase specific sites required for statutory functions and also areas for comprehensive development. Secondly, it defines sites for proposed public purposes and allocates areas for agricultural, residential, industrial, and other uses, but without necessarily providing for their public purchase.[7]

DESIGNATION

There are, of course, many statutory powers enabling public authorities to acquire individual sites: it will be sufficient to refer by way of illustration to such powers in relation to housing and highways. In the development plan, however, designation of land for compulsory acquisition is a special evolution in the general law of compulsory purchase, because the Minister's approval of the plan, after the holding of a public local inquiry, if demanded, at which objectors may be heard, can settle once and for all the proposed use of the land, so that, in dealing with a consequent compulsory purchase order, the Minister may disregard any objection which amounts in substance to no more than an attack upon that proposed use.[8] Designation thus acts as an anticipatory decision on the need to allocate the land for the particular public purpose. It gives something like an option to the local planning authority without, however, binding it to acquire the land at any given time or, indeed, at all.[9] For the owner, however, it can lie like a dead hand on the land, which may become virtually unsalable. Because of this "planning blight" land may be desig-

---

[6] New Towns Act, 1946, 9 & 10 Geo. 6, c. 68. The Town Development Act of 1952, 15 & 16 Geo. 6 & 1 Eliz. 2, c. 54, provides for the expansion of existing towns by the local authorities concerned; but this normally involves extensive acquisition.

[7] Town and Country Planning Act, 1947, 10 & 11 Geo. 6, c. 51, § 5.

[8] Town and Country Planning Act, 1947, § 45.

[9] Under the New Towns Act of 1946, § 1, the Minister himself makes a draft designation order, which he has power to confirm after holding a local inquiry at which objectors may put forward their objections: Franklin v. Minister of Town and Country Planning, [1948] A.C. 87.

nated for compulsory purchase only for relatively short periods of time,[10] and special provisions generally enable an owner-occupier to require the purchase of land which cannot be sold save at substantially lower prices than would obtain if it were not subject to designation.[11]

The availability of public funds places an obvious practical limit on the extent of compulsory purchase, but the Town and Country Planning Act of 1947[12] extends at least the theoretical existence of the power, since it authorizes proposals for the designation for compulsory purchase by a Minister, local authority, or statutory undertaker of any land allocated by a plan for the purposes of any of their functions. Approval of a plan containing such a designation confers power for the compulsory acquisition of the land, even if, apart from the plan, there is no statutory power to acquire land for that purpose. This is a wide extension. But much has happened to weaken any sentiment for the sacrosanctity of land ownership. The common law has long struggled against attempts to render land inalienable, and the nineteenth century brought legislation designed to facilitate its transfer. This movement culminated in the property legislation of 1925, which took as its model the simplicity, cheapness, and expedition of the transfer of stocks and shares, which had come to rival land as a permanent investment, and attempted, so far as the differing nature of their subject matter could permit, to reproduce them for interests in land. The means were necessarily complex and the identity in result imperfect, but the Law of Property Act of 1925 and the Settled Land Act of 1925 did succeed, at any rate, in ensuring the free marketability of land even when settled, the interests under the settlement being transferred automatically to the proceeds on a sale. Land, therefore, can always be reduced to a common value in money, for which in effect it is no more than a temporary investment. In this the property legislation has made it less difficult to accept the notion that liability to compulsory purchase can be a common incident of ownership.

In form, at any rate, that liability is not inconsistent with ownership.

---

[10] The Minister must not approve a designation proposal unless he is satisfied that the land is likely to be acquired within ten years, or, if agricultural, within seven: Town and Country Planning Act, 1947, § 5. If not acquired within twelve years, or, if agricultural, within nine, the owner may call on the local planning authority to purchase within six months, and if this is not done the designation automatically lapses. Town and Country Planning Act, 1947, § 9.

[11] Town and Country Planning Act, 1959, 7 and 8 Eliz. 2, c. 25 §§ 39–43. These provisions also apply to cases where land is allocated for public use or is affected by a highway proposal without specific designation.

[12] Section 37.

The mere power of compulsory purchase does not deny ownership of the land over which it may be exercised. When a compulsory purchase order has actually been made, there is still no change in position. Even its confirmation leaves the legal ownership untouched, since not until the acquiring authority serves notice to treat and the price has been agreed upon or fixed by arbitration does the relation between the parties reach something analogous to that between vendor and purchaser under a contract of sale.[13] Indeed it is not until the transaction is completed by conveyance — or by a statutory equivalent where a conveyance cannot be obtained — that the ownership vests in the acquiring authority.

PLANNING CONTROL

Apart from the designation, the other main component of the development plan is planning control. It is based in its present form on section 12 of the Town and Country Planning Act of 1947, which provides that "permission shall be required . . . in respect of any development of land,"[14] and "development" is given a wide definition to include "the carrying out of building, engineering, mining or other operations in, on, over or under land, or the making of any material change in the use of any buildings or . . . land."[15]

Earlier attempts to confer comparable powers had proved largely ineffective because the liability to pay compensation could not be balanced by any practicable method of collecting the corresponding betterment felt by lands benefited by the restrictions. However, the Committee on Compensation and Betterment, under the chairmanship of Mr. Justice Uthwatt, which reported in 1942,[16] pointed out that the value of a piece of land was frequently a compound of two elements: first, its value for the use to which it was actually being put, and second, the value which could be attributed to it because it might be more profitably used for some other purpose. Upon this analysis were based the financial provisions of the Town and Country Planning Act of 1947.

The act imposed a well-nigh universal restriction by requiring that planning permission be obtained for any material change of use or other

---

[13] Tiverton & North Devon Railway Co. v. Loosemoore, 9 App. Cas. 480 (1884).

[14] Development orders made by the Minister of Housing and Local Government provide for the grant of planning permission: Town and Country Planning Act, 1947, § 13. The Town and Country Planning General Development Order, STAT. INSTR., 1950, No. 728, grants permission for other forms of development.

[15] Town and Country Planning Act, 1947, § 12. This definition is amplified and qualified in certain particulars.

[16] CMD. No. 6386 (1942), *supra* note 4.

development. It then provided for a once-for-all payment of compensation, to be based on the development value of the land as of July 1, 1948, which, when established, was to be met pro rata out of a fund of £300 million. The grant or refusal of permission to develop land would thus no longer be hampered by further considerations of compensation, while betterment could properly be claimed as a development charge, so far as the value of land was enhanced by the grant of permission. The landowner was left free to continue the existing use of his land. Hence, insofar as planning control interfered with existing use it still gave rise to compensation.[17] But on compulsory acquisition by a public authority only the existing use value was payable.[18] On the other hand, any enhancement in the existing use value accrued solely to the owner.

The development charge was assessed at the full increase in value due to the permission to develop. Consequently all profit on development was, in theory at least, taken away, thus leaving no incentive to develop. In practice private purchasers often found themselves forced to pay more for land than its existing-use value — which in logic was all they should have been ready to pay — and a development charge in addition. Thus the charge came to be treated as no more than an arbitrary tax on development. For this reason it was abolished by the Town and Country Planning Act of 1953, and distribution of the £300 million fund was likewise postponed.

In the following year Parliament sought a permanent solution for the instability thus created. The Town and Country Planning Act of 1954, by a piece of rough, if somewhat illogical justice, confirmed the established claims for loss of development value but further postponed their payment until the loss was actually felt in the form of compulsory purchase or refusal of planning permission. At the same time it excluded claims for many refusals or conditional grants of planning permission so long as the land could continue to be economically exploited in other ways. One strange result of this legislation was the existence of two standards of value to determine the purchase price of land. A public authority still paid only existing use value plus any unexpended balance of an established claim for loss of development value; but a private purchaser paid market

---

[17] For example, Town and Country Planning Act, 1947, § 19; Town and Country Planning Act, 1954, 2 & 3 Eliz. 2, c. 72, § 70; Town and Country Planning Act, 1959, § 35 — purchase notice where land is rendered incapable of reasonably beneficial use; Town and Country Planning Act, 1947, § 20 — refusal of planning permission for Third Schedule use; §§ 21 and 22 — revocation of planning permission, §§ 26 and 27 — alteration of existing use.

[18] Town and Country Planning Act, 1947, § 51.

value. This anomaly was removed by the Town and Country Planning Act of 1959.[19] But market value is now a somewhat artificial concept, being dependent in part upon whether planning permission has been granted, or is likely to be obtainable, for uses other than the existing use. Hence the act of 1959 has to lay down what assumptions about planning permission must be made in determining the market value and hence the price to be paid in purchases by public authorities.[20]

This illustrates sharply the wide impact that control of land use now has on all transactions in land. In practice, of course, the exercise of these wide powers is limited by the fact that in certain cases compensation will become payable, or the land affected may have to be purchased from the owner whose occupation is rendered unbeneficial in consequence. Moreover, planning control consists of specific powers which, however, lack any defined rules for their exercise. Thus, though the Town and Country Planning Act of 1947[21] requires a local authority, in considering an application for planning permission, to consider, among other things, the provisions of the development plan, it nowhere gives any binding force to the plan. Indeed, under the General Development Order of 1950,[22] a local authority is authorized to grant permission for development which deviates from the development plan, so long as the proposal, in the opinion of the authority, would neither involve a substantial departure from the plan nor injuriously affect the amenity of adjoining land. In other cases the authority must first refer the case to the Minister, who may require an amendment to the development plan. The development plan, in short, is no more than a declaration of the local authority's intentions. It is not mandatory: it does not bind or directly benefit landowners, and the local authority may not be compelled to follow it, nor be challenged in its interpretation of the plan's provisions.

Conversely there is no requirement that the development plan contain all the factors which may influence the local authority in exercising planning control. It may determine in a particular case that some other consideration is material or may lay down by its own simple resolution those standards which it will apply to all applications of a class. Thus standards prescribing the amount of parking space to be provided in a new development, or the bulk of building defined, perhaps, in relation

[19] Section 1.

[20] Sections 2–12.

[21] Section 14.

[22] Town and Country Planning General Development Order, STAT. INSTR., 1950, No. 728, art. 8, and Town and Country Planning (Development Plans) Direction, 1954.

to the area of the plot, have been established by some local planning authorities. These standards are of even more attenuated legal force than the provisions of the development plan: to change or depart from them does not require the complexity or the publicity of an amendment to the development plan.

Supervision over these wide administrative powers is itself administrative. Where a proposed new use is concerned, appeal to the Minister of Housing and Local Government is available from a refusal of planning permission, merely conditional approval, or failure to decide.[23] Where the action affects an existing use, much the same result is achieved, because in one form or another an order or notice will come before the Minister for his confirmation or approval.[24]

Nonetheless these powers remain wide and uncertain in definition. Their exercise necessarily tends in practice to deviate from any formal pattern of presentation and decision. Developers concerned with more than the simplest proposals naturally consult with the officers of local planning authorities about both the form and substance of their applications. This is indeed encouraged by the opportunity to apply for outline planning permission, so that the principle of a particular proposal may be settled without the delay and expense of preparing final plans.[25] These consultations sometimes lead to what are in effect bargains between the developer and the planning authority under which the developer may agree, for example, to surrender land for a road improvement free of cost to the authority in consideration of being permitted to count the surrendered area as part of his total plot for the purpose of calculating the bulk of building he may erect.[26]

[23] Town and Country Planning Act, 1947, § 16; Town and Country Planning General Development Order, Stat. Instr., 1950, No. 728, art. 5.

[24] For example, Town and Country Planning Act, 1947, § 19 (amended by 1954 Act, § 70; 1959 Act, § 35) — purchase notice; § 21 — revocation of planning permission; § 26 — alteration of existing use; § 28 — tree preservation order; § 29 — building preservation order.

[25] Town and Country Planning General Development Order, Stat. Instr., 1950. No. 728, art. 5; Hamilton v. West Sussex County Council, [1958] 2 Q.B. 286.

[26] See 622 H.C. Deb. (5th ser.) 58 (1960): "Sir H. Butcher asked the Minister of Housing and Local Government . . . if he is aware of the growing tendency of local authorities to use the planning laws to obtain valuable considerations in the shape either of the acquisition of land below its true value or the compulsory user of premises or part of premises for specific and often unremunerative purposes as a condition precedent of granting planning permission; and whether he will take steps to restrain such practices. Mr. H. Brooke: I am not aware that local authorities are misusing their planning powers in the way suggested. If my hon. Friend will send me particulars of any cases he has in mind, I will investigate them."

Other forms of consultation also take place. The General Development Order of 1950[27] requires local planning authorities to consult with specified authorities or departments when considering certain types of applications. The Town and Country Planning Act of 1959[28] requires an applicant who has no legal interest in the land concerned,[29] to give notice to all owners or to publish a notice in local newspapers, and, where agricultural land is concerned, any applicant, even if owner, must give notice to all agricultural tenants.[30] Similarly, an application relating to certain types of development likely to injure the amenity of neighboring property must be advertised.[31] In all these cases the local authority must take into account any representations received from persons likely to be affected. These steps all take time and therefore add to the total delay to development which planning control imposes; and delay not only causes frustration and criticism of the whole mechanism and principle of planning, but also means expense and a waste of resources. Even discounting these special requirements for consultation and notice, the developer must allow up to two months for a decision from the local planning authority. If the decision is not to his liking or if no decision has then been given he can appeal to the Minister.[32] But appeals are lodged in something like 2 per cent of the 400,000 applications made each year throughout the country, and an average six months elapse between the filing of an appeal and the issue of the decision. He may well think it worthwhile to continue negotiating with the local authority in the hope of obtaining permission, even if it does not give him all he would otherwise like.

And in so doing he may not be without powerful arguments in his favor. The property condemned may carry rights under the Third Schedule of the Town and Country Planning Act of 1947,[33] which can only be disregarded by the local planning authority at the risk of having to

[27] STAT. INSTR., 1950, No. 728, arts. 7 and 9; Town and Country Planning (Airfields) Direction, 1949.

[28] Section 37.

[29] An applicant need not have any interest in the land in question: Hanily v. Minister of Local Government and Planning, [1952] 2 Q.B. 444; however, permission is not purely personal, but inures for the benefit of the land: Town and Country Planning Act, 1947, § 18.

[30] Because under the Agricultural Holdings Act of 1948, 11 & 12 Geo. 6, c. 63, the grant of planning permission for some other use is a condition precedent to giving notice to quit an agricultural holding.

[31] Town and Country Planning Act, 1959, § 36.

[32] Town and Country Planning Act, 1947, § 7; Town and Country Planning General Development Order, STAT. INSTR., 1950, No. 728.

[33] Which, for example, gives a claim for full compensation if planning permission should be refused for replacement of an existing building for the same use by a new one of the same cubic content plus ten per cent.

pay compensation. Again, the authority may be deterred by fear lest a purchase notice[34] should become a possibility.

EFFECTIVENESS OF PLANNING CONTROL

A large volume of development has been proceeding in England for some time — in the public sector in the development of new towns and the extensive housing schemes of local authorities, and in the private sector in industrial and speculative building, the latter taking the form mainly of suburban housing and central area redevelopment. The policy of rigidly controlled greenbelts around towns, at a time when modern transport and a rising standard of living are encouraging people to live nearer the country, is creating a building-land famine, forcing prices to a startling height, and causing a denser form of development than may be really desirable. There is, however, no incentive — and indeed a number of deterrents — to the redevelopment by private enterprise of the standard housing of the older urban residential areas, built a century or so ago and now ripe for redevelopment. This task therefore falls more and more to public authorities. There are strong incentives for private enterprise to engage in redeveloping the commercial centers of towns, but the most profitable forms of building are not necessarily consistent with the policies of the planning authorities. Thus congestion in central London has been aggravated by a substantial increase in employment, and it is the policy of the planning authorities to discourage the building of more offices there. But this official discouragement, besides perhaps having maintained the rental level of office accommodations, has tended to deflect the pressure of redevelopment into those areas in central London which contain buildings with high ceilings and existing office uses. Under the Third Schedule of the 1947 act, unless the authority pays heavy compensation, these buildings may be replaced with an addition of 10 per cent to their cubic capacity and, by rebuilding with modern low ceiling heights, a much greater increase in the floor space available for office letting can be obtained.

Indeed, the growing needs of urban renewal afford a current test of planning legislation. Planning should ensure that redevelopment of central areas is better than it would otherwise have been. If left uncontrolled,

---

[34] Town and Country Planning Act, 1947, § 19; Town and Country Planning Act, 1954, § 70; Town and Country Planning Act, 1959, § 35. Demolition is not development and so does not require planning permission; it may be difficult to find a reasonably beneficial use for a cleared site whose development in the manner desired by the applicant for planning permission has been refused.

the accidents of separate ownership would have tended to reproduce much the same pattern of development as at present, save insofar as the demand for or efficiency of bigger buildings made it profitable for developers to face the delay and expense of acquiring larger sites. It is, however, the task of planning to secure redevelopment in accordance with comprehensive schemes more convenient and more pleasing architecturally than might otherwise be expected. This may entail disregarding present ownership boundaries, perhaps pooling values, and altering street alignments. The planning acts do of course provide machinery for just such an operation in the provisions permitting designation of whole areas for comprehensive redevelopment. But this method almost inevitably involves the local authority in purchasing the whole area, and the cost of this in central areas ripe for redevelopment can be so heavy as to be prohibitive, at least if the local authority is expected to keep pace with developers. One alternative is for the authority to prepare a plan indicating to developers what sort of planning permission would be readily forthcoming. But such an "advisory plan" is weak in the face of resistance, can be reasonably effective only if large developers able to acquire substantial blocks of property are willing to engage in redevelopment, and is likely to involve the authority in acquiring the unprofitable portions or the property of uncooperative owners without being able to set off against their cost the profits which may be made in the other portions.

This issue of comprehensive redevelopment in central areas came into controversy in connection with a proposal for a building in Piccadilly Circus, a well-known and important center in London. The Minister has called for a comprehensive plan for its redevelopment, but has apparently accepted the fact that this cannot be carried out by compulsory purchase and that an advisory plan should suffice. The attempt to do this may well lead to further consideration of the whole problem of urban renewal and, possibly, to new legislation.

NATURE OF PLANNING POWERS

Control of the use of land under the planning acts by local authorities is copied in origin from the powers of the owner of a large estate to control the development of his land through leases and covenants. This is a field within which the law does not seek to operate: the owner's discretion is absolute. To afford this control to public authorities by analogy is to confer upon them defined and specific powers, which, however, must stand without the underlying support of ownership. Moreover, these powers of their very nature must be imprecise in form and discretionary in content. In England (and I cannot speak of what may be the position in a country in which the existence of a written constitution may exert other influences) the courts have been diffident in controlling the exercise of discretionary powers conferred by statute. Partly this flows from the omnipotence of Parliament, partly from a difficulty in fitting bare discretionary powers into a pattern of legal thinking which is focused mainly on rights and duties and which reflects the nineteenth century laissez-faire outlook dominant in the period when the rule of strict precedent had recently been accepted and was forming the foundations for the development of the modern law. This judicial attitude recognizes that freedom of action exists in certain fields, perhaps flowing from rights. Such a field, however, is not defined positively, but merely represents an area of possible action not prohibited by duties or contravening the rights of others. Mere powers are difficult to fit into this setting. Some statutory powers can, of course, be regarded as doing no more than removing an internal bar in the constitution of the body upon which they are conferred. Other statutory powers which have an external operation cannot be so simply dealt with, but many are not only carefully defined but their exercise is made dependent upon a definable standard or the existence of some set of circumstances. The power, for instance, to condemn property for clearance as unfit for human occupation is related to a specific norm, the existence of which could, if necessary, become a justiciable matter. Such statutory powers, therefore (though still difficult for the courts to accept), are not wholly alien to judicial patterns of thought. But statutory powers which are discretionary and cannot be related in their exercise to anything approaching a legal rule, but on the contrary are to be exercised in accordance with such indeterminable ideas as policy and expediency, are almost incapable of judicial control.

In the end the courts have shown extreme reluctance to interfere with the exercise of statutory powers of a discretionary nature. Appeal, moreover, is the creature of statute and is not inherent in the grant of a discretionary power, even where the decision of an administrative body involves a point of law.[35] In the absence of a statutory right of appeal the courts will do no more than consider whether the exercise of the power was *ultra vires,* whether it was exercised in good faith, and, where it is of a quasi-judicial type, whether the rules of natural justice were observed in reaching the decision, having regard, however, to the nature of the

[35] Racecourse Betting Control Board v. Secretary for Air, [1944] Ch. 114 (C.A.).

deciding body.[36] Such review provides no appeal on the merits and only a limited scope for controlling the more outrageous departures from reasonable practice. Dissatisfaction with this led to the appointment of a committee under the chairmanship of Sir Oliver Franks, whose report urged greater safeguards and more scope for control through resort to the courts.[37] These recommendations were largely adopted in the Tribunals and Inquiries Act of 1958, and in parts of the Town and Country Planning Act of 1959.[38] The latter in general provides a limited right of appeal to the High Court from the Minister's decision on a planning application and from his confirmation of those orders and notices which may affect a property owner. The appeal is available only on the ground either that the Minister's action was not within his statutory powers or that the interests of the appellant were substantially prejudiced by a failure to comply with any of the statutory requirements for exercise of the power. Subject to this, the act expressly declares that the validity of the decision, or action, or order "shall not be questioned in any legal proceedings whatever."

PLANNING AND OWNERSHIP

The law of land-use control is thus still largely exercised by purely administrative bodies following in great measure no prescribed procedure and bound in their decisions only by the extralegal concepts of policy and expediency. The system shows strains, since in a sense it attempts to reconcile the irreconcilable by permitting public authorities to control the use of land through the exercise of powers copied from an ownership not vested in these authorities themselves. In broad terms, the situation illuminates the difficulties which can flow from a divorce between the requirements of layout and the pattern of ownership. If so wide a degree of public control is needed as the planning acts attempt to create, then from the purely legal point of view this could most logically and satisfactorily be achieved by vesting ownership in the public authorities who are to exercise the control. But simple legal technicalities are not the only consideration. The nearest approach to this solution was attempted by the Town and Country Planning Act of 1947, which could be said to have provided for the compulsory acquisition by the state of the de-

---

[36] See Board of Education v. Rice, [1911] A.C. 179; Local Government Board v. Arlidge, [1915] A.C. 120.

[37] Report of the Committee on Administrative Tribunals and Enquiries, CMD. No. 218 (1957).

[38] Section 31.

velopment right over all land. It may be objected that to regard ownership as capable of division into two distinct "rights" — the right to continue the present use of the land and the right to change its use — is a
false analogy drawn from the two elements which may be material in
assessing the value of land. In any event the recognition of such a right
to develop would merely be a restatement in another form of the fact of
planning control and would not provide any valid explanation or legal
basis for its existence or scope. Indeed, though the Town and Country
Planning Act of 1947[39] specifically requires permission for development,
it nowhere takes away the right to develop or directly forbids development. It merely provides for dealing with contraventions by means of an
enforcement procedure — and that procedure assumes that permission may
still be granted.[40]

There is manifest advantage, however, in continuing as far as possible
to deal in long-established and well-understood legal concepts, rather than
attempting to mutilate them into unrecognizable forms. It may be that
gradually the position may right itself in this direction. Planning legislation is young and the circumstances which have given the occasion for it
are relatively new as compared with the length of time which wide
changes of layout and the consequent ownership pattern have previously
taken. Increasingly, more housing development, and especially redevelopment, is being undertaken by local authorities. Outside of housing, pressure for comprehensive redevelopment in central urban areas may well
effect the extension in some form of the procedure for public acquisition.
And once acquired, the ownership of this land is unlikely to return to
private hands. The new towns illustrate this: it can be a positive embar-
rassment to dispose of the ownership of a complete town vested in the
development corporation which built it. So far the solution proposed is
to transfer the ownership of all the new towns, once initial development
is complete, to a statutory commission which, though it may dispose of
items of its property, seems likely to operate primarily as a holding corporation.[41] Because it reunites the strange, unusual powers of planning control with the ownership from which they ought not logically to be divorced, and because it tends to restore the equilibrium between the layout and the pattern of ownership which should subserve and support it,

---

[39] Section 12.

[40] Town and Country Planning Act, 1947, §§ 23 and 24; Town and Country Planning
Act, 1959, § 38.

[41] New Towns Act, 1959, 7 & 8 Eliz. 2, c. 62.

it may be that in time planning control will be merged in leasehold control based on some new form of public feudalism.

PLANNING AND FREEDOM

To some the main object of planning is to allocate in the national interest the use of land between various competing, or potentially competing, claimants; to others it is the instrument for regulating the living and working environment; to some it is the means by which the haphazard machinery of commercial competition can be controlled in the interest of amenity; to others again it is the mechanism for preservation. While all these carry weight in actual planning decisions, there can be a temptation to give too much attention to minor points and to interfere paternally in too great detail. This accounts for much popular criticism of planning.

Planning control implies regulation not only for landowners but also for other would-be land users. The industrialist must expect to be told where he may manufacture, the ordinary man where he may live — or, at least, where they may not manufacture or live. The imposition of such decisions by a public authority may seem to be an interference with personal liberty. But even if these autocratic powers did not exist, men's effective freedom would be limited within a framework of practical choice, even though that framework might be set more widely and established by other agencies. One may doubt, however, whether the effective choice for the ordinary man would often be much greater than at present. This criticism of planning is, however, perhaps based at least as much on the source as on the content of the decisions which form the framework of personal choice. The alternative carries the attraction that those decisions would be produced by the interaction of innumerable acts of unknown individuals, each pursuing his own interest without consideration of its effect on others, this in total conferring upon them the anonymous and impersonal quality of the products of an irresponsible natural force. These can, and indeed must, be accepted without criticism or complaint, since there is nobody to whom either could be usefully addressed. Just as the heavy weight of responsibility can be more easily borne by a jury of twelve than by a single judge, so hard decisions limiting a man's freedom of action are more willingly accepted when their authors are unidentifiable than when they flow from a single and known source.

In any event the broad justification for planning control must rest on the fact that the need to control the use of land in the public interest has become intense because of the mounting pressure on land in the United

Kingdom. This not only at the one extreme requires a national control over the allocation of land to various uses, but at the other extreme makes possible some more effective protection for the individual in the enjoyment of his land against the inconvenience and loss of amenity which he might suffer from neighboring property than the law of nuisance can afford.

The present system can claim the merit of introducing some sense of public responsibility into the making of decisions about the use of a commodity essential to the life of every member of the community. But this implies that there are people equipped by training and experience and inspired by public spirit who are able to make objective and disinterested decisions. However, this is not purely a technical problem. Planning may be necessary, but it must not become an end in itself nor be allowed to retard development. Just as it has been unkindly said that war is too important a business to leave to generals, so planning control is too important a business to leave to planners. This is what justifies — and, indeed, makes essential — the traditional pattern of public administration, in which the professional expert must work to and obtain the approval of the popularly elected representative, in whom alone reposes the legal power and the political responsibility for decision.

The exercise of planning control can profoundly — and unevenly — affect property values. Now that the system of development charge has been abolished the right to claim betterment has disappeared, and a planning decision may make a very great difference to the sum land will fetch in the market. Because planning decisions are concerned with considerations incapable of reduction to lawyerlike rules, they cannot be made by agencies working in the way in which courts of law are used to work. Some other mechanism for ensuring honesty and probity of decision is required. This is to be found perhaps not so much in the formal requirements of procedure, of application and appeal, as in the pressure which public opinion can exert, and hence in the publicity which can be given to the matters coming before planning agencies. In this connection the recent notice and publication provisions of the 1959 act are perhaps significant. Bureaucracy needs the light of publicity.

PROPERTY AND PLANNING

The control of land use involves a much greater degree of public intervention than — in peacetime at any rate — occurs in any other form of economic planning. There are obvious practical reasons why this should be so in England. Land is one of the basic requirements of life and society. But unlike the other basic requirements, such as air and light, it is capable of individual and exclusive occupation, and its amount is constant and cannot for practical purposes be increased. As the pressure of population on the available land increased, first, no doubt, private ownership became recognized, and later, restrictions in the interest of the community inescapably increased. Perhaps it is not too far-fetched to claim that this is dimly reflected even in international law in the concept of sovereignty as requiring a physical control over a defined area of land. In any case it can be argued that the degree of public control varies directly with the pressure on land.

In parallel with these practical considerations lies the fact that English law has always treated rights in land in a manner sharply different from rights in other forms of property. In part this derives from the physical nature of land as opposed to chattels. Land is immovable and indestructible. Because it is immovable the law has had to recognize the needs of neighbors, giving rise to what may be called third-party rights, such as easements. Because it is indestructible the law has had to recognize successive rights to its enjoyment, and has accomplished this through the peculiar doctrine of estates and the rules of waste. Because it is both immovable and indestructible the law has recognized that land — in contrast to chattels — can always be recovered in specie, and has provided the real actions for this purpose. From this last fact is, of course, derived the term "real property," which in the mind of the layman denotes another sense of "realness," even in these days when land is no longer the only, nor the most attractive, form of investment. But this popular idea is very wide of the mark. The English law of real property never developed a true theory of ownership: title was, and still is in essence, possessory and, moreover, relative rather than absolute.

As if these complexities were not enough, land has long played an important part in public law and, indeed, was the basis of government in the feudal state. Though the economic gradually came to dominate the political importance of land, tenure retained some practical effects and remained at least the formal frame for private rights until the modern property legislation came into operation in 1926.

These peculiarities of English real property law help to explain why intervention by the state in this field has been accepted on a scale greater than in other economic matters. To discuss planning as an interference with ownership, however, requires clarification of two other points: first, that the state has been interfering all along in various ways with the use and exploitation of land and, second, that the word "ownership" in this context is used in a political, or economic, sense. In this sense the practical freedom to exploit land — the content of the right, in other words — has never been absolute, and in modern times has necessarily become more restricted as the pressure on land has increased. Planning control is only one aspect of this restriction. Mines of gold and silver were always reserved to the Crown; now coal, petroleum, and uranium have joined them. In the interests of fire prevention and public health, restrictions are placed on the type and location of buildings that may be erected; in the interest of traffic decongestion, the use of roadside land is in many ways restricted; in the interests of tenants, the Agricultural Holdings Acts and the Landlord and Tenant Act of 1954 provide a high degree of security of tenure, in some cases amounting to a virtual freehold. No doubt these and similar limitations can be grouped, if not explained, as analogies to various other legal concepts, such as nuisance or contract; but in fact they arise from the nature of land, and they reflect the mounting pressure on it. The growth of an urban, industrial society has thus removed land from its earlier pre-eminence as practically the sole form of investment and the foundation of social position, and has converted it into an exploitable commodity. And this in turn has made it the more necessary to limit the power to exploit such a precious and scarce essential of living. It is, however, only comparatively recently that anything even approximating absolute ownership of land has been an accurate conception in English law, which for long has been forced by its doctrine of estates to be familiar with what nineteenth century legislation christened the "limited owner." Restrictions on the practical content of ownership are thus not so startling in English law as might be the case elsewhere.

English law has now had fifty years' experience of the restrictions imposed under planning. The aim of this legislation has grown from a limited control over the layout and development of new building areas to providing machinery capable of supporting important national policies. Throughout, its effectiveness has been retarded by failure to find a satisfactory solution for the interrelated problem of compensation and betterment. Without this, planning control alternates between over-reaching itself and failing to meet the avowed ends for which it was created. Perhaps this merely echoes wartime experience, where attempts to impose public control over particular economic acts generally ended in extending public control over the whole economic process. But public ownership of land is not likely to be quickly established, even though it would presumably involve no more than public ownership of the freehold, leaving the leasehold interest as the sector in which private dealings would still continue.

Whatever critics may currently say of planning control as it is in fact exercised in England, they must recognize that the important half of the 1947 Town and Country Planning Act, which sought to provide a solution for the problem of compensation and betterment, has been repealed: planning control limps along, as it were, on one leg. The brave theme of development rather than control, since it was so proudly elaborated in the 1947 act, has lost impetus. The provisions have gone for ensuring the availability of land at reasonable prices for approved development by private enterprise and the retention by the state of the profit arising from development. In the main, it is true, they failed to work satisfactorily, but instead of modification they have suffered annihilation. In consequence, positive planning is much weakened. Comprehensive development areas may still be designated, but they necessarily tend to involve full acquisition by the local authority, whose financial resources may not be commensurate with the cost of the areas needing redevelopment. But useful provisions in the 1947 act, which permitted compulsion to overcome reluctance to sell or unreasonable demands for land needed for an approved private development, have been repealed. Consequently the incentives for private development, necessarily based on the possibility of profit, have often been limited and deflected from those developments, or redevelopments, which the planning authority desires, to others which the authority may be actively seeking to discourage.

Current planning problems therefore include urban renewal and traffic on the one hand, and greenbelts and the price of land on the other. Traffic congestion presents opportunities for urban redevelopment and adds point to the demand that it be comprehensively planned and architecturally worthy. Finance is a limitation on the possibility of urban redevelopment being undertaken by public authorities under the procedure of comprehensive development areas, even if such a concentration of activity were socially or architecturally desirable. Unfortunately the incentives for private redevelopment point at present toward rebuilding of enlarged office blocks in central areas, which increase congestion and worsen traffic conditions. There is thus a growing demand for special control over the location of offices comparable to that exercised by the Board of Trade over the location of industry. If such a plan should be introduced, or if the market for office accommodation should become saturated, a further step might be to facilitate and encourage private enterprise to take a major part in redevelopment of the vast residential areas which are now at the end of their useful life. This might take the form, little used in England, of public authorities undertaking the clearance and replanning needed to make the site ready for rebuilding by private enterprise.

Urban renewal — at any rate, where existing occupiers must be decanted to permit clearance of the site — involves what the planners call "overspill," and the policy of decentralization of population and employment from cities to new towns has in part been intended to provide for this. But population has increased faster than expected and is tending to break into more and smaller family units than formerly. In consequence, the affluent society in which we now live has also produced a strong stream of voluntary outward migration. Greenbelts are designed perhaps not so much to stem this movement as to prevent it from stopping so near to the city boundary as to create an amorphous and limitless urban sprawl. Unless, however, greenbelts are balanced by adequate building land available for homes and employment beyond their limits, they can become harmful rather than helpful.

In the last few years, as building land inside the greenbelts has become exhausted, the price of land has risen very steeply and rapidly. So far as responsibility can be laid at the door of planning, it illustrates the need for planning machinery sufficiently well informed and flexible to meet the effective demand for land and steer it in the desired directions. Perhaps it also illustrates the need for a more effective coordination of the development plans of local planning authorities over wider areas than at present — if, indeed, not for a regional approach to the broad issues of settlement and employment. Almost inevitably it foreshadows a movement for a more intensive use of land than at present.

In any event, underlying and accentuating all these problems is the unsolved problem of compensation and betterment. The Minister of Housing and Local Government has emphatically repeated that a free market for land is to be maintained. But values and, therefore, market prices for land depend on whether planning permission is granted or refused. There may well be reluctance to retrace steps and try once more a solution on the lines of the development charge of the 1947 act. Development charge inflexibly fixed at 100 per cent of the increase in value attributable to the grant of planning permission proved ineffective. But the original idea had been a variable development charge, which could be adjusted to the circumstances of the particular case, giving an incentive where development was desired and none where it was to be discouraged. This would, of course, have meant still another discretionary power incapable of judicial control. It would have required complex administrative arrangements and demanded the highest integrity. But in its effect it would have been no more outrageous than the present power to grant planning permission which, without effective mechanism for balancing compensation and betterment, can so often decide whether a particular individual shall reap what may amount to a fortune which, once granted, must be denied his neighbors. A variable development charge could offset this and, if coupled with the power to compel sale at a proper price to meet the needs of approved development, might be effective. The alternative would logically appear to be public control of land use through ownership rather than under statutory planning powers. But to introduce this by legislative enactment would involve many problems. Perhaps the future will for some time continue to hold alternating periods during some of which planning control will be popular and particular difficulties will be met by specific legislation, and during others will be unpopular and will lose force. In this way planning control may itself suffer from that piecemeal treatment which it is currently accused of allowing in place of the comprehensive planning which should be its aim.

PROPERTY, CITY PLANNING, AND LIBERTY

ALLISON DUNHAM
PROFESSOR OF LAW, UNIVERSITY OF CHICAGO

Planning literature in the United States has, on the whole, been unconcerned with the relationship of city planning to private property and to liberty.[1] Aside from the professional articles about how to plan, about needed factual research, and about the use by planners of the techniques of economic analysis used by private owners in making their own land-use decisions, the planning literature shows three phases of intellectual thought: there is, first, the phase, heavy in the first twenty-five years of planning but still an undercurrent in the literature, of trying to demonstrate the need for planning controls from the picture of chaos and squalor with which our nineteenth century cities leave us in the twentieth century;[2] there is, second, a great deal of theorizing about the place of the city planner in the power structure of urban government (is he, for example, to make governmental decisions himself, or is he only to make advisory plans on the basis of which action may or may not be taken by municipal officials as they choose?);[3] third, there is something in the literature from time to time about the need to permit the people to participate in planning in order that plans may be democratically arrived at.[4] Thus the planner has not been concerned about what should constitute

[1] If the 1950 issues of the Journal of the American Institute of Planners can be taken as a fair sample, the following is revealed: out of 17 main articles two dealt with general principles none of which concern the subject at hand, eight with specific planning, three with the need for research, one with the problem of putting plans into effect, that is, with governmental machinery, and the balance were general articles. The editorials consisted of exhortations on the need for planners to formulate agreed objectives, on how to get citizens to participate in planning, and on the danger of rigidity and the like.

[2] Illustrative of this approach is Lewis Mumford, The Social Foundations of Post-War Building (London, 1943).

[3] The best general treatment of this problem may be found in R. A. Walker, The Planning Function in Urban Government (Chicago, 2d ed. 1950). For the analysis of the place of a particular city planning commission in the power structure of government, see W. S. Sayre and H. Kaufman, Governing New York City (New York, 1960).

[4] See generally 1 Coleman Woodbury, The Future of Cities and Urban Redevelopment, and Coleman Woodbury, Urban Redevelopment Problems and Practices, both published by the University of Chicago Press in 1953. See also George Duggar, Urban Renewal Reexamined, 1957 Planning 209.

the respective spheres of private decisions concerning land use and of decisions centrally arrived at, but rather has proceeded with theoretical discussion on the assumption that centrally arrived-at decisions are made, and the problem from the planning point of view is to have the planner participate and yet to have the people participate as well through governmental machinery. About the turn of the century a satirical German weekly said that an economist should be defined as a person who went around with a ruler measuring workers' cottages, finding them all too small. A modern paraphrase of this might be that a city planner in the United States is a person who goes around taking pictures of all of the chaos in our cities and of all of the good things in our cities, finding the chaos due to private decisions and the good things due to centrally arrived-at decisions, at least if the planner and the people participated in the decision making.

My topic is more or less virgin territory for American planning. It is my impression as well that not until the catastrophe of the Town and Country Planning Act of 1947 did British planners exhibit any real interest in the delimitation of a sphere for private decision making.

In fairness to professional planners it must be admitted that until recently economists[5] and lawyers[6] gave regrettably little attention to the different aspects of urbanism. Theoretical economists on the whole followed Adam Smith's view that the problems of municipal government, "to wit, the proper method of carrying dirt from the streets and the execution of justice [in city regulation] . . . though useful, are too mean to be considered in a [theoretical] discourse of this kind." [7] Lawyers, too, are to blame. We have recognized the untruth of Blackstone's statement that the right of property is "that sole and despotic dominion which one

[5] While we have in the United States a school of "land economists," Professor Anthony Scott of the University of Toronto has pointed out that this whole school largely traces back to the concern of America for particular land problems such as conservation, see SCOTT, NATURAL RESOURCES: ECONOMICS OF CONSERVATION (Toronto, 1955).

[6] While it is true that much of the land planning in the United States can be said to be the product of lawyers such as E. M. Bassett, Alfred Bettman, Philip Nichols, and Frank B. Williams, the legal profession as a whole did not become interested in the theoretical aspects of the relation of law to city planning until much more recently. The earliest theoretical discussion may be found in ERNEST FREUND, THE POLICE POWER (Chicago, 1904). More recently see the articles by C. M. Haar referred to in notes 13 and 17 *infra* and my own articles, Allison Dunham, *Legal and Economic Basis for City Planning,* 58 COLUM. L. REV. 650 (1958), *City Planning: An Analysis of the Content of the Master Plan,* 1 J. LAW & ECON. 170 (1958), and *Flood Control via the Police Power,* 107 U. PA. L. REV. 1098 (1959).

[7] ADAM SMITH, LECTURES ON JUSTICE, POLICE, REVENUE AND ARMS 154 (Oxford, Cannan ed. 1896).

man claims and exercises over the external things of the world, in total
exclusion of the right of any other individual in the universe";[8] from
time immemorial the common law and statute law in England and the
United States have regulated land use.[9] It was a true statement only in
the sense that all of the great legal texts on property concentrated on the
transfer of rights and the creation of estates and left to others, primarily
to writers in torts, the task of dealing scantily with land use,[10] which the
property writers treated as analogous to assault and battery and other
personal injuries.

In constructing a theory about the relation of property law to planning,
we are not interested in the formal shape of property law — in such
matters as estates, future interests, and formalities of transfer. Bentham
tells us that property is nothing more than the expectation of deriving a
certain advantage from a thing which the law allows us.[11] We cannot be
interested in the technical legal aspects of property, for, under Bentham's
definition, private property today includes whatever limits on expectations
planning law has imposed, rightly or wrongly, during the past fifty years.
We must be concerned with a deeper question: what expectations should
the law allow a private citizen? To answer this question, in relation to
planning, we must think a bit about economics and the philosophy of
liberty.

A first point is this: If property is the established expectations which
the law gives an owner, then as long as the owner is not commanded
to use his property in a particular way and is secured some freedom of
choice as to its use, it cannot be said that government restriction on land
use has in it any denial of private property. Prohibition on the use of a
person as a slave, on the private use of land as a fort, military establishment, brewery, or as a factory in a residential district, may or may not
be wise economically, may or may not be a serious interference with

[8] 2 BLACKSTONE, COMMENTARIES 2 (15th ed. 1809).

[9] For examples of early legislation, see An Act for Rebuilding the City of London, 19
Car. 2, c. 3 (1679): An Act for Prevention of Common Nuisances arising by Slaughter-
houses, etc., Acts and Resolves of the Province of Massachusetts Bay (1692).

[10] More recently property books deal to some extent at least with the problem of land use
control. See, for example, GEOFFREY C. CHESHIRE, THE MODERN LAW OF REAL PROPERTY
116–137 (London, 8th ed. 1958); R. E. MEGARRY, A MANUAL OF THE LAW OF REAL
PROPERTY (London, 2d ed. 1955); R. R. B. POWELL, REAL PROPERTY (Albany, 1949), particularly vol. 6 (1958). It should be noted, however, that a standard treatise on real
property published in 1952 treated land-use problems as an afterthought in a separate
volume published in 1954, and even then had no material on city planning: AMERICAN
LAW OF PROPERTY (Boston, A. J. Casner, ed. 1952), vol. 6a (1954).

[11] See JEREMY BENTHAM, THEORY OF LEGISLATION 111–113 (London, Etienne Dumont,
ed., R. Hildreth, transl. 1864).

personal liberty, but such prohibition merely subtracts from an owner's expectations of enjoying a thing. Any particular use an owner can or cannot make of his property is not of importance to the existence of private property. This does not mean that a governmental decision to remove some one or more expectations from those which an owner previously had may not be costly to the individual or to society. We shall have more to say on this later.

A second point is this: society's objective in imposing a restriction of land use would likewise seem irrelevant to the system of private property. However wise or unwise for reasons of liberty and economic well-being it may be for a government planner to impose the ideas of a Geddes, Mumford, Stein, or Howard on the physical and social organization of a city, it is of little concern to the system of private property. That there is such a restriction is not important, but, and this is my main thesis, how that restriction is imposed is important for a system of property, and, as we shall see, how it is imposed, what the restriction is, and for what reason it is imposed may be important for liberty as well.

PRIVATE PROPERTY AND PLANNING

Prior to the advent of planning legislation about fifty years ago there was in the United States a great deal of land-use regulation (much more than many of us are inclined to credit), which on the whole presented no serious problems for private property as an institution. The regulation was stated abstractly, providing that in certain circumstances the actions of individuals must satisfy certain conditions. Thus a fire district would prohibit wooden buildings beyond a well-defined line in a municipality; or the regulations specified that a saloon could not be located within a given distance of a church or school. So far as private property was concerned, these regulations merely subtracted from the owner's possible expectations one or more methods of land use. So far as the owner was concerned, they became part of the data upon which he could base his decisions. So far as the lawmaker was concerned, he did not try to foresee the effect of these laws on particular people or for what purposes he would use them. The law prohibited wooden houses; it did not prohibit them unless the owner was building a house for his widowed mother or low-cost housing or a house of religion. Neither did the application of the law turn on the lawgiver's ends. It prohibited saloons near a church even if the operator of the saloon was determined by all observable standards to be a good churchgoer, even a member of the adjacent church. The owners built brick houses or buildings because they, not the lawgiver, wanted brick houses. These laws provided fixed features in the owner's environment, and although they eliminated certain expectations previously open to him they did not, as a rule, limit the choice to some specific action that somebody else wanted him to take.

The other type of restriction on private land use was judge-imposed through such common-law rules as nuisance. While these restrictions were admittedly less certain than the legislation previously referred to, the ideal was the same predictability and objectivity. Witness the requirement of written opinions containing reasons applicable to other situations, the principle of *stare decisis,* the assertion that judges were not making law but following previously established general principles and, most importantly, the principle that the judge had no purpose in mind when he imposed a restriction.

In its origin in the United States about fifty years ago planning law also was in the tradition of this legislation. The municipality was divided into districts, with the permitted and prohibited uses and structures fairly clearly set forth. While the ordinance might delete one or more expectations of an owner, thereafter within the bounds set by the zoning law the owner's choice was unlimited, not subject to the will or objective of any other person. Thus one of the fathers of planning in the United States, Edward M. Bassett, could object to a zoning ordinance which authorized an administrator to adjust the regulations at district boundary lines, on the ground that "every owner is entitled to know the exact boundary line. In building he can take into account the likelihood of the boundary being altered at some future day." [12] This principle of certainty and limited administrative discretion was also found in the official map acts and the early subdivision regulations. This attitude toward the form of the zoning regulation may also explain the unwillingness of our courts to be concerned with the requirement in almost all enabling acts that zoning be done in accordance with a "comprehensive plan." While such a plan might be useful in a constitutional argument as to reasonableness, it had no other value, for the governing law was the zoning ordinance passed by the legislative body [13] and not the asserted objectives or policies on which the planning officials had based the ordinance.

This general attitude toward law was also shown in the original

[12] E. M. Bassett, Zoning 51 (New York, 1940).
[13] See C. M. Haar, *In Accordance with a Comprehensive Plan,* 68 Harv. L. Rev. 1154 (1955).

legislation authorizing creation of master or comprehensive plans. Bassett objected very strongly to the adoption of the plan or policy by the legislature, and thought it proper that it should be adopted, if at all, by the planning commission. To him, the plan was policy on which law *could* be based, but it was not law because it was policy of the moment.[14]

More recently there has been a shift in attitude. Two instances may set the problem: the rise of a list of special uses for which development permission is needed,[15] and the increase in clauses in subdivision regulations which permit the administrator, usually the planning commission, to refuse permission on the ground that the proposed development does not conform to its master plan or policy.[16]

This raises serious implications for a system of private property. While private property does not presuppose freedom to engage in any particular action, it does presuppose an area of activity within which the private volition of an owner is free of arbitrary decision by others, that is, free of a decision based on another's policy.

This is one important aspect of the discussion initiated by Professor Haar of the master plan as an "impermanent constitution." [17] Although it moves quickly into another important question concerning democratic ideals such as the propriety of a plan having coercive effect if not adopted by the legislature, much of Professor Haar's discussion concerns the need for a rule of law by which to judge action.

He seems to recognize that a plan should be more than advisory so that it may become part of the owner's arsenal of facts on which to exercise choices concerning land use and, more importantly, part of the material which a court may use to determine whether the administrator is acting in accordance with law. This can mean only that it is more important for private property that an owner have a set of expectations

[14] See E. M. BASSETT, THE MASTER PLAN (New York, 1938); E. M. BASSETT, FRANK B. WILLIAMS, ALFRED BETTMAN, AND ROBERT WHITTEN, MODEL LAWS FOR PLANNING CITIES, COUNTIES, AND STATES (Cambridge, Mass., 1934).

[15] See Walter H. Blucher, *Is Zoning Wagging the Dog?* 1955 PLANNING 96; Richard F. Babcock, *The Unhappy State of Zoning Administration in Illinois,* 26 U. CHI. L. REV. 509 (1959); Note, *Zoning Amendments and Variances in Illinois,* 48 NW. U.L. REV. 470 (1953). For a judicial discussion of the matter, see Ward v. Scott, 11 N.J. 117, 93 A.2d 385 (1952).

[16] See H. W. LAUTNER, SUBDIVISION REGULATIONS (Chicago, 1941); see also Washington Revised Code (1951), § 58.16.060, which authorizes the planning commission in approving or rejecting a subdivision to "consider all other facts deemed by it relevant and designed to indicate whether or not the public interest will be served by the platting, subdividing or dedication."

[17] C. M. Haar, *The Master Plan: An Impermanent Constitution,* 20 LAW & CONTEMP. PROB. 353 (1955).

on which he can act than that he be permitted to do any particular thing. I might add that as far as private property is concerned it is not material whether the master plan be adopted by a legislature or a planning commission; the important thing is that it be adopted without knowledge of any particular case of land use; that it be definite enough so that it can be objectively determined whether administrative action conforms to it or not; and that it be adhered to when government action is taken.

We have developed various constitutional rules about unauthorized delegation of power — that there must be standards imposed on an administrator, and the like. While many cases have been decided on the basis of the ordinance giving the administrator standards by which to judge an application for a special exception or use, the important point of policy is that there must be some standards in order to give private property any meaning.

So far I have not been concerned with the merits of any planning scheme because the merits are not particularly relevant to the institution of property. That the town planning schemes of an Olmstead or Geddes are part of an antieconomic movement or present serious implications for personal liberty does not necessarily mean that the system of private property is endangered if the scheme is adopted by some government authority.

ECONOMIC POLICY AND LAND-USE RESTRICTIONS

If we shift from thinking about the nature of private property to thinking about the relationship between land-use restrictions and economic policy, then the character of the governmental restriction rather than its extensiveness or form becomes important. The institution of private property can survive if Lewis Mumford's conception of land use is adopted with certainty and inflexibility, but if we consider economic policy we must pass judgment on the merits of his plan. Judgment must be passed not only from an economic point of view, but also from the point of view of liberty.

Planning legislation in the United States, as distinguished from its administration, has made no frontal attack on the historic method of obtaining the optimum social welfare; it has accepted the principle that market prices are on the whole the best signals toward optimum welfare. This is not to say that the market pricing system, utilizing a host of individual decisions made for one's own ends, always operates at its optimum; price signals for example may not be received by those who make the decisions.

Urban living is a case in point. The enormous increase in productivity made possible by urban industry has been obtained at great costs which are to a large extent communal: they do not always fall on those who cause them and may have to be borne by all. A level of poverty perhaps tolerable in a rural atmosphere produces outward signs of squalor which are shocking to fellow men; the squalor and lack of amenities in urban living may make demands on community services beyond those for which the community is paid. Thus in many respects the contiguity of city life invalidates the assumptions underlying the market-pricing system. We have a proposition then which fits into the assumptions of the market system: the completely unrestricted use of urban land by its owners according to what each deems to be in his own interest leads to results injurious to all owners and consumers as a group. For the market to bring about an efficient coordination of individual endeavors, both private owners and the authorities controlling communal property must be compelled to take into account the effects of their action on other property. Insofar as planning legislation is negative and denies an owner a particular use in a particular location because of the cost which it imposes on others, it is operating within market principles by making the restricted activity settle in a more costly location and thus bear the costs formerly thrown on others.

The main theoretical difficulty comes in distinguishing restrictions imposed for this purpose from those imposed in order to secure a desired development, such as a Mumford plan. Are planning restrictions imposed on residential construction in industrial districts designed to relieve industry of the adverse effect of proximity to residences, or are they designed to obtain the advantages of reserving land for future industrial growth? Are the requirements in a subdivision development for long curving blocks with lots of greenery imposed because any other layout will cause harm to persons and property in the community who do not choose to live in the subdivision, or are they imposed because the planning authority desires that kind of layout for its own sake, or because it will enhance the value of neighboring properties?

The practical problem in the United States comes from the fact that under our written constitutions, as interpreted, we have not as yet been able to subject planning decisions by government authority to the tests of the market place. Most planning measures will enhance the value of some individual properties and reduce that of others. If the measure is to be beneficial to society the sum of the gains must exceed the sum of the losses, and to assure ourselves that this calculation is made as accurately as possible, the gains and losses must accrue to the planning authority. Why not impose a Mumford plan on private landowners if the governmental decider has no costs to bear? And if a Mumford plan is indeed beneficial to neighboring land why not coerce an owner to use the plan so as to benefit persons who happen to own the neighboring land?

An effective system would require that the government authority have the power and responsibility to charge the individual owner for the increase in value of his property due to a planning scheme (even if the benefit accrues against the will of some of the owners) and the power and duty to compensate those whose property has suffered. That we do not as yet have an effective way of achieving this balance is in part due to our constitutional history.

Although our colonial and postrevolutionary legal system offered many devices to offset these gains and costs, sometime in the early 1800's our courts adopted a set of rules which made this all but impossible.[18] In the first place, the courts tried to prevent government from expropriating property even though government was willing to pay a fair market price. They did this by adopting a rule of constitutional law that property could not be taken unless the end result was public enjoyment of the property taken in the same physical sense that a public highway or public building results in enjoyment by the public at large.[19] The effect of this requirement of "public use" was to prevent government from charging an individual owner for the benefit of a planning measure by expropriating his property at market price, then imposing the planning measure, and finally reselling the property to him or others at a price which reflected the benefit conferred. True, some of this could be accomplished through use of special improvement districts, but these operate only where a physical improvement is made.

The second legal difficulty imposed by the courts was a narrow interpretation of the government's duty of compensating those whose property had suffered from governmental action. Unless land was taken in a physical sense, many of our courts said, there was no constitutional

---

[18] See 2 PHILIP NICHOLS, EMINENT DOMAIN, §§ 7.1–7.21 (Albany, 3d ed. Julius L. Sackman and Russell D. Van Brundt 1950); Note, *The Public Use Limitation on Eminent Domain: An Advance Requiem,* 58 YALE L.J. 599 (1949).

[19] See NICHOLS, EMINENT DOMAIN.

requirement of compensation for damage which was called "consequential." [20]

The first of these two legal difficulties is the more serious because it imposes a real limitation on governmental power, but we are beginning to extricate ourselves by interpreting "public use" to be equivalent to public purpose. Thus, the United States Supreme Court recently permitted the federal government in the District of Columbia to condemn land near the capitol for the purpose of resale to a developer who would, by providing newer buildings and better arrangement, improve the amenities of the capitol.[21] Presumably because of other doctrines now worked out, the government in this case could have purchased the neighboring area not to be redeveloped and sold it back to the present or other owners at the increased value caused by the first redevelopment project.

The second of the legal difficulties is less serious because even if there is no duty to pay for consequential damage, there is no serious limitation on the power of government to choose to compensate those who suffer loss from a planning decision.[22] Government could, if it wished, establish a procedure similar to some provisions in English planning acts providing for a reverse expropriation — in certain circumstances a private citizen injured by a planning decision could compel government to buy his land.

The need to have gains and losses accrue to the same deciders is all that is necessary to have a proper accounting. Nothing is needed as complicated as the British Town and Country Planning Act of 1947, which attempted to secure for government not only the increase in value attributable to a planning decision but any increase in value, while at the same time putting all risk of loss on the owners, nor as monopolistic as that same act which gave government sole power to decide new uses of land in England.

The danger to economic policy and probably to private property and certainly to liberty comes in our system from not coordinating gains and losses, and also from the desire of many planners to be released from the necessity of counting all the costs of the scheme. We do not have anything comparable to the British planning acts, which compel the planning authority to buy land from a private owner if planning permission is

[20] *Id*. ch. 6; FREUND, POLICE POWER, §§ 507–510 (1910).

[21] See Berman v. Parker, 348 U.S. 26 (1954).

[22] Many states have amended their constitutions (for example, ILL. CONST. art. II, § 13) or have by statute given a right to damages for injury in some cases (for example, MASS. GEN. LAWS, Ter. Ed., 1936, ch. 79, § 9, as amended, St. 1938, ch. 172, § 7; MASS. GEN. LAWS, Ter. Ed., 1936, ch. 79, § 10).

refused. If I read the British planning literature correctly, this provision has had a salutary effect on planning decisions because of the necessity of counting costs; but I also read it as reflecting the same desire to be relieved of this necessity.

This desire, current in the planning literature of both countries, to be released from the necessity of counting all costs of a scheme ought, in my opinion, to be treated with great suspicion. If it is democracy we seek, nothing can be better calculated to induce voters to make rational choices than to compel them to ask: Do I really want this kind of development, considering its costs? If it is equality we seek, the necessity of government's counting costs assures that the costs will be borne equally throughout society. Although it is generally made to appear that reducing the costs which government must bear effects an absolute reduction of costs, in reality such a scheme merely transfers the costs to the shoulders of some private owner and then disregards them. The problem here, although often couched in the language of law, is in reality an ethical one of determining whether government should pay for the external costs which its decisions impose on others to the same extent that other planning legislation seeks to compel private decision makers to pay for the dis-economies which their decisions, made in the market, impose on others.

FREEDOM AND LAND-USE RESTRICTIONS

While the planning literature has expressed little interest in the economic, humanitarian, and private-property implications of planning decisions, it does abound with the terminology and criteria of private property — albeit used in another context. The literature of private property and of economic policy at times judges the merits or demerits of a proposal in terms of the security, protection, and predictability which it brings, and at other times in terms of its flexibility and adaptability. Thus it is said that the security and protection of private property in a market economy gives the economic system its flexibility and adaptability. Planning literature, too, talks about the need for flexibility and adaptability of plans, and about measures to secure and protect plans against inroads. The problem is that the more flexible and adaptable the planning scheme the greater may be the restriction on liberty; or to state it conversely, the more coercive the system may become.

I am not at this point using liberty or freedom as a function of the number of courses of action open after a planning decision has been made; rather I am using it to indicate the extent to which the pattern of conduct is of a man's own design and directed toward his own ends rather than toward positions created by others in order that he do what they want. In this sense, whether a man is free depends not on the range of his choice but on whether he can expect to shape his course of action in accordance with his own intentions. The range of physical possibilities from which a person can make an effective choice at a given moment thus has no relation to the freedom we are discussing. The driver of an automobile faced with impending danger who sees only one way to save his life is unquestionably free, though he may have no effective choice.

It should likewise be clear that liberty in this sense is not political liberty. I may enjoy the political liberty to turn the rascals out who have prevented me from building a gasoline station because they do not like gasoline stations, but I would not have freedom or liberty in the sense used here if I nonetheless need the consent of some government official. Nor is liberty used in John Dewey's sense as power to do specific things. In this sense a modern planner, at least quite frequently, has liberty, since he may under a subdivision regulation have power to effect his desire that all subdivisions resemble Radburn.

The problem of liberty or freedom in relation to planning is the inability of a property owner to anticipate the restraints which are to be placed upon him. As Maitland, the great legal historian, said, "Known general laws, however bad, interfere less with freedom than decisions based on no previously known rule." [23]

As suggested earlier, it is in relation to liberty that we see the real importance of the debate initiated by Professor Haar with our planners concerning the master plan as an impermanent constitution.[24] Whether restrictions on administrative action should be laid down by the general legislature or whether this function may be delegated bears on the question of democratic control of government but not on the question of freedom. The important point is that there be known rules announced prior to application to which the administrator must adhere. This, I take it, is what Professor Haar is asking for in matters where administrators can approve or reject private decisions concerning land use.

The problem of freedom is also involved in Bassett's very limited conception of city planning, which, as evidenced by his writings and the model city planning enabling act drafted by him,[25] emphasizes the location

---

[23] I E. W. MAITLAND, COLLECTED PAPERS 80 (Cambridge, Eng., 1911).

[24] See Haar, *The Master Plan.*

[25] SEE UNITED STATES DEPARTMENT OF COMMERCE, A STANDARD CITY PLANNING ENABLING ACT (Washington, D.C., 1928). See also BASSETT, THE MASTER PLAN.

of public improvements and minimizes the regulation of private land-use decisions. In the one case where the plan deals with major private decisions, the master plan is to be only the basis of the zoning ordinance. This conception reflects the differences in areas of permissible discretion in relation to freedom. Where government is directing and allocating resources put at its disposal, the professional administrator properly enjoys unlimited discretion in deciding what tasks to undertake and the means to be used in undertaking them. Here policy, meaning the aims of the government of the day, is important. Decisions as to upkeep, design, and location of roads and public buildings are necessarily of this kind and may be as flexible as the public administrator wants. Here government has little coercive power over the acts of private citizens and their own decisions concerning land use. Where this type of administrative decision impinges on the private sphere, the principle of no expropriation without just compensation serves as an important restraint on infringements on liberty. This is the case not because the landowner is paid, which justice may require, but because compensation tends to restrict the administrator's interference with the private sphere to cases where the public gain is clearly greater than the harm done by the disappointment of normal individual expectations.

The recent hassle in Illinois, where a community park board decided to condemn land for park purposes after the private developer had decided to build racially integrated housing, is illustrative of the difference. Assume that the purpose of the board's action was the dubious, if not illegal, policy of coercing the owner into adopting the community aims rather than his own. How much greater is the potential restraint on liberty if the community could deny permission to develop on the ground that "public welfare" would not be served or that the development is "not in accordance with community plans for development" than if, when it entertains these views, it must compensate the disappointed developer for loss of his development rights!

The difference in the two situations is illustrated also by the difference of the ideal in the two types of community action. The ideal where the administrator can deny permission to develop has been that his action is reviewable by a court in order to determine whether the action is in accordance with a rule of law; but in the case of expropriation the power of a court to control the decision to expropriate is ideally much less, actually not much more than a concept of *ultra vires*.

From the standpoint of freedom an administrator's decision need not be reviewable by a court if it is reviewable by someone as to its conformance with a previously announced rule. We do not have in the United States any procedure for a review of local planning regulations, and decisions under those regulations, by another administrator. The fact of review is not enough, however; the scope of the review is important. We do have in our subdivision control decisions in many states (and even in zoning decisions) a procedure whereby the decision of the administrator may be reversed by the local legislative body. But if the reviewing body, be it another administrator or a legislative body, merely substitutes its aim for another, our private citizen is still coerced into doing something because some other person wants it; only if he is reasonably free to do what he wants within the confines of a known rule of law can he be said to be free.

The tendency in American, as in English, planning has been away from these relatively simple concepts of Bassett. From the idea that law, be it legislation or previously announced regulation, should coerce private persons to do or not to do something, we have moved toward wider and wider administrative discretion. Thus many subdivision regulations are so indefinite that the administrator can reject a subdivision unless the private citizen agrees to the administrator's conception of amenities, appropriate layout, or even timing of development. This development parallels the "special exception" or "special use" development in the zoning ordinance to which I have referred.

From the standpoint of freedom or liberty it is no defense of this development to require that the administrative discretion be exercised only on the basis of the official's estimate of community sentiment, desires, or aims. Liberty in this sense requires that there be some sphere where a private citizen may serve his own ends and not the ends of state.

Another aspect of freedom or liberty is not as yet involved with planning in the United States, for we have no planning worthy of the name governing areas larger than counties.[26] True, the statute books authorize various forms of regional planning; these almost without exception permit, but do not require, the smaller units of government to participate in such planning if they wish. Insofar as the decision of a small unit of government to restrict certain kinds of private activity within its borders imposes external costs on neighboring areas, a case can be made for planning by some larger unit in order to minimize or

[26] See C. M. Haar, *Regionalism and Realism in Land-Use Planning*, 105 U. Pa. L. Rev. 515 (1957).

equalize the costs. Insofar as the small unit of government provides services of lesser quality than neighboring units, this may increase demands for the services of the neighboring unit and accentuate its governmental problems. It is not uncommon in the United States for prospective home purchasers to shop for schools and other services in deciding the suburb in which to live. This factor would not seem to justify a larger unit of government compelling a community with lesser services to increase the quality or quantity of its services, nor compelling one more attuned to consumer demands to reduce its quality and quantity. Insofar as there is economy in providing services such as water and sewerage for a larger group there is an argument for provision of these services by a larger unit. The question is whether economic forces can be allowed to induce the needed centralization or whether the smaller units should be compelled to join together. Undoubtedly there may be situations where circumstances require such coercion, but they would seem to be very few. Popular literature for regional planning of a coercive variety presents anew the question of individual liberty which we have been discussing, and perhaps another important liberty: freedom to associate with individuals of one's own choosing. The small unit of government serves as an effective check on tendencies to interfere with private choices, just as does the requirement for compensation on expropriation. For if the local unit plans or fails to plan itself so that it discourages economic development or community stability, economic pressures are likely to be a check on its extravagances.

In this paper I have not discussed one topic that interests many American planners, that of the relation of planning to democracy, although I think it could more accurately be termed the relation of planning to the principle that all men should have the same share in making governmental decisions. I have done this because it seems necessary to distinguish political liberty from the ideal of freedom and of private property. It provides no answer to what ought to be the relation of planning to private property and freedom to assert that the coercive decisions are democratically arrived at. We can agree that whenever coercive rules have to be laid down the decision ought to be made by the majority. We can also agree that where there is administrative discretion as to the use of resources subject to governmental control, democratic majorities are a useful method of allocation. When it comes to decisions about how private land ought to be used, democratic procedure is a useful and perhaps the only method available for determining whether a particular decision affects persons other than the deciders. But when it comes to such questions as whether development in a particular area should be sparse, as in a green-belt (as distinguished from a park or public recreation area), or whether industry which has no external effects should be located in an area already heavily developed, we have a question of which procedure best records the wishes of the consumer of the service — a Gallup poll by an administrator, a vote by a representative assembly, or the price signals in the market.

Planning in the United States does not yet seem too conscious of the possibility that the price mechanism is a more adaptable and flexible method of land-use allocation than a flexible plan administered by an inflexible administrator. Publicity of bureaucratic decisions is not enough; some philosophy about the relation of planning to liberty and to private property seems in order.[27]

[27] The best attempt at presenting the problems of liberty, democracy, and property is the imaginary dialogue by Professor Haar in LAND-USE PLANNING 730ff. (Boston, 1959).

The Making
and Effect of the Land Plan

THE DEVELOPMENT PLAN AND MASTER PLANS: COMPARISONS

JAMES B. MILNER

PROFESSOR OF LAW, UNIVERSITY OF TORONTO

THE EXPRESSION "development plan" is enshrined in a single British statute[1] and needs no justification or explanation beyond that which it is the purpose of this paper to unfold. The corresponding expression "master plan," however, has no universal statutory home in the United States, and some opinion has been expressed that the term is obsolete.[2] It is used here for convenience, and is intended as a generic term that includes all of the plans provided for in planning enabling acts throughout the United States.[3] "Master plan" is probably the most commonly used expression, but among the other terms "comprehensive development plan" is used at least once. The multiplicity of terms probably signifies no difference in meaning, particularly as the concept of community planning is far from settled. Indeed, these comparisons reflect throughout an inarticulate tension between the view that we can produce a settled plan to build and rebuild our cities closer to our heart's desire and the view that although we can engage in "planning" we cannot produce anything

---

[1] Town and Country Planning Act, 1947, 10 & 11 Geo. 6, c. 51, § 5, applicable to England and Wales [hereinafter referred to as the British Act]. Similar but separate legislation applies to Scotland: Town and Country Planning (Scotland) Act 1947, 10 & 11 Geo. 6, c. 53.

[2] See, for example, V. B. Stanberry, *Is the Term Master Plan Obsolete?* 15 AMERICAN SOCIETY OF PLANNING OFFICIALS NEWS LETTER 49 (1949), where the author objects to the rigidity implied by the term and defines a plan in fact as "a series of plans (as they exist at a particular date in the office of the planning agency) for various types of physical improvements in which efforts have been made to take into account the present and probable future needs of the community for such improvements together with some consideration of the interrelationships, especially spatial relationships, among the various physical features."

[3] Planning enabling acts in the United States are state statutes and are probably not available to English readers. Reference is made to a convenient summary, PLANNING LAWS (2d ed. 1958), a comparative digest of state statutes for community, county, regional, and state planning through December 1957, prepared by the Housing and Home Finance Agency, which may be obtained from the Superintendent of Documents, U.S. Government Printing Office, Washington 25, D.C. See also C. M. Haar, *The Master Plan: An Impermanent Constitution,* 20 LAWS & CONTEMP. PROB. 353 (1955), where different aspects of the various statutes are set out in tables for synoptic and comparative study.

reliable or durable that also has precision. Both law and practice vary
according to the degree of sophistication reached by the professional
planners, the legislators, and the body politic in any planning community
of whatever jurisdiction, local, county, regional, or state. An attempt to
reduce "planning" to a common denominator in the United States would
only be misleading.

It is customary to distinguish between planning and implementing the
plan, and this paper is limited to the first aspect of the planning process,
the preparation of the plan and the legal effect of the document or
documents comprising the plan. Only where it is necessary for the understanding of this aspect will reference be made to the legal devices for
implementing the plan: "planning permission," [4] as it is called in
England, the zoning ordinance,[5] subdivision control [6] and the public
works programs and the official street map,[7] as they are called in the
United States and Canada.

GENERAL PERSPECTIVE

The relative roles of the development plan and the master plan can be
better appreciated if some perspective is kept in mind about the two
systems generally. In particular, the central (national) government plays
a notably more important part under the British Act than the corresponding role played by the central (state) government under the American
acts. The mere fact that the British Act runs to over 200 pages in the
King's Printer edition, while the usual planning and zoning enabling
acts total about ten or twelve pages, indicates a much larger measure of

[4] Section 12 of the British Act requires permission to be obtained from a county council,
a county borough council, or where the authority has been delegated, under § 34(1) from
a county district council, for any development carried out after June 1, 1948. The meaning
of "development" is all-embracive, but subject to restrictions and special provisions too
elaborate to be mentioned here.

[5] English readers will find the zoning ordinance a rather optimistic document that
purports not only to divide the whole of a city into areas precisely defined, usually with
maps, where specifically listed uses only are permitted, but also to regulate the uses in great
detail, such as the setback of houses, the minimum side yards, and the like.

[6] The subdivision problem is particularly acute in the agricultural areas around cities,
where the land is owned in large parcels, perhaps 100 acres, and its sale is prohibited until
the design of subdivision is approved by some public authority.

[7] Public works programs are sometimes overlooked as planning control devices, but the
construction of a street and the supply of utilities at a strategic time may have more influence
on the private development of land than an easily amended zoning ordinance by an indifferent planning commission. The street map shows road widening and establishment
programs.

central dictation on details that are left entirely to local authorities in the United States. There is, of course, a whole scheme for the nationalization of development rights in the British Act on which all American acts are silent, and there are many provisions respecting the expropriation of land and the compensation to be paid that are not to be found in general planning legislation on this continent. But apart from this extra detail, the greater role of the central government is principally apparent from the powers given to the Minister to "approve" the development plan, along with which run subsidiary powers to direct the preparation of the plan by regulation. The scope of state executive regulation in planning is almost unexplored in the United States at the moment.

The degree of central control under the British Act is further exemplified by the fact that planning is compulsory and, subject to ministerial extension of the time, every planning authority was under a statutory duty to prepare a survey and development plan for approval by July 1, 1951, three years after the act took effect in 1948. In fact the Minister reported at the end of 1951 that 60 plans had been submitted and three approved.[8] By the end of 1959 there were still 12 plans or partial plans outstanding. Thirteen plans were approved during 1959, bringing the total to 142, comprising 64 county plans, 76 county borough plans, and two planning board plans.[9] The notion of compulsory planning is also almost unexplored in the United States, where planning may be described as voluntary, although there are many indirect pressures brought to bear on local governments to exercise their powers under the state enabling acts, where there are enabling acts.[10] Apart from the usual political pressures from the local inhabitants, an important incentive to plan comes from the operations of a federal agency, the Housing and Home Finance Agency, which grants money for housing, urban planning assistance, and urban redevelopment and renewal, and which requires that the grant be spent in fulfillment of some comprehensive plan. Despite these influences, however, planning has been undertaken by surprisingly few communities, although zoning, the principal device of planning control, early became popular in many municipalities. Planning is resorted to in perhaps half

[8] Report of the Ministry of Housing and Local Government for the period 1950/51 to 1954, CMD. No. 9559 at 150 (1955).

[9] Report of the Ministry of Housing and Local Government 1959, CMD. No. 1027 at 91, 192–193 (1959).

[10] PLANNING LAWS, *supra* note 3, indicates that 43 states had enacted enabling acts by the end of 1957, and Alaska and Hawaii, now states, as well as Puerto Rico, the Virgin Islands, and the District of Columbia had authorized community planning.

as many municipalities as zoning, although planning might be thought of as a rational basis for zoning and necessarily to precede it.[11]

The Schuster Report [12] gave prominence to a distinction between "positive planning" and "negative planning," which, if it has any validity, would suggest that the implementation of the development plan, and, to some extent, the plan itself, was "positive" and the master plan "negative." The distinction, however, seems to turn, not on the plan proposals, which are usually positive in both countries, but on the means taken to implement them. Negative planning seems to consist of setting forth positive proposals and then waiting until the proposals are carried out by private enterprise. In fact, the proposals in any plan will be to a large extent public undertakings, and whether the undertaking is commenced or not will depend upon the earnestness of the public authorities executing the plan. In this sense planning in the United States could often be said to be "negative," because the initiative to carry out the positive side of the plan is vested in a different body from the planning agency. In England, because of different political traditions, positive planning by local authorities is carried further than public works, for much of the residential building since the war has been so-called "council housing," erected by a local authority. Moreover, more elaborate programs for the location of industry have been undertaken by both the central and the local governments in the United Kingdom.

Any comparison of the British with the American legal system must take account of the difference between a unitary state and a federal state. Moreover, the Bill of Rights in the American Constitution, which renders every legislative, judicial, and executive act subject to judicial review, has no clear parallel in the United Kingdom. The so-called police power, under which planning legislation is said to be justified, appears to be a blurred statement of the residual power to legislate, vested in the states, coupled with the due-process requirement of the Fourteenth Amendment. The oversimplified proposition may be made that the state can legislate on planning and land-use control, but its legislation, and local delegated legislation, may be reviewed and may be upset on the ground that it is "unreasonable." In addition, of course, the local legislation may also be attacked on the ground that it is *ultra vires* the enabling acts.

[11] According to the International City Managers Association, of 1,347 cities over 10,000 in population reporting in 1953, 791 had enacted zoning ordinances but only 434 had adopted master plans showing the approximate location and alignment of future streets; but 756 cities had official planning agencies. THE MUNICIPAL YEARBOOK 283 (Chicago, 1953).

[12] Report of the Committee on Qualifications of Planners, CMD. No. 8059 (1950).

Although planning is a state rather than a federal function, the federal government influences planning indirectly. Mention has already been made of the program of the Housing and Home Finance Agency. Additional influences may be found in federal public-works projects and other national activities, including road building.

As to the scale of operation in America and Britain, the comparison should be between states and England and Wales. In terms of density of population, no state could compare closely with England and Wales, which have a population of about 44,000,000, and an area of about 58,000 square miles. New York State has a population of about 16,000,000, and an area of some 49,000 square miles. The state of Georgia is close in area to England and Wales, about 59,000 square miles, but its population is only about 4,000,000. Despite this lower density and the common notion that North America has land to spare, the urban land market in many parts of North America is as high, or, in some cases, higher than in England and Wales.

CONTENTS OF PLANS

If a comparison of development plans and master plans is to be anything more than idle chatter of a transcendental kind, it is essential that the content and legal effect of the plans be closely analyzed. In fact, such an analysis provides a basic perspective for any further analysis of planning and land-use control. And such an analysis should provide insight into the concepts of planning. Just as it is impossible to understand the concept of contract without a close examination of the remedies available for breach of contract, so it is impossible to understand the concept of planning without knowing the legal sanction and extralegal significance of plans, as well as their content, which is, of course, inextricably bound up in the analysis of their legal effect.

The British Act distinguished between the survey and the plan, but the survey is required to be made by law.[13] Although earlier planning acts in England had not given the same prominence to a survey, the importance of surveying before planning was well understood by that part of the planning profession that had come under the influence of Sir Patrick Geddes, whose *Cities in Evolution* (London, 1915) had predicted the evils of planning without surveying back in the early years of the century.

[13] Section 5(1).

This compulsory survey dictated by the Minister[14] requires maps and tables showing existing land use, the age and condition of buildings, quantities of building uses (the floor space devoted to a particular use), residential density, and land unsuitable for building purposes. In addition, information has to be collected respecting ancient monuments and buildings of architectural or historic interest, rural community structure, population change and movement, industry and employment, mineral assets, agriculture and forestry areas available for development with minimum economic loss to agriculture, road, railway, water and air transport, public utilities, social services, conservation and open areas, "holiday development," and proposed developments by government authorities. The extent of this survey can be easily imagined, and the personnel required to do it was probably not available between 1948 and 1951, which may account for the tardy appearance of most plans. By contrast, the Standard Planning Enabling Act,[15] adopted in many states, imposes the duty in very general language to make "careful and comprehensive surveys and studies of present conditions and future growth of the municipality and with due regard to its relation to neighboring territory"; most states have no provision at all; and none require the survey to be reported to any state authority. It cannot be concluded that because the enabling act does not demand a survey no such survey is in fact undertaken. Only an examination of the files in a planning commission office would show to what extent planning is intelligently carried on, but couple the absence of a statutory duty with a possible lack of zeal (North American planning agencies are quite obviously more zealous about land-use control than about land-use planning), and a foreigner may be forgiven if he suspects the worst.

Were it not for this curious silence in many of the enabling acts, further comment on the importance of the survey might be rather superfluous, but it should be clear that although the British Act may be totally impractical in making such onerous demands, the danger of planning without a proper foundation of fact can easily lead to gross injustices to the inhabitants of the planned area if the plan has either a

[14] Ministry Circular No. 40 (April 16, 1948). The information required is set out in some detail in C. M. HAAR, LAND PLANNING LAW IN A FREE SOCIETY, 58–59 (Cambridge, Mass., 1951).

[15] U.S. DEPARTMENT OF COMMERCE, A STANDARD CITY PLANNING ENABLING ACT (Washington, D.C., rev. ed. 1928). According to Haar, *The Master Plan, supra* note 3, table 3, the model act has been adopted in this respect by some 15 states. Some 26 states had no provision at all, and the remaining states have equally general provisions.

specific legal effect or a practical effect unsupported by legal sanctions. Just as the finding of facts in litigation may determine the outcome on the merits of the case, so may the basic facts determine a planning proposal. While combative trial techniques would be hopeless as a way of determining facts for a survey, the problems of adequate fact determination should not be ignored. The degree of accuracy itself is a matter for consideration, and the English practice is understood to accept approximation of an unspecified, and probably unspecifiable, degree. If a comparison with statutory interpretation may be permitted, the survey may be of help in interpreting the plan itself, if the implementary law requires the plan to be referred to. The survey then becomes part of the "legislative history" of the plan, history at which English courts forbid themselves to look!

Although the British Act requires a report of the survey as well as the plan to be submitted to the Minister, approval is required only of the plan. The ministerial control of the survey seems to be limited to ministerial circulars and orders[16] and to some unrecorded amount of informal control through departmental pressures and advice to local planning authorities. While the development plan must be published and sold at "a reasonable cost," there is no indication that the survey must be made available to the public at any time. It could, of course, be useful to private developers as well as to the local government. As a matter of drafting, the distinction between the survey and the plan is hard to draw and the plan may appear rather arbitrary without the survey data and explanations.

It is impossible to discuss with any sense of reality the content of plans. It is only possible to examine what the enabling acts either require or suggest about content, and, in explanation of the content, what the acts indicate to be the purpose served by the plan. Some notion of the intended purpose of both the development plan and master plans can be had from an examination of their intended contents, about which the British Act is more specific than the state acts.

A development plan shall indicate "the manner in which . . . [local planning authorities] propose that land in that area should be used (whether by the carrying out thereon of development or otherwise) and the stages by which any such development should be carried out." [17] So much is compulsory, but in addition the British Act authorizes the plan-

---

[16] See Town and Country Planning (Development Plans) Regulations, STAT. INSTR., 1948, No. 1767, and Ministry Circulars Nos. 40, 59, 63, 92, 95, and 97.

[17] British Act, § 5(1).

ning authority to show in its plan (1) the sites of proposed roads, public *and other* buildings and works, airfields, parks, pleasure grounds, nature reserves, and other open spaces; (2) the allocation of land for use for agricultural, residential, industrial, or other purposes of any class specified in the plan; (3) a designation of any land subject to compulsory acquisition by any Minister, local authority, or statutory undertakers (if the acquisition is likely to take place within ten years, or seven years in the case of agricultural land); (4) a designation of land in a defined area of comprehensive development in which designated land may be compulsorily acquired, the area being either "blitzed" or "blighted" or merely for replacement of open space or relocation of people or industry, or for the purpose of securing its use in the manner proposed by the plan; and (5) a designation of any other land which, in the opinion of the local planning authority, ought to be subject to compulsory acquisition for the purpose of securing its use in the manner proposed by the plan.[18]

The form and content of the development plan are further defined and circumscribed by the Town and Country Planning (Development Plans) Regulations of 1948,[19] which provide for a basic map and a written statement together with special maps, as applicable, showing comprehensive development areas, designated land, street authorizations, and a required "programme map."

Except for the difference in detail, the form of plan provided for in state enabling acts is not materially different, although the emphasis on the written statement is rather less evident. One early writer on master plans, Edward M. Bassett, conceived of a master plan as only a map: "Each of the elements of the plan set forth in this book . . . can be shown on a map." Elements that "cannot be shown on a map . . . do not constitute elements of the plan."[20] This view could hardly be said to prevail today, but only an examination of the plans themselves could show to what extent practice has kept up with changing fashions in planning.

Professor Haar's table[21] should be consulted for a list of the subjects for whose coverage explicit provision is made. The Standard Planning Enabling Act lists land use, size and use of buildings, population density, streets, public utilities, public structures, and recreation areas. While the majority of states include most of these subjects, some omit land use (!),

[18] Sections 5(2)–(3).
[19] *Supra* note 16.
[20] EDWARD M. BASSETT, THE MASTER PLAN 50 (New York, 1938).
[21] Haar, *The Master Plan, supra* note 3, table 3, "Contents of the Master Plan."

and some list one or more of conservation, slum clearance, urban redevelopment, public housing, public works programs, and government
expenditures. The subject of land use in the Standard Act is reflected in
the component of a zone plan, which should not be confused with the
zoning ordinance, a very different document. All that is intended in the
master plan is no more than is intended by the words "allocate areas of
land for use for agricultural, residential, industrial or other purposes" in
the British Act.

THE SCOPE OF PLANNING

There is every indication in the expanded lists of the subject matter of
planning that the new British comprehensiveness is gaining favor on this
continent; one of the potential factors strengthening this trend is the
indirect influence of the Housing and Home Finance Agency's requirement that its federal aid will only be made available if there is locally a
"workable program" which includes a "comprehensive plan for the
community as a whole." [22] The interest of the agency is obvious. It is
handing out money to local governments and private developers, and it
wants some assurance that the money will not be wasted.

Two features of the Housing and Home Finance Agency's requirements
point to a concept of planning more like that of the British Act and
foreign to the Standard Act. The first is the inclusion of the zoning and
subdivision control regulations in the comprehensive plan. To a limited
extent, this merging of the plan and its implementation, which is rather
out of step with American tradition, is characteristic of the actual operation
of the British development plan, which is really the closest parallel in
the British Act to the zoning ordinance.

The second feature is the requirement that the plan show the programming of public works and redevelopment. This notion was rejected by
Bassett, who, in his chapter on "What is not community land planning"
expressly considered "fixing the time for beginning various improvements" and discarded it as not planning.[23] The development plan must
indicate the stages by which the development should be carried out. Some
American opinion can be cited that good planning requires careful
attention to timing. Henry Fagin has advanced five planning bases for
timing control: (1) the need to economize on the costs of municipal

---

[22] See the Housing Act of 1949, 63 Stat. 414 (1949), as amended by the Housing Act
of 1954, 68 Stat. 622 (1954); 42 U.S.C. §§ 1451–1460 (1958).
[23] BASSETT, THE MASTER PLAN, at 51.

facilities and services; (2) the need to retain municipal control over the eventual character of development; (3) the need to maintain a desirable degree of balance among various uses of land; (4) the need to achieve greater detail and specificity in development regulations; and (5) the need to maintain a high quality of community services and facilities. Mr. Fagin suggests that suitable regulations be designed to set up zones of building priority and to regulate the tempo of building, to be "administered pursuant to soundly based municipal planning policy." [24] This growing concept of the planning function has led Professor Haar to comment that the province of city planning "is now extended to almost unlimited horizons." [25]

The trend to all-inclusiveness brings with it two dangers. The first Professor Haar pointed out himself, the danger that the plan may "be rendered diffuse, ambiguous, and meaningless as a base for action when land development and redevelopment actually occur . . . The 'big picture' may be blurred by the insistence on handling all factors." [26] The extent of this danger will depend on the legal significance of the plan, which is not so material as to make this danger very real.

The second danger has been pointed out from time to time by economists and legal commentators more concerned with economic theory than most lawyers or planners tend to be. Perhaps the most stimulating presentation is Professor Dunham's recent attack[27] on all-inclusiveness of plans, and his interesting attempt to justify Bassett's much narrower view, by advancing reasons which Bassett himself never articulated. Professor Dunham's theory seems to be that so far as the elements of economy and efficiency are concerned in public works, municipal departmental planners can be counted on to make as good decisions as the central planner, but when the decision of one department may be incompatible with that of another, the central planner coordinates so that, in his opinion, the gain to total welfare exceeds the loss to consumers of municipal services resulting from a departure from the most economic and efficient first choice

[24] Henry Fagin, *Regulating the Timing of Urban Development*, 20 LAW & CONTEMP. PROB. 298, 300–302 (1955). See Professor Dunham's criticism of this view in *City Planning: An Analysis of the Content of the Master Plan, infra* note 27.

[25] C. M. Haar, *The Content of the General Plan: A Glance at History*, 21 JOURNAL OF AMERICAN INSTITUTE OF PLANNERS 66, 68 (1955).

[26] *Id.* at 70.

[27] Allison Dunham, *City Planning: An Analysis of the Content of the Master Plan*, 1 JOURNAL OF LAW AND ECONOMICS 170 (1958) and in a slightly different form, 58 COLUM. L. REV. 650 (1958). Subsequent references are to the article in the JOURNAL OF LAW AND ECONOMICS.

of the departmental planner. In this view the city manager, if there were one, would presumably do all the necessary planning, and a planning commission would be supernumerary.

Professor Dunham's view of the planning of land uses rejects the notion that the state should control a private development solely for the benefit of the ultimate consumers of its services because this control would amount to an "extraordinary power of meddling with the choices of the sovereign consumer." [28] He draws an analogy, which I find difficult to follow, with the supposed impropriety of a possible control of automobile color design. Two differences are at once apparent. First, it is easy to have an abundance of choice in automobile colors, and second, the automobile is easily repainted, it has a probable life of ten years, and its ownership is easily transferable during that life. If tastes change, no great economic cost is involved in satisfying new tastes. Variety in housing style or location is not great, and changes are expensive. Housing is relatively permanent, its life expectancy is around fifty years, in some cases one hundred, and it is very nearly stationary. For these reasons the choice of the private developer (which is more significant than the supposed choice of the sovereign consumer, who has to choose, usually, from limited offerings) not only has an impact on space but also in time. It is hardly necessary to apologize for a concern over the impact of development on succeeding generations since this is a first principle of ethics and politics as well as planning. The private developer's interest in time may be limited to the mortgage term. By this time consumers' choices are predetermined, a little short of "sovereign," and the case for state participation in the predetermination is stronger than Professor Dunham suggests.[29]

[28] *Id.* at 177.

[29] Professor Dunham has defended his illustration in a letter to me: "I picked the car paint job as an illustration for several reasons. First it is an area of our economy where the financial loss due to obsolescence or change in styles is fantastic. There is nothing in housing comparable to the 50% loss in the first year of a new automobile, a loss due to style changes rather than depreciation. While it is true that housing represents a greater share of the consumer's savings, if he owns his house, than does an automobile, it is not clear to me that the 50% loss in the value of a car in the first year is for most car purchasers less of a drain on his savings than is the 5% to 25% loss in the value of housing. Secondly I picked the color job on automobiles to compare with housing because this, like the housing situation, is an area where the loss or "cost" to the individual buyer is completely economic. I excluded from consideration losses to health and the like where the housing is improperly located. Since the loss is completely economic, the permanence and life expectancy of the house is irrelevant, no house purchaser must remain in his house as long as its economic life expectancy, just as no automobile purchaser must own an automobile until it becomes salvage in the physical sense. There are very few areas of our legal society where we interfere with consumer choices solely for the purpose of protecting him against rash economic decisions. The automobile was picked for a third reason, and indeed this is

Professor Dunham concedes that when the design of private development affects surrounding lands in the community the central planner may
control the development, but only if his government has intervened for
the purpose of benefiting the surrounding lands by the impact of the gov-
ernment-aided development. There may be cases where the government
may be aiding the development solely for the benefit of the consumers,
in which case he thinks the central planner has no role to play. Thus if
housing subsidies are provided, without requiring integration of the
scheme into a comprehensive plan, it could be because the housing is
wanted regardless of its impact on the surrounding lands.

That a government should undertake housing subsidies of this sort
without first consulting the central planner would seem to risk investment
in an area destined to redevelopment later. In any event, some aspects of
any development would seem to risk harm to neighboring lands: changing
road patterns, increasing density of population, and the like, which should
concern the central planner.

In the direct control of land use by zoning, Professor Dunham's restrictive theory would produce a much lesser degree of control than is often
supposed to be justified under more liberal theory. He distinguishes between "restricting a private decision concerning land in order to prevent
an external harm and restricting a private decision in order to confer a
benefit on persons other than the property owner." [30] In the first case,
the external harm is prevented as much by nonuse of the private land as
by a positive use permitted by the law. This position could be coextensive
with the common law of nuisance. In the second case, it is positive use
that is desired, because use of the land in a particular way is necessary to
confer the benefit. The serious objection, of course, arises when positive use

the most important one, because it was an area where I thought society had on the whole
indicated that it would allow the consumer to make his free choice either on the assumption
that it was not worth protecting him or on the assumption that there was no reason considering the characteristics of the consumer to protect him against ignorance and the like. All of
the studies which I have seen of the characteristics of the house buyer indicate that he is
better educated, has a higher income, and uses services available to make the most rational
possible choice in housing purchases than the public as a whole. While I have seen no
studies made of the characteristics of the automobile consumer, I would have no hesitance
in asserting that the housing consumer is, according to all the standards we have used in
other areas to impose regulations on consumer choice, better able to take care of himself
than is the automobile consumer and the consumer of other services where we have regulated
the quality of the supply. The issue, it seems to me, is whether the housing consumer as a
class is so likely to make irrational choices that he needs protection. I know of no principle
which asserts that a class of persons should be protected against mistaken choices simply
because the cost of the mistake is high."

[30] *Supra* note 27, at 180.

of the land, demanded by the state for the supposed external benefit, is wholly paid for by the owner, who is required to assume this cost rather than share it with those benefited. This problem is implicit in the use of the zoning device, and the general assumption that zoning advances the public good should be reconsidered in terms of compensation and betterment. Clearly, as Professor Dunham says, the British Act is more concerned about this question. It should be pointed out, however, that there is an easy assumption that the costs and benefits to which Professor Dunham refers can be measured, but he says nothing about how it is to be done.[31]

The difference seems to be that in an area where judgments must be made of unmeasurables, Professor Dunham prefers a major premise of "hands off," and Professor Haar is reporting on the planners whose major premise is that every land use is inextricably related to every other land use. In these circumstances the personnel and procedures of decision making are as vital as its rationalization, but Professor Dunham's wise caution should not be underestimated; it means that the Americans must worry more about compensation and betterment. In particular, Professor Dunham draws attention to the unsatisfactory state of the tax laws.

One further aspect of the contents of the plan is raised by confusion of the notion of planning with prediction. There are strongly divergent views about planning that stem not from confusion, perhaps, but from conviction, that a planner must submit to the inevitable. The *plan* then becomes a mere *prediction,* and the planners are content to establish one authoritative predicting body. Other planners are equally convinced that planning should consist of a choice of competing courses that the community might take, and they reject the view that man's communities are made for him by some new brooding omnipresence over which he has no control. Nothing in the legislation of the English Parliament or the various states would compel a planner to take either view, assuming the dichotomy could be as sharp as it is presented here, but the regulatory detail of the British administration and the traditions of its planning profession suggest that there is more faith in choice of action there than in the United States.

[31] *Ibid.* Professor Dunham quotes J. J. Dukeminier, Jr., *Zoning for Aesthetic Objectives: A Reappraisal,* 20 LAW & CONTEMP. PROB. 218, 224 (1955): "According to our basic social hypotheses, this intervention should occur only when community values are *seriously* damaged or threatened by specific uses of land." So far as I am aware one cannot measure "community values," and "*seriously* damaged" reminds me of tort talk about being *grossly* negligent.

One of the inescapable characteristics of the English planning profession is its origin in the related professions of architecture, engineering, and surveying. This bias, which some observers have thought would exclude appropriate consideration of economic, political, and social aspects of planning,[32] may account for the greater emphasis on design in British town planning writing. Assuming that design means the physical coordination of buildings, streets, and other open spaces so as to help achieve the social ambitions of a community, the location of buildings and even their architecture may be a concern to the planner, who may agree with a remark of Winston Churchill that "we shape our buildings and afterwards our buildings shape us."[33] Anyone familiar with Thomas Sharp's *Oxford Replanned* (London, 1948) will realize to what a considerable extent that distinguished planner was concerned with the three-dimensional approach. These planners start their thinking with the premise that a city consists of buildings and space, and any planning of the city must therefore plan the buildings and the spaces. This view does not exclude consideration of the social factors, but the emphasis of the design school is very different, or is believed to be, from the emphasis of the economic school.[34]

In one respect the development plan differs from almost all master plans, so far as the enabling legislation reveals; the development may designate lands as subject to compulsory acquisition. This does not amount to expropriation, but it does announce to the landowners affected that their land may be taken within the statutory period. It also encourages coordination of compulsory acquisition policies, a desirable end in itself. But the effect of this device on the landowner can only be surmised. Since development plans must be reviewed every five years, owners of land are never quite sure whether they are free from designation (and possible acquisition) in the next ten years, or, having been designated, whether they may be dropped from the list. The effect of this uncertainty on market values is equally uncertain. The British Act protects the owner if his land is in fact acquired after being designated, and "no account shall be taken of any depreciation in the value which is attributable to the designation."[35] But the injury to the owner's interest during designation and before acquisition is not provided for. Maintenance and alienation present

---

[32] See, for example, *The Achilles Heel of British Town Planning,* app. A in LLOYD RODWIN, THE BRITISH NEW TOWNS POLICY (Cambridge, Mass., 1956).

[33] 393 H.C. DEB. (5th ser.) 403 (1943).

[34] See the Schuster Report, *supra* note 12, esp. paras. 66–72; and RODWIN, BRITISH NEW TOWNS POLICY.

[35] Section 51(3).

very real problems. The relief, if any, lies in the opportunity to be heard at the time of the five year review.

THE LEGAL EFFECT OF PLANS

Whatever may be the content of a plan, and the directed content of the development plan is more likely to be realized than the suggested content of the master plan, there remains the question of its legal effect. A good comprehensive plan could be produced by a community in a state that has no enabling legislation, and the plan would have no appreciable legal effect. It does not follow that it would have no operative effect. No sanctions would attach to its disregard in the future development of the community. But its operative effect might be just as burdensome, or confer just as real benefits on landowners, depending upon its voluntary acceptance by the community. A good plan, imaginatively presented, could easily take hold in a community whose local sentiment was strong and directed sympathetically with the plan's goals. But advisory plans of this sort rarely have a chance to be proven in the United States, where most communities, if they decide to plan, invoke local planning legislation.

Under the compulsory planning system in England the legal effect of the plan is apparent, if not real. Although nowhere said to be binding on anyone, the development plan is not easily disregarded in the subsequent development of the community. The British Act "froze" land uses as of July 1, 1948,[36] and except where development is permitted by special order, or is deemed not to be development, "planning permission" must be obtained from the local planning authority or its lawful delegate. In dealing with the application for planning permission the local planning authority "shall have regard to the provisions of the development plan, so far as material thereto, and to any other material consideration."[37] Having regard to a plan hardly makes the plan binding on the local authority, but since the Minister could make a development order[38] authorizing the local planning authority in certain circumstances to grant permission for development that does not accord with the provisions of the development plan, it was implied that the authority must do more than "have regard." The Town and Country Planning General Development Order of 1950,[39]

---

[36] Section 12(1). The act does not prohibit development, it merely requires the developer to ask permission. This produces curious results where development is undertaken without permission. These matters are discussed in detail under another topic.
[37] British Act, § 14(1).
[38] British Act, § 14(3).
[39] STAT. INSTR., 1950, No. 728, art. 8.

limited the occasions to those which the Minister directed, subject to such conditions as he chose to prescribe in the directions. With this added discouragement, one might conclude that the development plan at this stage was binding on the local planning authority and the local authorities within the area of the plan in respect of future development.

In 1954, however, the Minister issued the Town and Country Planning (Development Plans) Direction, which permitted a local planning authority to grant planning permission that did not accord with the plan, provided the authority was of the opinion that the development would neither involve a substantial departure from the plan nor injuriously affect the amenity of adjoining land. This language would appear to preclude judicial review, and the Minister did not impose any sanctions administratively.

Perhaps the Minister did not have to add to existing procedures, since he could "call in" any application for planning permission and decide it himself.[40] Of course, he would have to hear about it first, and the local planning authority had no duty to report applications that in *its* opinion accorded with the plan. Neighbors could hardly be expected to inform on each other or on the planning authority. The Minister did require other applications (that did not accord in the authority's opinion) to be submitted to him, and he allowed himself three weeks to refuse them or to give further directions before the local planning had authority to grant the permission. Whenever the local planning authority did grant permission that did not accord they were required to send the Minister a copy. Furthermore, the Minister could always revoke or modify any planning permission before building operations had been completed or a change of land use had taken place,[41] but such an unusual retroactive power would presumably be exercised only in extreme cases.

Both of these procedures, of calling in and of revoking or modifying, were in the original act and could not have been thought of as especially applicable in a situation only arising after the 1954 Direction was introduced. No further legal or psychological limitation seems to have been imposed on the freedom to disregard the plan, except that in the accompanying explanatory circular[42] the Minister exhorted the authorities not to abuse their new privilege.

[40] British Act, § 15. The Minister called in the notorious Piccadilly Circus application. For an account of the earlier history of the application see Bernard Levin, *The Monster of Piccadilly Circus,* Spectator, Dec. 11, 1959, p. 861.

[41] British Act, §§ 21 and 100(2).

[42] Ministry Circular No. 45/54, June 25, 1954, reprinted 1954 JOURNAL OF PLANNING AND PROPERTY LAW 581.

In practice, of course, legal effect depends on how the plan is drafted, whether it is silent on a crucial matter, whether there is any built-in flexibility, or whether it is rigidly written. Since land use has to be allocated to areas, the definition of those areas is most important. The basic map presumably outlines the area, but on a scale of one inch to one thousand feet the lines would not be very precise. It also matters to what extent, if any, the plan contains any regulation of use, as distinct from allocation of use, or whether this is left to be settled as a condition of granting planning permission. Yet most plans are singularly silent on these vital details.

In the United States, the Standard Act provides for a very limited legal effect. Because of the fragmented local jurisdiction it is necessary to determine what the legal relation of the master plan is to public works, the official street map, subdivision control, and zoning.

To the extent that the master plan governs the public-works program or the official street map, it may be said to fetter the freedom of the legislative body — the local council — in the regular course of its activities. A common provision states that when the commission has adopted the master plan no street, square, park, or other public way, ground, or open space, or public building or structure, or public utility, whether publicly or privately owned, shall be constructed or authorized in the municipality or in a planned section or district until the location, character, and extent thereof shall have been submitted to and approved by the commission, but the commission must give reasons for its disapproval and the council may overrule the disapproval by a two-thirds vote.[43]

The adoption of the plan by the *planning commission,* regardless of its contents, operates to confer a power of review and approval on the commission that the council can only avoid by a two-thirds vote. In one case the suggestion was advanced that even if the vote was secured, the commission could only be overridden if the council found that it was wholly arbitrary.[44] The extraordinary vote is a frequent provision, but in some states only a majority of the entire council is required (not a majority of a quorum), and in some cases the requirement is only that the council's proposal be submitted for review. In California, where the master plan has to be adopted by the council,[45] there is no power in the planning commission to delay action pending an extraordinary majority vote; the pub-

[43] Cf. The STANDARD PLANNING ACT, *supra* note 15. The section paraphrased is from the Alabama act, PLANNING LAWS, *supra* note 3, at 1.

[44] Gratton v. Conte, 364 Pa. 578, 73 A.2d 381 (1950).

[45] PLANNING LAWS, *supra* note 3, at 7.

lic works proposal is merely to be submitted to and reported on by the planning commission. What happens if the commission decides to delay its report is not provided for, but since no particular status is given the report, its absence after a reasonable time is presumably irrelevant. A number of states specify a number of days — for example, New Jersey specifies forty-five days — after which the works authority may proceed without the planning commission's recommendation. The New Jersey provision contains the interesting addendum making it apply to "action by a housing, parking, highway or other authority, redevelopment agency, school board, or other similar public agency, Federal, State, county or municipal." [46] Just how far a municipal planning commission could delay a federal agency acting within its constitutional jurisdiction is not clear. The provision might, of course, operate in a practical sense for political reasons. Indeed the sanction of the commission's planning point of view in most cases is no more than the effect of publicity, but experience has shown, particularly in times of political crisis, that the advice of an advisory planning commission secures a good deal of public support, and a council disregards it at its peril, even by extraordinary vote. The curious result is that even if the council complies with the plan it has no assurance that it will not have trouble from the commission.

The 1955 Indiana legislation is the most detailed in its delineation of the master plan's contents, and the plan has a more precise effect. After adoption by the commission the council "shall be guided by and give consideration to the general policy and pattern of development set out in the master plan" in public works programs, and within the corporate limits of a city, and on unincorporated lands within the jurisdiction of the commission, "A structure shall not be located and an improvement location permit for a structure on platted or unplatted lands shall not be issued unless the structure and its location conform to the master plan and ordinance." [47] This master plan apparently operates only as a guide to the council, but binds the private developer in the same fashion as a zoning ordinance. In its effect on public works the plan, then, is of secondary importance, both to the council and the private developer. At the most, it can only require the council to take second thought. As for the developer, it is no more than a suggestion of the course of future action by the council and the planning commission.

Of primary importance, when there is one, is the official map. Unlike

[46] *Id.* at 43.
[47] *Id.* at 19–20.

the plan, the map has a clear, specific legal significance and it parallels the development plan's designation of land: it designates the land to be acquired for streets and parks. The municipality protects itself against the higher cost of acquiring land for streets by providing that no compensation will be paid for structures erected on the "designated land." This street map is rarely a part of the plan, the Bassett fetish for plasticity having led him to distinguish the carefully drawn map, imposing liabilities on landowners, from the master plan, an innocuous document in the files of the planning commission for its own guidance in the exercise of its power of approval. Moreover the street map is an old institution, having been in use for almost a century before planning became fashionable.[48] Most planning commissions are authorized to plan streets, and their master plan, containing an "unofficial" street map, may warn developers away from building on land shown as a future road or park. Even though the developer may know that he is entitled to compensation if he builds and the street is later established, he will not likely be interested in building anything substantial that he or his purchaser may be forced to sell in a few years. Of course neither the plan nor the official map obliges a municipality to carry out any projected development, and the developer under the official map system has perhaps less protection than the British developer, whose land must be taken within a specified period or the designation removed.

Apart from street plans, the whole character of a subdivision and development of a large parcel for multiple neighborhood uses may come within the influence of the master plan. The Standard Act requires a subdivision to be approved by the planning commission before filing with the land registry, and it requires the commission to adopt general regulations before exercising approval, but it is clear that the master plan does not dictate the terms of the regulations, which are themselves, therefore, a kind of special plan, and the subdivision platting, upon approval, constitutes an addition or an amendment to the master plan. Far from being controlled by the plan, it becomes an integral part of the plan. Only Illinois appears to require that the subdivision plat must conform with the master plan.[49] In many states, the platting regulations are enacted by

[48] I accept Professor J. H. Beuscher's statement of history. See his excellent account (with J. C. Kucirek) of the street map, *Wisconsin's Official Map Law: Its Current Popularity and Implications for Conveyancing and Planning*, 1957 WIS. L. REV. 176.

[49] Haar, *The Master Plan, supra* note 3, table 4. Professor Beuscher tells me that Wisconsin controls subdivisions by the master plan. For a review of current legislation, see *An Analysis of Subdivision Control Legislation*, 28 IND. L.J. 544 (1952–53), especially the tables at 574–586.

the local council, sometimes with the recommendation of the planning commission.

The control of major significance to the private developer of land is the zoning ordinance, which made its appearance long before master planning became fashionable. Many states have adopted the Standard State Zoning Enabling Act.[50] After authorizing councils to regulate land use, the act provides that "such regulations shall be made in accordance with a comprehensive plan." It might be thought that the "comprehensive plan" referred to was the master plan. This view would be buttressed by the Standard Planning Act's provision that the plan should include "a zoning plan for the control of the height, area, bulk, location, and use of buildings and premises." Most states have this or a similar provision. The interlocking requirements of two model acts produced by the same body might have led to the conclusion that the comprehensive plan in the Standard Zoning Act was the zoning plan in the Standard Planning Act. Had this view been taken by the courts the master plan would have become a much more important document legally, for no zoning ordinance would have been valid unless it were preceded by a master plan with which it accorded. The operative effect would have been rather limited, for the zoning ordinance could always be accorded with the master plan by changing the master plan. Since the council is usually required to adopt the zoning ordinance (although the planning or zoning commission may prepare it), the private developer seeking an amendment would have to obtain it from two different public bodies.

In fact, however, the courts have not taken the view that the "comprehensive plan" must be the master plan.[51] The historical sequence of events ran counter to the logical sequence of planning and then implementing the plan. The zoning ordinance preceded planning in most municipalities. The variations possible on the term "comprehensive plan," once it is accepted that the master plan is not meant, are almost infinite, but cannot be discussed here.

Under the British Act, where no provision is made for the regulatory provisions of the zoning ordinance, the local planning authority, not having any detailed rules, will study each application for planning permission

[50] ADVISORY COMMITTEE ON ZONING, U.S. DEPARTMENT OF COMMERCE, A STANDARD STATE ZONING ENABLING ACT (rev. ed. 1926).

[51] Professor Haar points out that by the end of 1927, before the Standard Planning Act was published, 29 states had adopted zoning legislation based to a large extent on the Standard Act. C. M. Haar, *In Accordance with a Comprehensive Plan*, 68 HARV. L. REV. 1154 (1955).

on its merits, "having regard to the development plan." The legislative body is thus not expected to exercise the wisdom of Job and to make decisions on potential applications in advance by general rules, which is the function of the zoning ordinance. The British method, however, produced an estimated 400,000 applications for planning permission in the year ending March 31, 1958, of which 360,000 were approved, with or without conditions. From the 40,000 refusals 9,068 were appealed to the Minister.[52] The degree of discretion and the applicability of the development plan is illustrated from this case referred to in the Ministry's report for 1959:

The Leicestershire County Council refused permission for a house to be built on the main street of the small, charming village of Swithland within Charnwood Forest — an area described in the development plan as one of outstanding landscape value.[53] The grounds for refusal were that the materials chosen for this building — straw coloured bricks and purple roofing tiles — were unsuitable in a place where the traditional materials were Swithland stone and slate. The council said that they would be ready to give permission if the walls were finished in stucco or colourwash, the roof clad in grey slates, and some features finished in local stone.

At the local inquiry . . . The appellant argued that a previous appeal concerning a house he was building on an adjacent plot had been allowed by the Minister, although the council had stipulated exactly the same conditions about building materials. Local stone and slate would add materially to the cost of the house. The village, he considered, was very drab and needed brightening up.

The Minister did not agree that the two cases were identical. In allowing the previous appeal he had said that grey bricks and tiles were not out of keeping with the character of the village; this proposal was concerned with straw-coloured bricks and purple tiles. The design, which was similar to that of the other house, was suitable for a single isolated dwelling . . . The Minister . . . dismissed the appeal.[54]

The existence of a comprehensive zoning ordinance does not guarantee a complete domination of the "rule of law," however, because zoning ordinances may be amended in respect of individual properties, although the amended ordinance must still accord with some unidentified comprehensive plan. Such amendments may be dubbed unconstitutional "spot zoning," that is, zoning a small parcel of land for some profitable use apparently incompatible with surrounding uses. There may, however, be

[52] *Supra* note 9, at 98.
[53] It is not clear that the development plan said anything else relevant to the application.
[54] *Supra* note 9, at 99–100.

good planning reasons for creating such zones, and where the reasons are set out in the master plan attack by aggrieved landowners will be less likely to succeed. If the master plan is adequately publicized and understood the attack might be avoided altogether. Although it has no positive legal connection with the zoning ordinance, the master plan thus has a potential value if the council and planners can agree to use it. Whether the future course of enabling legislation should give the plan a greater status depends largely on the development of planning concepts. If the master plan can be made in fact a thorough study and a reasonably stable statement of the long-term needs and goals of the community, conformity with such a plan might be a valuable limitation on the council's freedom of judgment. While strong political pressures would be brought from time to time to change the plan to permit a rezoning, the redirection of the council's thinking from the immediate demand to the long-term requirement would probably protect the long-term interest adequately. Of course, such good judgment can be exercised by councils without the trappings of planning legislation; the trappings are only important because they guide the more short sighted councils in the "right" direction.

Such being the tenuous legal effect of the development plan, and the rather more tenuous legal effect of the master plan, the cogency of the effect is still subject to another factor, the ease with which the plan can be amended to change its operative effect. Generally speaking, in both countries the plan can be amended as it was made, by the same agencies and with the same procedures. The procedure under the British Act makes amendment less convenient, but a regular five-year review of the survey and the plan is mandatory, again with the requirement of ministerial approval. By the end of 1959 a total of 72 approved plans had been amended, but the frequency of submission of "proposals for alterations or additions submitted under section 6" of the act seems to be increasing: there were 15 in 1955 and 82 in 1959.[55] In the four-year interval the number of approved plans increased considerably. The development plan thus seems to be a somewhat more stable instrument than the master plan, judging, as far as one can, from the legislative schemes whereby each is set up.

The intending developer will be more concerned with the implementary laws than with the master plan if he is buying the land he intends to develop and is taking the prudent course of investigating planning controls along with the traditional dangers of defects in his title. The master plan will present no encumbrance to his title, if it is proper to describe

---

[55] *Id.* table A, app. XIV, at 176; Report, 1955, *supra* note 8, table A, app. VI, at 122.

any burden on land imposed by planning controls, that is, by a public law, as a defect of title or an encumbrance. Although the typical contracts for the sale of land carry a warning about the zoning ordinance and the requirements of plat approval are well known, it appears from Professor Beuscher's study[56] that the legal effects of the official street map are often not properly ascertained in a title search. So far as the planning controls are concerned, once it has been ascertained that the master plan has no unusual effect[57] the purchaser can confine himself to some fairly clear questions.

Has his contract any clause permitting him to cancel it if there is a zoning ordinance prohibiting his intended use? This question is frequently impractical, where the purchaser does not wish to disclose his intended use, since it might adversely affect his bargaining position.

Has the vendor misrepresented the uses permitted? Although the permitted use is a matter of public law, it is conceivable that a court would treat a misrepresentation as a ground for cancellation.

Has he asked for a deed free of encumbrances? Such a contract, which the lawyer seems to like, requires a court, in order to do justice, to distort new ideas and language to fit the traditional language of the conveyancer. It is surprising that standardized forms using functional language or at least contemporary jargon have not come into more common use. If there is a building built on the land in violation of the zoning ordinance can it be regarded as an encumbrance, as it would be if it were in violation of a restrictive covenant? It is common practice in an offer to purchase to accept restrictive covenants and zoning ordinances, provided they are not violated. Is the land affected by a proposed street shown on the official map? Is there a building on the land? Was it built before or after the official map was adopted? Was a permit issued because of unnecessary hardship? None of these questions can ordinarily be answered by looking at the master plan; the implementing ordinances must be read, and the risk run that the form of offer will be construed to protect the intending purchaser. An honest and efficient real-estate dealer might protect the average purchaser by more specific terms in the offer.

Under the British Act the position of the purchaser is somewhat dif-

[56] *Supra* note 48. See also Allison Dunham, *Private Enforcement of City Planning,* 20 LAW & CONTEMP. PROB. 463, 468–475 (1955). American courts seem to accept planning control violations as title defects, but title searchers seem less concerned.

[57] Professor Haar cites, for example, the case of The Pennsylvania Planning Act, PA. STAT. ANN. tit. 53, c. 48 (1953), as one where the master plan itself is the regulatory measure for laying out streets and parks. Haar, *The Master Plan, supra* note 3, at 365.

ferent. He knows, although he is looking at a fairly stable guide to council action, that apart from the designation of land, which tells him even more than the official map tells the American purchaser, and the allocation of areas of land use, from which he will learn far less than the American purchaser learns from the zoning ordinance, he is pretty much at the mercy of the local planning authority.

Professor Harold Potter early expressed the view that the development plan forms part of the vendor's title in just the same way as do restrictive covenants imposed by a building scheme.[58] If this view is accepted, as it appears to have been, then an Englishman now owns the fee simple in the existing use of his land, since the right to develop the land, that is, to make a material change in its use, has been vested in government hands, and the local planning authority must be approached for permission to develop. How one determines existing use is a bit uncertain. Presumably no land-use maps would be produced by the planning authority that would establish the *lawful* existing use for judicial purposes. Consequently, the matter of effective title searching under the British Act is probably even more difficult than it is in the United States under the complex of zoning ordinances, platting regulations, street maps, and the general registry system of the various states. Conveyancers are doubtless grateful that the development charge, with its incredibly complicated requirements, is slowly disappearing. Planning considerations will continue to be of major importance, however, and the forecasting of permitted uses must create peculiar problems when the development plan is quite devoid of the detail of a zoning ordinance. Apparently the best the prospective purchaser can do is to inquire in advance to see whether his development would be permitted. The Minister has recently allowed an appeal on the ground that the developer twice consulted the local authority and was assured of planning permission.[59]

It is a rather striking fact that general legislation in neither country gives much indication of how land that is in use for a purpose that the plan considers inappropriate should be dealt with by public authorities or private developers. Such nonconforming use could often be accounted for in the master plan as one that is expected to prosper because of its strategic location, or one that is expected to wither away. Where authority

[58] Harold Potter, *Dealings with Land Under the Planning Acts,* 1948 JOURNAL OF PLANNING LAW 440.

[59] Notes on Planning Decisions, 1960 JOURNAL OF PLANNING AND PROPERTY LAW 440.

exists to permit the improvement of a nonconforming use the plan ought to be some sort of guide to a prospective purchaser.

THE AGENCY RESPONSIBLE FOR PLANNING

The most striking contrast between the British Act and the majority of American acts is the identity of the bodies responsible for making plans, adopting them, and carrying them out. Two aspects of this contrast are especially significant, the degree of central government control, which has already been observed, and the degree of representative political control.

The British Act places the responsibility for preparing plans squarely on the county councils and on county borough councils, who may delegate their powers to a committee of their members and others, provided their members are a majority.[60] Judged by earlier planning acts, this was a tremendous improvement, the number of authorities concerned in planning being reduced from 1,441 to 145. The same councils have the responsibility of granting planning permission, unless it has been delegated to a county district council, which under the 1947 regulations could be arranged by agreement subject to ministerial approval. In 1959 new regulations gave county district councils with a population of 60,000 or more a right to a wide measure of delegation. A district council must obtain the county council's concurrence before granting permission for development that does not accord with the development plan. The Minister may also in certain circumstances require delegation to a district council with a population less than 60,000. Otherwise the new regulations are the same for the smaller district councils, but the county councils are now encouraged to delegate where the district council has "adequate technical advice" available. Responsibility for the original development plans could not be delegated, but the smaller councils are now to be encouraged to cooperate in preparing amendments.[61] The local planning authorities are thus representative bodies politically responsible to the community for whom they are planning.

The planning authority in the United States is rarely the council of the municipality for whom the planning is done. Although in a few cases the plan is adopted by the local legislature, in most cases it is prepared and adopted, or at least prepared, by a body known as a planning com-

---

[60] Sections 4(1) and (4), and pt. II of the First Schedule.
[61] *Supra* note 9, paraphrased from pp. 96–97.

mission. The members of a planning commission are appointed. The appointing authority is very often the mayor, but sometimes the council has the power, occasionally the chief executive officer, and in one or two cases some named official. The Standard Act envisaged a commission of nine members, and several states provide for a nine-man body, but some are smaller, as low as three (to seven), and five is a popular size, while some commissions run to ten or twelve members, and one case runs to fifteen. Some members hold office ex officio, usually the mayor and certain senior officials, and the others hold offices for terms varying from three to six years which are staggered so that not all terms expire at once. Usually a member must be resident in the planning area, a taxpayer, and very often he cannot be an employee of the municipality. Where provision is made for removal from office it is usually only for cause. No compensation is offered in most cases, although actual expenses, sometimes a per diem allowance, can be claimed, and expenses may be paid to members attending planning conferences and the like.[62] Since the citizen lacks the ballot-revolt control available under the British Act, the general competence of the planning commissioners may be of more interest. One study by Professor Walker[63] has indicated what is probably the contemporary picture, although the study is the result of a prewar investigation. Seventy-nine per cent of the membership came from nine groups: general businessmen, manufacturers, bankers, contractors, and officers of utilities representing 35.1 per cent of the total; realtors 15.4 per cent, lawyers 11.1 per cent, architects 10.1 per cent, and engineers 7.7 per cent. The disproportionate number of realtors reflects their great interest in zoning. The lawyers' interest is also in zoning, or was when the count was made. The architects and engineers reflect the fact that at least in 1937 the predominant professional interest in planning came from those professions. This representation of the real estate and construction interests makes the planning commission a special-interest body in more senses than one. It has an interest in fostering building whether the conditions are such that development is needed or not. It also has a special interest in planning, which is intended to assure that planning will get the attention it deserves. The view seems to be that the council has other interests that predominate. It was the fond hope of those who first conceived the planning commission that it would take planning "out of politics." It hardly

---

[62] Haar, *The Master Plan, supra* note 3, sets out very full particulars in table 1.

[63] ROBERT A. WALKER, THE PLANNING FUNCTION IN URBAN GOVERNMENT 150 (Chicago, 2d ed. 1950).

succeeded, but the objection is not, however, that planning has not in fact been taken out of politics, but rather that although it is in politics, where it belongs, it is not in so that the voter can control it the way he does the legislative body.

Although Walker convincingly criticizes the "semiautonomous planning board," the planning commission should be understood in its historic setting as part of a form of government with which Americans are very familiar and perhaps prefer to a more centralized form. In his table of "local governments" in the metropolitan region of Chicago, Walker[64] lists a total of 1,642, comprising, in addition to 384 cities, counties, and townships, 978 school districts, 70 park districts, four mosquito-abatement districts, and one health district. The American voter in local government is thus familiar with and accepts this fragmented local government, and it would be a mistake to suppose that it is as ineffectual as it appears to someone accustomed to a unitary state and a council-dominated local government.

Both the British Act and the various American acts make inadequate provision for regional planning. The county unit in England and Wales is no more valid as a *regional* planning area than it is in the United States, where county or regional or both planning areas are provided for in all but seven states.[65] A simple illustration can be had from an analysis of the Merseyside conurbation. The Board of Trade's development area ("the greater part of the conurbation") includes the county boroughs of Liverpool, Bootle, Birkenhead, and Wallasey, together with a number of boroughs and county districts,[66] which means that the county council of Lancashire would have to be added to the four county boroughs, making a total of five local planning authorities in the conurbation. The region could easily include the Manchester area, which would add another six local planning authorities. Although the British Act provides for joint planning boards, apparently only two have so far been established. The local planning authorities have not been united in any of the great conurbations.

The United States' experience offers no more encouraging example.[67] For the most part, regional planning, at least beyond the county area, is dependent upon voluntary cooperation among affected municipalities, and

[64] *Id.* at 260.
[65] PLANNING LAWS, *supra* note 3, Comparative Analysis.
[66] WILFRED SMITH, ED., A SCIENTIFIC SURVEY OF MERSEYSIDE (Liverpool, 1953).
[67] See C. M. Haar, *Regionalism and Realism in Land-Use Planning,* 105 U. PA. L. REV. 515 (1957).

even if they are cooperative, the constitution and aims of the permissible planning agency are vague and ill-defined, and the legal consequence of a regional master plan is even more unsettled than that of the planning commission for a city.

One reasonably simple, perhaps too simple, solution to the problem of regional planning lies in the greater use of state planning. This solution is more apt for Britain, where there are no abutting states and the existing law provides the machinery of national coordination of plans at the time of ministerial approval. Such a program of state planning in the United States would cut across some dearly held notions of "checks and balances" and the decentralization characteristic of a federal state.

Regional planning may not be consciously practiced by the central government, but regional administration is its business, and in this area public works of vital planning significance are planned, one way or another, every day. The location of a superhighway can easily change the character of various communities, dividing this one into unrelated halves, introducing new industrial land to that one, opening up recreational land in another. If there is no adequate process of consultation the security in decentralization may have been bought dearly with a loss of freedom for effective planning.

A sensible assessment of a planning agency cannot be made if it is accepted that the planning will be done by the lay members of the planning commission or the elected members of the county and county borough councils. Whatever may have been the complexity of planning in the 1920's, when Bassett was inventing the planning commission, few people today would expect the exercise of the ubiquitous planning controls to be more than supervised by laymen, who can be trusted to slow up their exercise by zealous professionals. The question remains, therefore, what kind of person is doing the planning? In 1950 the Schuster Report[68] indicated that out of 153 planning authorities of all types, senior responsibility was held in 81 cases by engineers, in 34 by architects, in 32 by surveyors, and in six by so-called professional planners with no other professional qualification. About half of the architects, engineers, and surveyors had also qualified as members of the Town Planning Institute. Probably the same sort of personnel is to be found in the United States, but there is a chronic shortage of planners. One survey[69] showed almost

---

[68] *Supra* note 12, para. 83.

[69] In 1959 there were said to be 436 positions advertised and 247 graduates expected from planning courses in United States universities. AMERICAN SOCIETY OF PLANNING OFFICIALS, JOBS IN PLANNING, January 1, 1960, p. 5.

twice as many jobs available as there were graduates of planning courses to fill them. To the extent that the goal of the planner is the civil service, the prejudices against such a career are well enough established that many able students will be deflected to other professions. If good students are not attracted to the planning profession the accumulation of additional and wider legal controls should be regarded with some suspicion that effective planning may be only a paper illusion.

THE OPPORTUNITY TO BE HEARD

Of major importance to the lawyer is the opportunity these planning agencies present for citizen participation. Perhaps the more important function of citizen participation in planning was that stressed a half a century ago by Patrick Geddes: the education of the citizen to a greater understanding of his city's growth and change and his possible contribution. But the lawyer's special concern in community planning is the organization of the planning agency to the end that individual interests can be effectively presented. This can only happen if the legislation or the practice of the local planning authority or the planning commission provides opportunity for hearings. The form of hearing is important, and it can be directed to *three* purposes.

There is, first, the gathering of basic data for the survey. Neither country prescribes any procedure for this kind of inquiry, as it probably cannot be formalized. Yet in the drafting of the statutes, lawyers tend to think in terms of formal hearing procedures and to underestimate the value of promoting public understanding. It is not enough to suppose that the planning commission, or even the local planning authority, will bring forward all the criticism, valid or otherwise, and all the alternative suggestions that can come out of a widely advertised public gathering and from the press and television.

Even when the Minister is about to approve the development plan the British Act leaves it to him to decide whether it is necessary to hold a hearing, but opportunity must be given for written representations to be made, which will be considered by the Minister, and if he dispenses with a public local inquiry he must give the private objectors who want it a private hearing before an inspector, at which the local planning authority shall be heard.[70] When the British Act was passed in 1947, *Local Government Board v. Arlidge*[71] was still respectable but much criticized law,

[70] Section 10(2) (b) and the Town and Country (Development Plans) Regulations, STAT. INSTR., 1948, No. 1767, art. 17.
[71] [1915] A.C. 120.

and the reports of inspectors who held local public inquiries were not usually made public. After the government had announced that it had accepted many of the recommendations made by the Committee on Administrative Tribunals and Enquiries,[72] new arrangements provided that the inspector's report would be made available at the same time and place as the approved amendment of the plan.[73] One criticism of this "reform" is that the report comes too late to be of practical value to the applicant, although there is also provision that if "new factual evidence" is brought to the Minister's notice from any source after an inquiry on an appeal from refusal of planning permission and might in his view be a material factor in the decision, the parties would be given an opportunity of commenting on it. If necessary, the inquiry would be reopened.[74]

One cannot help wondering whether the inspector's report has changed its character now that it can be seen, and whether opinions of the inspector are passed informally to the Minister. It is one thing for a civil servant to write a confidential report to his Minister, it is quite another to write a public decision, or a recommendation with an articulate rationalization, directed to making the local planning authority or the aggrieved citizen believe that the inspector acted "reasonably." The Minister has reported that he has differed from his inspector in about 5 per cent of the cases.[75]

If the Minister chose to listen to the inspector's informal comment he evidently could with propriety because he is allowed the unusual privilege (in the context of judicial review cases) of consulting any person he thinks ought to be consulted without affording any opportunity for further objections, representations, or inquiries.[76]

The British Act, many state enabling acts, and the Standard Act afford an opportunity for judicial review, a constitutional right in the United States in any event. The British Act limits the right to review to the grounds that some aspect of the development plan or an amendment is not within the powers of the act or that some regulation has not been

---

[72] Report of the Committee on Administrative Tribunals and Enquiries (Franks Committee Report), CMD. No. 218 (1957); see ch. 23 at 71–74, esp. paras. 343 and 344.

[73] Report of the Ministry of Housing and Local Government, CMD. No. 737 at 51 (1958). See also Ministry Circulars 8/58 (1958) and 51/58 (1958), reproduced in 1958 JOURNAL OF PLANNING AND PROPERTY LAW 266 and 814.

[74] Ministry Report, 1958, *supra* note 73, at 50. Apparently the government did not accept the Franks Committee recommendation in para. 345 (*supra* note 72) that the parties have an opportunity to see the inspector's findings of facts before he reports to the Minister so that they can propose corrections.

[75] *Id.* at 51. This percentage held true for 1959 as well. *Supra* note 9, at 99.

[76] British Act, § 10(3). Cf. Errington v. Minister of Health, [1935] 1 K.B. 249.

complied with, and there is also a limitation period of six weeks after the notice of approval, within which the action for review must be started. The High Court may quash the plan or any provision on the specified grounds, but otherwise a development plan should not be questioned in any legal proceedings.[77]

In the actual operation of events after 1947, and until 1960 no applications to the High Court seem to have been started, and the cases in review of master plans in the United States are very rare.

CONCLUSION: SOME QUESTIONS

These comparisons have raised, and left unanswered, a number of questions, some of which may be worth restating as a basis of further analysis.

First, what sort of plan should enabling legislation provide for? Somewhere between the utter plasticity and comparative secrecy advocated by Bassett and the classical city plans of the architectural school with their threat of "fearful symmetry" there must be some middle course. Can this course be discovered abstractly and a suitable legislative device worked out to embody it? Or must we learn planning from experience by trial and error?

Second, can the kind of analysis suggested by Professor Dunham be stated in legislative form? Is there some value in the direction in the British Act that the local planning authority "have regard to the development plan"? Could the list of factors that the planners, as well as the implementers, should have regard to be written in more specific detail than is fashionable in American planning enabling acts?

Third, should a plan have any legal effect? Planners often describe the plan as a "legal document," but the course of legislative history and interpretation in both countries seems to favor a minimal sanction. If the plan has no real legal consequences can one provide against the danger that the land-use controller will become arbitrary?

Fourth, if planning is to be self-conscious and articulate, should the central state not be a partner in the planning process with the local municipality? If so, should there not be a much more systematic process for consultation among the principal partners and the private developer?

Fifth, does existing legislation in either country provide a satisfactory opportunity for "citizen participation" in planning? Should there be, in addition to formal hearings at an advanced stage, mandatory consultation

[77] British Act, § 11. See also Town and Country Planning Act, 1959, 7 & 8 Eliz. 2, c. 53, § 31.

and the occasion for discussion of competing planning proposals at an earlier stage?

Sixth, is the land tax, which is commonly emphasized as the chief source of revenue for municipalities, an adequate tax base for municipal development? Can the planner hope to make a wise allocation of land use if his government has to compete for industrial taxation? Is something like the English system of "derating" industry feasible in American states?

ENGLISH DEVELOPMENT PLANS
FOR THE CONTROL OF LAND USE

DESMOND HEAP
COMPTROLLER AND SOLICITOR TO THE CORPORATION
OF THE CITY OF LONDON

The next portion of the Bill is that portion which deals with town planning. This is a new departure in the legislation of this country. I regret that it has come so late. No one can go through the East End of London, or to places like Liverpool, Leeds, Manchester and Glasgow, and see the effect, both on the physique, morale, happiness, and comfort of men, women, and children, through lack of some such condition as this a hundred, or at least fifty, years ago, but will come to one definite conclusion, that, late though it is, it is better late than never. — The President of the Local Government Board (Mr. John Burns) in the House of Commons, April 5, 1909, when moving the second reading of the Housing and Town Planning Bill of 1909.

Notwithstanding the great care, courtesy and skill which has been shown by the Lord Chancellor on this Bill . . . I am going to call a spade a spade and not a shovel. So far as I am concerned, this Bill might as well be printed in Chinese; I simply do not know what it means. — Lord Meston in the House of Lords, May 7, 1959, during the committee stage of the Town and Country Planning Bill of 1959.

THE OBJECTS of this paper are, first, to consider the legal background and framework of the English law into which there is fitted, by town planning experts and technicians, the administrative instrument known in England as a development plan, the object of which is, briefly, to sketch out the shape of things to come in the foreseeable future in the matter of land development; and, second, to consider the making, effect, and functioning of a development plan when it has come into operation.

It is imperative to sketch the legal framework out of which the concept of the development plan has sprung and without which a development plan could not function, if one is fully to understand the intent and purpose of such a plan. In short, without the impelling force of the law behind it, a development plan could, in a free society, have neither status nor effect.

A development plan is a flexible instrument indicative of planning policy; it is a guiding factor to those who have the duty of controlling development; it does not itself control development, but acts as a disciplining influence upon those who have this grave responsibility.

The art, science, or mystery of town planning is, of course, as old as the hills, but town planning with the sanction of the law behind it has, in England, existed for only half a century. The year 1960 saw the beginning of the second half century of town planning law. The year 1959 was the jubilee year, for it was on the third day of December 1909 that the first English statute to deal with the subject of town planning control over the use of land received the Royal Assent. This was the Housing and Town Planning Act of 1909, and that part of it which related to town planning comprised fourteen sections and two schedules.

How the legislation has been fruitful and multiplied over the half century! The faltering fourteen sections of the 1909 act have long since been repealed, and today, in their place, there stand on the statute books five acts dealing with the town planning of land and comprising some 271 sections and 31 schedules of statutory pronouncement. Nor is this all, for the statutes have spawned an enormous brood of subordinate legislation in the form of orders, regulations, and directions running into hundreds of pages, the whole supplemented by scores of ministerial circulars giving advice, suggestions, and guidance on the administration of this branch of the law. It is, indeed, a far cry from the happy-go-lucky days of *sic utere tuo* . . . (use your own land in such a way as not to injure another's), when the Englishman's home really was his castle, to the intricate provisions and controlling sanctions of, say, the Written Statement to the County of London Development Plan of 1955.

But if town planning law has proceeded from simplicity to complexity it is not irrelevant to remember, on the occasion of its jubilee, that so also has the matter with which it purports to deal, namely, the substitution of a controlled form of land use for the laissez-faire attitude to development of the previous century. The society into which this control seeks to inject itself today is also a good deal more complex than it used to be, and this does not make it any easier for town planning law either to say what it wants to say or to do what it wants to do. In short, things are not by any means what they were in the days when town planning enactments first appeared on the legal scene; indeed, they are not merely different, but amazingly different, when one recollects that the changes which have brought about the difference have themselves all occurred in less than the lifetime of many a man living today.

Statistics can, of course, be made to prove anything (depending on which expert witness is handling them), but perhaps a few of them, not wholly unconnected with the concept of town and country planning, may here be allowed to tell their own story in their own way, and thereby help to illustrate the gulf which separates the beginning and the end of the first half century of town planning control under the sanction of the law.

In 1909 the population of the United Kingdom was 44,507,100 and the expectation of a male life at birth was 41.35 years. In 1958 the population of the United Kingdom was 51,680,000 (and it is still growing) and the expectation of life at birth had risen by as much as 26 years to 67.52 years.

From the motoring point of view, England in 1909 must have been a land not only of wide open spaces but of open and empty highroads. Even in 1909 the internal combustion engine was making its presence felt to the tune of 48,109 private motor cars, a figure which had changed by the time 1959 came along to 4,736,000. If all the horseless carriages of those early days are to be taken into account, then there were 143,877 of these in 1910 compared with 8,030,000 in 1959. One estimate was made that the figure for road vehicles of all kinds on the roads in 1962 would be around 11,000,000, nearly four times as many as there were but twenty years ago.

Between 1909 and 1947 a number of Town Planning Acts were passed. Of these it is important to mention that the Town Planning Act of 1932 projected the concept of the planned control of development and redevelopment both *inward* into the centers of already fully developed towns, and also *outward* into the open, undeveloped, rolling countryside. Though it is still popular to speak of *town* planning, it should not be forgotten that the expression embraces the control of land use not only in towns but also in country areas; in short, throughout the whole of the land in the realm.

Another important date to be mentioned is 1943, which saw the creation of the Minister of Town and Country Planning (now called the Minister of Housing and Local Government), who is responsible to Parliament for all matters associated with town and country planning. He is charged under the 1943 Act with the duty of "securing consistency and continuity in the framing and execution of a national policy with respect to the use and development of land throughout England and Wales." In pursuance of his policy, the Minister has had conferred upon him, by subsequent legislation, an increasing number of powers, until his centralized control over the use of land in town and country is now striking.

Four years later came that dramatic and monumental town planning enactment, the Town and Country Planning Act of 1947. This act wiped the slate clean of all previous town planning enactments (except the aforementioned Minister of Town and Country Planning Act of 1943), re-enacted a variety of earlier provisions, but broke entirely new ground by enacting principles which were completely novel to town planning law. It was, and still is, the principal act relating to the control of land use throughout the whole of England and Wales.

TOWN AND COUNTRY PLANNING ACT OF 1947

It is impossible to exaggerate the importance of July 1, 1948, from the point of view of the local planning authority, the landowner, or the building developer, for the Town and Country Planning Act of 1947, which came into full force and effect on that date, contains some of the most drastic and far-reaching provisions yet enacted affecting the ownership of land and the liberty of an owner to develop and use his land as he thinks fit. Indeed, since that date, ownership of land, generally speaking, carries with it nothing more than the bare right to go on using it for its existing purposes. The owner has no *right* to develop it, that is to say, he has no *right* to build upon it and no *right* even to change its use. Until the 1947 act was amended by the Town and Country Planning Act of 1954, a landowner selling his land could expect to obtain (in theory, at least) only its existing-use value, because whatever development value the land had was expropriated by the State under the 1947 act. The 1947 act did not nationalize the land; what it did do was to nationalize the development value in land — a state of affairs which is reversed by the 1954 act, under which development value in land returns to the landowner though it was only development values that had accrued to land before January 7, 1947, which are compensated under the 1954 act on the imposition of planning restrictions or on the compulsory purchase of land under a notice to treat served *before* October 30, 1958.

The objects of the 1947 act may be grouped under seven headings and summarized briefly as follows:

(1) to replace the former system of planning control through the medium of rigid schemes by a new system of control through the medium of flexible development plans prepared by a greatly reduced number of planning authorities and subjected to constant review;

(2) to prohibit (with exceptions) the carrying out of any kind of de-

velopment whatsoever, and whether before or after the coming into operation of a development plan, without the consent of a local planning authority;

(3) to provide for the levying by a new body, the Central Land Board, of development charges payable (with exceptions) on the carrying out of any kind of development;

(4) to expropriate for the State the development value in all land and, in consequence, to enable landowners to make claims on a £300 million fund for loss of the development value of their land;

(5) to confer upon local authorities wider powers for undertaking development themselves than they have ever previously held and, as a corollary to this, to confer upon such authorities wider powers for the compulsory acquisition of land;

(6) to provide increased financial assistance to local authorities to enable them to discharge their functions under the act, including especially the acquisition of land and its development or redevelopment by the local authorities themselves;

(7) to amend the law relating to compensation for compulsory acquisition of land by abolishing the 1939 standard and substituting compensation based on existing-use value only.

Objects numbered (3), (4), and (6) above are substantially amended (1) by the Town and Country Planning Act of 1953, under which development charges are abolished; (2) by the 1954 act, under which the claims made on the £300 million fund are to be met in full but only as and when planning restrictions are imposed, or land is compulsorily acquired at its existing-use value under a notice to treat served *before* October 30, 1958; (3) by Part I of the 1959 act, whereby market value is to be paid on the compulsory purchase of land under a notice to treat served *after* October 29, 1958.

TOWN AND COUNTRY PLANNING ACT OF 1953

The financial portions of the 1947 act relating respectively to the making of claims on the £300 million fund for loss of development value and to the payment of development charge before undertaking development were the subject of criticism between 1948 and 1952, with the result that the government of the day produced the white paper of November 1952 entitled "Proposals for Amending the Financial Provisions of the 1947 Act." The new financial structure for town planning, as outlined in the white paper, was brought into being first by the Town and Country Planning Act of 1953, under which development charges were abolished for all development commenced on or after November 18, 1952, and the distribution of the £300 million fund to successful claimants (a distribution due, under the 1947 act, to take place in 1954) was suspended. The making of payments to those who suffered as a result of planning restrictions or requirements imposed in the public interest was left by the 1953 act to be dealt with by subsequent legislation, which duly followed in 1954.

TOWN AND COUNTRY PLANNING ACT OF 1954

The Town and Country Planning Act of 1954, which came into force on January 1, 1955, completed the implementation, begun under the 1953 act, of the provisions of the white paper of 1952 by replacing the financial provisions of the 1947 act with a new code of compensation payments. These payments are limited to the amount of the claims made under the 1947 act on the £300 million fund, and are to be paid not at one given time (as was the arrangement under the 1947 act), but only if and when a landowner is prevented from reaping the development value in his land by either (a) suffering the imposition of planning restrictions (subject to exceptions) which prevent or limit the development of his land, or (b) having his land compulsorily acquired at its existing-use value under a notice to treat served *before* October 30, 1958.

The main objects of the 1954 act may be grouped under five headings which provide briefly as follows:

(1) for the making of payments by the Central Land Board in respect of past matters and events (other than planning decisions) occurring before the commencement of the act;

(2) for the payment of compensation by the Minister of Housing and Local Government in respect of past planning decisions occurring before the commencement of the act;

(3) for the payment of compensation by the Minister in respect of planning decisions occurring after the commencement of the act;

(4) for the payment of compensation by public and local authorities in respect of any compulsory purchase of land under a notice to treat served after the commencement of the act but before October 30, 1958;

(5) for the payment of compensation by local planning authorities in respect of revocations or modifications of planning decisions occurring after the commencement of the act.

TOWN AND COUNTRY PLANNING ACT OF 1959

After the coming into operation of the 1954 act on January 1, 1955, there were two codes of compensation payable in respect of the acquisition of land. Development value in the land having been, in effect, returned to the landowner by the operation of the 1953 act in abolishing development charges, it followed that on a sale of his land a landowner clearly had, after the commencement of the 1953 act, the right to sell not only the existing-use rights in his land, but also the development rights. Thus on a sale of land by private treaty the vendor could demand the current market value of the land. But on a sale of land to a public body purchasing under compulsory purchase powers the acquiring authority was precluded by the joint effect of the 1947 act and the 1954 act from paying more than the existing-use value plus the 1947 development value of the land — in short, nothing was paid for post-1947 development values.

As time went on the discrepancy between the price payable under these two codes of compensation — the code applicable on a sale by private treaty and the code applicable on a sale under compulsory purchase powers — tended to become greater. This caused dissatisfaction, which was commented upon in the Report of the Committee on Administrative Tribunals and Enquiries, which declared (in paragraph 278):

> One final point of great importance needs to be made. The evidence which we have received shows that much of the dissatisfaction with the procedures relating to land arises from the basis of compensation. It is clear that objections to compulsory purchase would be far fewer if compensation were always assessed at not less than market value. It is not part of our terms of reference to consider and make recommendations upon the basis of compensation. But we cannot emphasize too strongly the extent to which these financial considerations affect the matters with which we have to deal. Whatever changes in procedure are made dissatisfaction is, because of this, bound to remain.

Accordingly, the government of the day decided in 1958 to bring to an end the double code of compensation payable on the acquisition of land. The result was the introduction into Parliament on October 29, 1958, of a bill which subsequently became the Town and Country Planning Act of 1959.

The Town and Country Planning Act of 1959 came into force on August 16, 1959, one month after it was passed. Its main objects may be grouped under six heads as follows:

(1) to provide for market value compensation (in lieu of compensation

at the rate, under the joint effect of the 1947 act and the 1954 act, of existing-use value plus 1947 development value) in the case of any compulsory purchase of land under a notice to treat served *after* October 29, 1958:

(2) to give local authorities and other public bodies greater freedom from ministerial control in the acquisition, appropriation, and disposal of land;

(3) to provide further opportunity for challenging in the courts certain orders made under the 1947 act and certain decisions and directions of the Minister of Housing and Local Government under the Town Planning Acts of 1947 to 1959;

(4) to secure greater publicity for planning applications and to ensure that owners and agricultural tenants are informed of any planning applications affecting land owned or occupied by them;

(5) to provide for the obligatory purchase by a local authority of an owner-occupier's interest in land detrimentally affected by town planning proposals;

(6) to give local authorities additional powers to buy land in advance of their requirements.

THE PRESENT TOWN PLANNING CODE

The act of 1947 still remains the principal act relating to land planning, but its financial provisions are now drastically altered by the 1953 act, the 1954 act, and the 1959 act, while Part V of the 1947 act (relating to compensation payable on the compulsory purchase of land) is supplemented by the 1954 act in respect of any compulsory purchase deriving from a notice to treat served after January 1, 1955, and is replaced by the 1959 act in respect of any compulsory purchase deriving from a notice to treat served after October 29, 1958.

These four acts of 1947, 1953, 1954, and 1959 (together with a short act of 1951), when conjoined with the host of rules, orders, and regulations made under them, together comprise the town and country planning code under which the use of land in England and Wales is controlled. It may be added that similar control is available in Scotland under the Town and Country Planning (Scotland) Acts of 1947 to 1959.

ADMINISTRATION OF PLANNING

The Minister of Housing and Local Government is, under the 1947 act, "the central authority for the administration of planning throughout

England and Wales." These words are of the greatest importance because they give the Minister the last word (subject only to Parliament itself) in all matters of policy relating to the control of land use in England and Wales.

The 1947 act draws a distinction, which needs to be carefully watched, between local planning authorities and local authorities. Local planning authorities are the councils of counties and of county boroughs, and local authorities are the councils of counties, of county boroughs, of noncounty boroughs, of urban districts and of rural districts, but the Minister may constitute, as a local planning authority, a joint planning board representing a united district comprising two or more counties or county boroughs.

The number of local planning authorities in England and Wales was reduced by the 1947 act from 1,441 to 145, and this latter figure will be further reduced as and when the Minister exercises his power of creating joint planning boards. A joint planning board has been constituted for the Lake District by the Lake District Planning Board Order of 1951, and for the Peak District by the Peak Park Planning Board Order of 1951.

It will be seen that while every local planning authority is also a local authority under the 1947 act, the converse is not always true. Speaking generally, it may be said that while all local authorities have powers with respect to the acquisition of land, only the local planning authorities may deal with the actual development of land, the making of land available to other parties for planning purposes, the making of development plans, and with applications for permission to undertake development of land. So far, however, as the latter applications are concerned, a county council was formerly authorized under the Town and Country Planning (Authorization of Delegation) Regulations of 1947 to delegate to any county district council within its area any of its functions under the 1947 act relating to the control of development, and many county councils have done this in accordance with schemes of delegation, which vary from place to place.

The Town and Country Planning (Delegation) Regulations of 1959, which supersede those of 1947, entitle a council of a county district having a population of sixty thousand or more to claim *as a matter of right* a wide measure of delegation of powers under the 1947 act, and also to authorize the Minister, if he is satisfied that there are special circumstances justifying such a course, to require similar delegation to the council of a county district with a population of less than sixty thousand. The 1959 regulations set out the procedure to be followed by a county district council wishing to claim delegation under the regulations. The 1959 regulations also repeat those parts of the revoked 1947 regulations, which related to the delegation of functions to county district councils without regard to population. It is to be noted that the functions of a county council relating to the making of development plans cannot be delegated at all, although a county district council must be consulted about the preparation of any development plan which will affect its own particular area.

A joint planning board may similarly be authorized by regulations to delegate any of its functions to any county council or county borough council within its united district.

Within the London area there are special and exceptional provisions dealing with the respective powers, under the 1947 act, of the London County Council, the Common Council of the City of London, and the councils of metropolitan boroughs, and regulating the relationships among these bodies in all matters pertaining to planning.

PREPARATION OF DEVELOPMENT PLANS

The town planning schemes of former planning enactments were re-placed under the 1947 act by development plans, and every local planning authority had to carry out a survey of its area, and within three years of July 1, 1948, had to prepare a development plan based on the survey indicating: (1) the manner in which the land covered by the plan is to be used (whether by the carrying out of development or not), and (2) the stages by which the development is to be carried out.

Generally speaking, a development plan consists of various maps (as, for example, basic map, town map, comprehensive development map, designation map, program map) together with a written statement, but there may be variations and additions to these two fundamental requirements in accordance with the needs of local circumstances. Details as to the form and content of development plans are given in the Town and Country Planning (Development Plans) Regulations of 1948, as amended by the Town and Country Planning (Development Plans) Amendment Regulations of 1954 and 1959, and in Ministry of Housing and Local Government Circulars Nos. 40/48, 50/48 and 54/59.

A development plan may (1) define the sites of proposed roads, buildings, airfields, parks, pleasure grounds, nature reserves, and other open spaces; (2) allocate areas for agricultural, residential, or industrial purposes; and (3) designate land as subject to compulsory purchase.

If a development plan covers land across which is to be constructed a trunk road by virtue of an order of the Minister of Transport (under the Highways Act of 1959) or on which a new town is to be developed by order of the Minister of Housing and Local Government (under the New Towns Act of 1946) the development plan is to have effect as if the provisions of the foregoing orders were included in the development plan itself.

REVIEW OF DEVELOPMENT PLANS

Before a development plan can come into operation it must be approved under the 1947 act by the Minister. The regulations of 1948 provide that notice of the submission of a development plan to the Minister must be given in the *London Gazette* and, in each of two successive weeks, in at least one local newspaper circulating in the locality where the land to which the development plan relates is situated. Persons who object to the plan may send their objections in writing to the Minister within whatever period is specified in the advertisement. This period may not be less than six weeks from the date of the first local advertisement, and while the Minister must consider all objections duly made he is not obliged to hold any public local inquiry. If he dispenses with such an inquiry he must afford a private hearing before one of his inspectors to any person who has made an objection, and at any such private hearing the local planning authority is entitled to be heard.

The Minister may approve the development plan with or without modifications. In doing so he will be acting administratively and not judicially or quasi-judicially and, accordingly, can permit himself, notwithstanding objections which have been made to him, to be influenced by matters of policy. He is expressly authorized to hold discussions with the local planning authority or any other authority or person "behind the backs," as it were, of objectors to the development plan. Provision is made as to the date of operation, and the right of an aggrieved party to challenge the legal validity of a development plan in the High Court.

A development plan must be reviewed by the local planning authority at intervals not exceeding five years, amended in the light of experience, and resubmitted to the Minister for approval. Thus a development plan never really achieves finality. The plan is under constant review, and in this way is the better calculated to represent what, at any given moment, are the latest concepts of good planning.

DESIGNATION OF LAND IN DEVELOPMENT PLANS

It will be seen that many things may be provided for in a development plan, but one of its most important features is its designation of land as being liable to compulsory purchase by a local authority. Landowners will be interested to note, however, that the Minister may not approve a development plan which designates land as liable to compulsory purchase if in his view the land is not likely to be acquired within ten years (seven years in the case of agricultural land) of the approval of the plan.

It does not follow from the foregoing that because a particular plot of land stands for the time being undesignated in a development plan that it will be immune from compulsory acquisition during the aforementioned periods of either ten or seven years respectively, because, in the first place, a development plan has to be reviewed at least once every five years, and, in the second place, the fact that land stands undesignated in a development plan does not in any way prejudice any power of compulsory acquisition otherwise available to a local authority.

The position, in short, is that while designated land may be said to be likely to be acquired compulsorily within ten years or seven years, as the case may be, it does not follow that undesignated land will not be so acquired, because the 1947 act does not affect existing powers of compulsory acquisition already conferred on Ministers or on local authorities. What the act does is to confer new and wider powers of compulsory purchase which are in addition to, and not in derogation of, those already available to local authorities. A new method of acquiring land compulsorily for almost any conceivable purpose is conferred by the 1947 act upon local authorities and other public bodies through the medium of designation as liable to compulsory purchase.

The following land can be designated in a development plan as liable to compulsory purchase: (1) any land allocated by a development plan for the purposes of any of the functions of a Minister of the Crown, any local authority, or any statutory undertaker; (2) any land within, contiguous, or adjacent to an "area of comprehensive development"; and (3) any other land which, in the opinion of the local planning authority, ought to be compulsorily acquired in order to secure that it will be used in the manner proposed by the development plan.

An "area of comprehensive development" is specially defined and includes any area to be developed or redeveloped as a whole for the purpose of (1) dealing with blitzed land (areas of extensive war damage); (2)

dealing with blighted land (areas of bad layout or obsolete development); (3) accommodating overspill consequent upon the redevelopment of a blitzed area or a blighted area; or (4) any other purpose specified in the development plan. Never have such wide powers of compulsory purchase been conferred by general enactment upon local authorities and other public bodies.

If land designated as subject to compulsory purchase is not in fact acquired by the authorized Minister, local authority, or statutory undertaker within twelve years (eight years in the case of agricultural land) from the date of the designation becoming operative, the landowner can *require* the purchase of the land to be dealt with within six months, and if it is not so dealt with the land is automatically made free of designation. This, however, is without prejudice to further redesignation in some amendment of the development plan made at one of the compulsory quinquennial reviews, or, indeed, at any time if the local planning authority so desires and the Minister approves.

DEVELOPMENT PLAN — NATIONAL OR LOCAL?

Notwithstanding the broadening of the area over which each individual development plan will function (consequent upon the drastic reduction of local planning authorities by the 1947 act) the fact remains that all development plans continue to be made locally and doubtlessly with a keen eye on matters of local concern. On the other hand, each development plan has been approved centrally by the Minister of Housing and Local Government. The Minister may approve each individual development plan, with or without amendment, and there is no doubt that in doing so he will not have erected each individual plan into a state of splendid isolation and viewed it wholly divorced from the context of other neighboring or adjoining development plans also before him for approval. The Minister will, to some extent, have coordinated one development plan with another. The intriguing question is: to what extent has this coordination been carried out? Idealistically, of course, the sum total of all development plans for England and Wales should add up to one national master plan for the whole of the country. If they did do so this would indeed be town planning on a national scale, but it is doubtful if coordination has ever gone as far as this.

Frankly, the view is irresistible that so long as town planning remains a local government function, the sum total of all the development plans put together cannot really add up to anything more than the mere sum total of a number of individual parts; in short, there is little chance of the sum of the parts being, as it were, something greater than the whole. On the other hand, if there were to be only one national plan made by one national centralized authority, then the plan would necessarily fail to embody within itself that respect for local detail, custom, and aspirations, which certainly go a long way to make the present individual development plans comprehensible to those two very important people, the man in the street and the woman on the No. 47 bus, without whose popular support town planning control (with its undeniable, yet basically essential, interference with the liberty of the individual) cannot expect to have the right to succeed in its purpose.

The Minister of Housing and Local Government was recently taxed in Parliament on his routine for dealing with development plans made, *locally,* by local planning authorities and then laid before him, *centrally,* for his coordinating approval. His remarks in the House of Commons on July 18, 1960, are illuminating, as showing the kind of thing which goes on all the time behind the scenes:

It is true that the 1947 Act is based on counties and county boroughs as the planning areas, but I am quite certain that these matters need to be looked at on a regional as well as on a county basis. This is just what the Minister has been doing. On top of our discussions with individual planning authorities, we are adopting a policy of regional conferences of central and local government officials. All this is already in hand. This, of course, is specially important and necessary in making sure that there is co-ordination and a common understanding between one planning authority and another and that the whole problem of outward migration and overspill movements is looked at realistically as between different planning authorities . . .

May I come back to what I was referring to just now — the flexibility of development plans? I should like to tell the Committee how the review of a county development plan goes forward. I will take an actual current case in a county affected by rising land values . . .

First of all, my Ministry furnished information derived partly from the Registrar General and partly from migration studies about population trends and numbers of households and so forth. The county council married all that with its own local knowledge and arrived at probable population figures for 20 years ahead. Then the council decide provisionally where to allocate land in various parts of the county to meet the whole needs of this additional population for the next 20 years. Now it is discussing with all concerned the agricultural, industrial and other problems involved and is keeping in touch informally with my Ministry. The final step will be for the planning authority to submit formal proposals to me for the amendment of its development plan.

This is the way in which we shall get the right pieces of land selected for housing development with proper regard for communications, agriculture and water supplies and all else which has to be taken into account . . . That is what wise planning means. It cannot be done by looking vaguely at a map and thinking that it would be nice to build here or there or in another place. The fact is that we in the Ministry have most cordial and close relations with planning authorities in these reviews which are going on the whole time and, as I have said, I have now extended it to regional forecasts as well.

In passing, it may be mentioned that there is one kind of development which *is* dealt with on a national, as distinct from a local, basis, and that is industrial development. Notwithstanding development plans and the powers of local planning authorities, the control of new industrial development is firmly vested in a national centralized authority (the Board of Trade — a government department), because any application for planning permission to erect an industrial building of more than 5,000 square feet is of no effect unless there has first been obtained from the Board of Trade a certificate saying that the location of the industrial site is satisfactory from the Board of Trade's point of view as distinct from the town planning point of view. Under the Local Employment Act of 1960, the Board of Trade, in considering the location of any development for which an industrial development certificate is required, is now under a duty to have particular regard for the providing of employment in localities where a high rate of unemployment exists or is imminent or is likely to persist, seasonally or generally. Subject to this, the Board of Trade must be satisfied that the proposed development is such as can be carried out consistently with a proper distribution of industry.

HOW FAR AHEAD ARE WE PLANNING FOR?

The 1947 act required a survey to be prepared by every local planning authority before it attempted to make a development plan. These surveys provided invaluable experience in the art of stocktaking — what has the county got in the cupboard and how should the ingredients be used? — and it was on the results of these surveys that the first development plans were prepared. The 1947 act came into force in 1948, but it was somewhere around 1951 before any planning authority, having completed the survey, got down to the job of drawing the development plan. It thereby became a sort of datum line from which local planning authorities looked forward, sometimes boldly and courageously, sometimes, perhaps, a little fearfully and timidly, into the future and endeavored to picture what would be the prospect before them if town planning control over land use was going to do its work properly.

The question arose as to how far ahead the local planning authority was to look. Was it to be five years, ten years, fifty years or, in a word, was the sky to be the limit? The view emerged that development plans should be an embodiment of the idealistic and the realistic. To look only five years ahead was obviously not far enough, but in a rapidly changing world, in which science was capable of producing a new boom every day and a new bomb every night, it would, on the other hand, be a wise man indeed who could look ahead and picture the state of affairs in, say, fifty years time. Accordingly, the Minister decided, as part of his responsibility for town planning, to instruct all local planning authorities to prepare their first development plans to cover a prospect of twenty years from 1951 to 1971.

Under the 1947 act there can be no development without planning permission being first obtained from a local planning authority. If the applicant for permission is aggrieved by either (a) the refusal of his application, or (b) the grant of his application subject to conditions, he has a right of appeal to the Minister, whose decision on these matters is final, as it must be if he is to be responsible for town planning. It was one of the fundamental principles of the 1947 act that this prior need of planning permission (which, of course, is the main decisive factor in the exercise of land-use control) was something which it should be necessary to obtain irrespective of the operation of a development plan. But in dealing with an application for planning permission, the act goes on to provide that the local planning authority shall have regard to the provisions of any development plan (so far as material thereto) and to any other material considerations. Thus, while a development plan does not itself grant planning permission, it is by no means an irrelevant factor in the consideration of an application for planning permission. It is, in short, a guide to those who have the responsibility of dealing with applications for planning permission.

Whereas the town planning schemes of earlier town planning legislation were immutable and binding upon all (until a succeeding town planning scheme was made), a development plan is not binding upon anybody and, indeed, it is open to a local planning authority to grant planning permission for development which is contrary to a development plan, though the Minister's consent would be required in such a case. The rigidity and the stiffness of the earlier town-planning schemes had come to be regarded by 1947 as an unduly restraining feature of planning control. Indeed, only some 4 per cent of the land in England and Wales was covered by operative town planning schemes when the 1947 act swept them away. A state of affairs had been reached shortly before 1947 where local authorities preferred to rely upon what was called interim development control of land use rather than scheme control, and the reason for this was greater flexibility. Indeed, flexibility was the deliberate object of the 1947 act, but, as that very distinguished town planner, the late Sir Patrick Abercrombie, said, "Whilst we want flexibility in town planning control we do not want 'jellibility.'"

It was, accordingly, for this, among other reasons, that the period of twenty years was decided upon as the right sort of period for which the new development plans should cater. If the period were to be less than twenty years, then it became questionable as to whether it was worthwhile making a development plan at all. If the period were to be longer than twenty years then the much desired flexibility in the development plan might pass over into a state in which provisions of the development plan would be so vague, nebulous, and imprecise that neither developers nor town-planning authorities would know with sufficient precision either where they were or where they were going.

It will be noted that 1960 saw the twenty-year period of the first development plans just about half expired, and in the reviews of the development plans under consideration the question again arose as to what period ahead we are planning for. Eight years ago suggestions were made that in any review of a development plan the plan should continue to pay attention only to the original twenty years. Many changes have, however, occurred since then, and if the development plans at this stage continue to look forward only to 1971, then it must necessarily follow that there will be, in the forthcoming years, an increasing number of applications for planning permission for development which does not conform to the plans. Accordingly, it seems that in the recent review of development plans the forward gaze should be for at least another period of twenty years, ending in 1981.

There is another, and even more cogent, reason for saying that at that time of review the forward glance should have been to 1981 rather than 1971: it is now clear that many of the premises on which the first development plans were drawn were inaccurate. For example, so strong has been the pressure on land for building purposes over the last decade that much of the land allocated in the first development plans for building development which was expected to take place over the years 1951 to 1971 has already been used up, and one of the big questions posed in the recent review is: where are the next areas of land to be allocated for building development to come from?

The fact is that at the present time everybody and everything seems to be, like June, "busting out all over." Everybody is more mobile, thanks to dieselization of the railways and petrolization of the roadways, and everybody wants more room for work, for play, for living, for everything. Over and above all this, it must be remembered that there is a good deal more of everybody than there used to be. In 1948 the population of England and Wales was expected to grow to 45.3 millions by 1971, but natural growth has been much faster, and there is already a population of something over 45 millions, which is expected to grow by a further 3 millions in the next 15 to 20 years. In short, the natural increase in population has turned out to be about twice as fast as the rate subject to which most of the first development plans were fashioned.

But in addition to increases in total population, there has been a rapid increase in the number of separate households brought about by earlier marriages and a consequent increase in the number of family units seeking separate living accommodation. Today's young married couple, receiving higher rates of pay and enjoying a higher standard of living, is no longer content to share a household with mother-in-law. This is a most pertinent sign of our times and one, incidentally, for which (by way of a refreshing change) town planning cannot be blamed in any way whatsoever! Thus, even though some places have ceased to grow in population there is still a continued demand for more houses. Towns and cities, accordingly, tend to broaden and take up more space even though population density may be declining.

All these were matters not as well understood as they are today when, a decade ago, the first development plans were in course of preparation. Today we know that the first development plans were based on data and assumptions not entirely correct. While no one can be blamed for these misconceptions, the fact that they were made itself requires, even if the 1947 act did not, that there should now be a review of the first development plans — a review which should not be superficial but should be one based on brand-new data, a review which, in a word, matches the impelling needs of the present situation.

EFFECTS OF DEVELOPMENT PLANS

No one should be left in any doubt that the making and coming into effect of a development plan can sometimes have dramatic effects on the value of land. While, as already stated, the development plan does not itself grant any permission for development, it does show the kind of thing for which permission may well be granted if it is sought. Thus, a development plan may, merely by coming into operation, drain away development value from land, or, conversely, may attract development value to land. The draining away of development value has been referred to, not very attractively, as "planning blight," and so important has this matter come to be regarded that the 1959 act makes special provision to deal with it. After all, a small symbol on a development plan might mean a great deal to the owner of the land to which the symbol is attached. If, for example, the symbol shows that a new highway is to be constructed across a man's land, then he may find it quite impossible either to sell his land or to get planning permission to develop it himself, assuming he wants to do so. But while the development plan may show a proposed road, it will not necessarily show the particular year in which the road is to be constructed. In the meantime, what is to happen to the landowner whose land is "blighted" in this fashion? The 1959 act makes provision for this by means of a procedure which may be termed "compulsory purchase in reverse."

The 1959 act enables certain owner-occupiers of property adversely affected by planning proposals to have their property purchased by the local planning authority. If the owner-occupier is a *resident* owner-occupier, and can show that, owing to the "blighting" effect of the planning proposals, he is unable, after making reasonable endeavors, to sell his residential property except at a price substantially below what it might reasonably have been expected to fetch had there been no such planning proposals, he may, by notice, require his residential property to be purchased by the "appropriate authority." The authority which receives such a notice to purchase may dispute its validity by serving a counternotice of objection, and the matter will then be dealt with by the Lands Tribunal. If the notice to purchase is upheld by the Lands Tribunal, or if no counternotice is served, the authority is deemed to be authorized to acquire the "blighted" property and to have served a notice to treat so to do. The purchase price will, by virtue of special provisions in the 1959 act, be the "unblighted" value of the property.

These provisions of the 1959 act make it important that any markings on a development plan which tend to show property as liable to compulsory purchase should be removed at the earliest opportunity once it becomes clear that the markings do not rightly reflect the intentions of the local planning authority, and that the Minister has drawn the specific attention of local planning authorities to this important point.

By exercising its discretion to acquire land at an earlier date than that on which they were formerly empowered to do so, a local authority may at one and the same time help the landowner by relieving hardship caused to him by planning proposals and help itself by acquiring the land before any general rise in land values occurs.

If it is true that the coming into effect of a development plan may, on the one hand, depress the value of land, it is equally clear that, on the other hand, the plan will, in certain circumstances, have the effect of raising the value of land.

The summer of 1960 saw a boom in land prices in England, and for this, planning controls in general, and development plans in particular, have been blamed. Examples of £8,000, £10,000, and £15,000 an acre have been quoted as having been paid for residential land situated near moderately prosperous industrial towns. It has also been estimated by contracting firms that the average values of building land are now between three and four times as much as they were five years ago. In July 1960 it was reported that an investment company had paid £25,000 for a site of just over half an acre now used as a parking lot in the center of Luton, a town of 114,500 inhabitants. This price is believed to be the highest price per acre ever recorded on a sale of land in Britain.

It is easy for those to whom the controlling influences of town planning are an anathema to suggest that it is town planning and all that it stands for that are solely responsible for these inflated land prices. It must be admitted that there can be no doubt that the effect of town planning legislation and development plans has contributed in some degree to this rise in prices. Indeed, if this were not so it would be a criticism of town planning and a suggestion that it was failing in its purpose. It is submitted, however, that the real reason for this spectacular rise in prices for land, while being partly due to the influence of town planning control, is much more substantially due to the general economic well-being of the country and to the evolving modern style of urban family life in which two adjuncts (both of which cost money and each of which is now regarded as a necessity), namely, privacy and space, are being sought after more and more by all sorts and conditions of people.

When questioned in Parliament on this matter of rising land prices the Minister of Housing and Local Government replied, on June 28, 1960, as follows:

What I am doing, is to ask local planning authorities, in the reviews of their development plans now proceeding, to allocate more land to building beyond the green belts. In addition to that I am seeking to encourage the fullest use of land within the urban areas. But we have to face the fact that the demand in and around the most prosperous towns will continue to exceed the supply, unless we are to abandon planning policies of restricting the growth of towns, preserving good agricultural land and protecting the country-side; and that I am not prepared to do. What this means is that builders must turn their attention increasingly to redevelopment of older areas within the towns, which is our chief need.

I am not prepared to modify the policy of a free market in land, without which of course we should not have had the vigorous building progress of the last few years. What the situation calls for is administrative action of the kind I have described, rather than more legislation.

There is another point, however, to be considered in connection with this rise in the value of building land. It would appear that the mere making of more building land available would not necessarily bring land prices down, because the land which would be made available might not be available in the places where people want to go. Speaking by and large, everyone in the North of Scotland wants to go to the South of Scotland, after which the increased numbers in the South of Scotland wish to pass further south into the North of England, after which the increased multitudes in the North of England wish to move further south again into the South of England. Population movements in the United Kingdom tend always to be from the north southward. The reason for this is not far to seek. It is the paramount magnetic attraction of the capital of London. It is clearly not in the interests of the United Kingdom as a whole that there should be undue pressures in the London area and unduly empty spaces elsewhere, though one must accept that there will always be higher population densities near the capital city. It is one of the problems of town planning control to reverse, at least to some extent, this ever growing pressure by making other areas equally, if not more, attractive for living and working in. This problem has not yet by any means been solved, because it would appear to be the case that thousands of people are prepared to go and live near the capital city and suffer daily the inconveniences, which to some might appear intolerable, of high rents, general congestion, and near chaos at peak travel times for the privilege of so doing. Town planning has already embraced the concept of the direction of industry, but it should not direct population otherwise than obliquely.

Until this problem of easing congestion in the Southeast of England has been solved, land prices will remain high and tend to get higher notwithstanding the making available of land for building elsewhere in the United Kingdom. It is, however, incorrect in these circumstances to blame, as some have sought to do, town planning controls and development plans for the high prices of building land now current. On this the words of the Minister of Housing and Local Government in Parliament on July 18, 1960, may be quoted again, when he said:

No power could prevent land prices from rising in a prosperous country where there is limited land. My business is to see that there is no artificial rise in prices through too little land being allocated for houses which are necessary and desirable.

That is what we are doing, and that is why I suggest that we do not panic or dash for quack remedies, that we use present trends as evidence, that we must put land to full use and not waste it, and that we press on with careful forecasts and research and make absolutely sure that we keep all our development plans right up to date both regionally and locally.

Above all I suggest that we work with the market forces and seek to harness them to serve national purposes, instead of acting like Canute's courtiers . . . vainly telling the tide that it ought to turn and threatening to tax it if it does not.

CONCLUSION

It is hoped that the foregoing will have done something to outline the legal framework of the English development plan and the procedure for its making; to show the relative functions of the local planning authorities and the Minister of Housing and Local Government in connection with development plans; the period for which they purport to plan; and finally, the effect of development plans on that highly important matter, the value of land.

The carrying out of the statutory, nationwide comprehensive surveys on which the first plans were based has produced a mine of valuable information on which sociologists, geographers, and economists, not to mention town planners pure and simple, can each exercise their own peculiar mystique to the general advancement of town-planning knowledge.

The making of the first development plans and the holding of the various public inquiries up and down the country — the public inquiry into the development plan for the County of London lasted about nine months of almost daily sessions — did a great deal to bring home to the public in general the real import of the 1947 act and to make clear not only the meaning of town planning control but also the imperative reasons, in a comparatively small country with a large population, for having to submit to it. The quinquennial reviews of the development plans now going forward serve as a sort of refresher course in this important business of public instruction.

The rapid changes of the postwar years in England would have been a testing time for any system of development control, but it is fair to say that the development plans have come through the first decade of their existence with credit. Much has naturally been learned and mistakes made in the preparation of the first plans can be rectified in the reviews that have recently taken place. This having been said, one feels entitled to submit that nothing has emerged to suggest that the concept of the development plan and the basic principles of land control on which that concept is founded (and as enacted in the 1947 act) are wrong. To put the matter the other way round, one can but shudder at what might have occurred in this tight little island of Britain had the reconstruction of war damage and the general accommodating of the public to a more bounding, spreading, postwar way of life not been subjected to the refining influences of town planning control through the medium of flexible development plans made locally by local planning authorities but approved centrally by the Minister of Housing and Local Government.

*The Individual
and the Machinery of Planning*

PLANNING DECISIONS AND APPEALS

F. H. B. LAYFIELD
BARRISTER AT LAW, INNER TEMPLE

THE LAND PLANNING system of England and Wales is based largely on the provisions of the Town and Country Planning Act of 1947, although many other statutes also are involved. An explanatory memorandum which accompanied it stated the object of town and country planning to be "that all land in the country is put to the use which is best from the point of view of the community." [1] This aim is forwarded by requiring that no serious change in the use of land may take place without permission from the appropriate authority.[2] If approval is not forthcoming the intending user often may appeal to the responsible Minister, now the Minister of Housing and Local Government. Naturally the outcome of such appeals is likely to and perhaps should have an important influence in shaping future decisions of the responsible authority.

It is at the stage of decision and appeal that, in the words of Mr. Desmond Heap, "the pinch of planning" is felt. If planning in England and Wales has a bad image it is created in large measure at the planning appeal stage. Few who get what they ask for are likely to be discontented with the administration of planning; it is those who are denied planning permission and who appeal from that decision who are the potential malcontents. Moreover, few people are involved in the initial planning decision; on the other hand, large numbers of people attend the hearings of planning appeals. For many, it is their only direct and real contact with the machinery of planning. For the planners, as well as for the administration, planning appeals are, in a real sense, the shopwindow of planning. These attributes invest planning appeals with an importance beyond their mere numbers, which are, in any event, significant.

[1] Town and Country Planning Bill, 1947, Explanatory Memorandum, CMD. No. 7006 (1947), and see H.C. DEB. 947, 989, 1001 (5th ser. 1947).
[2] Amendment of Financial Provisions, CMD. No. 8699, para. 5 (1952).

APPLICATIONS TO THE LOCAL PLANNING AUTHORITIES

The 1947 act requires that anyone wishing to develop land in England and Wales must apply to the local planning authority for permission to do so.[3] Development is defined broadly as "the carrying out of any building, mining, engineering or other operations in, on, over or under land or the making of any material change of use of any buildings or other land." There are some important exceptions; the act itself sets out a number of exempted activities such as certain maintenance works and the use of land for agriculture.[4] Several ministerial orders have considerably widened the field of exemptions. Nonetheless, almost all serious changes (excepting certain works by government departments) require prior consent by the local planning authority. In the rural areas, the county council is the local planning authority, but in the vast majority of cases the power to handle applications has been or will be delegated to the county district councils.[5] In the big towns, the county borough council is the authority concerned. The applications cover a wide range from matters as trivial as the use of a room, such as a doctor's consulting room, to developments as large as that of a nuclear power station. There are an average of 400,000 of them per year.

The initial handling of these applications usually is delegated to the planning committee of the recipient council (also consisting of elected representatives) or to a committee whose tasks include responsibility for town and country planning. In either case the initial decision usually is made by the committee in the form of a recommendation, which is then submitted to and normally approved by the council.

Both committee and council are, in the majority of cases, advised by a technical officer on their staff who is responsible to them for planning matters. In the case of the larger authorities, he is normally expressly trained for the post and employed solely as a planning officer. Smaller councils are, in many instances, advised by their engineer or surveyor, who deals with planning matters as well as other work.[6]

The authority is required to decide on the application within two months of its receipt; there are exceptions when difficult problems are involved or extensive consultations are necessary.[7] The authority is en-

---

[3] Town and Country Planning Act, 1947, 10 & 11 Geo. 6, c. 51, § 12.

[4] Section 12(2), provisos (a)–(c).

[5] Town and Country Planning General Development Order, 1950, art. 5(5).

[6] Report of the Committee on Qualifications of Planners, CMD. No. 3059, at 26 (1950).

[7] Town and Country Planning General Development Order 1959, art. 5(8).

titled to request of the applicant any further information it needs to come to a decision and, of course, it may ask the applicant to grant an extension of time whenever that seems appropriate.[8]

Having considered the application, the local planning authority may take one of three courses: it may refuse to grant the application; it may allow it outright; or it may give it qualified approval,[9] attaching to the grant of permission "such conditions as [it] think[s] fit." Although there are no reliable figures about the handling of planning applications, it has been estimated that about 40,000 were denied in the year ending March 31, 1958, while conditions were attached to about 290,000 consents. If the authority refuses to grant permission or grants qualified approval or fails to notify the applicant of its decision within the statutory period, the applicant automatically has the right to appeal to the Minister[10] within one month of the ruling or the expiration of the statutory period.[11]

The Minister is empowered to "call in" any planning application or any particular class of application; by so doing he directs the local planning authority to refer the matter to him for initial decision.[12] This course is most commonly adopted when the Minister anticipates considerable public criticism of a proposed development which he thinks the authority may be disposed to allow. Since third parties have no right to appeal from a grant of permission, this procedure enables the Minister to allow interested parties a public hearing before any decision is taken. Both the authority and the applicant have a right to be heard, as in a normal appeal.

Criticisms frequently are voiced about the way local planning authorities deal with the applications made to them. They are of some relevance because they shed light on difficulties encountered at the appeal stage. First, it is said that the authorities show a chronic inability to reach a decision within the two months allowed them. Three years after the 1947 act was passed the Minister set the two-month maximum, no doubt choosing that length after careful deliberation. More than ten years later it clearly has not been thought unreasonably short, since it has never been changed. It is nevertheless true that a large number of straightforward applications are not dealt with within the two-month period.

[8] Town and Country Planning General Development Order, 1959, art. 5(1) and 5(8).
[9] Town and Country Planning Act, 1947, § 14(1).
[10] Town and Country Planning Act, 1947, § 16(1).
[11] Town and Country Planning General Development Order, 1950, art. 11(1).
[12] Town and Country Planning Act, 1947, § 15(1).

Second, the authorities display a surprising reluctance to indicate to applicants, before they become appellants, what kind of development they would allow in those cases where they are unable to assent to the application as it stands. Although the Minister's policy is that "in planning cases, where the application cannot be immediately accepted as it stands, the local planning authority should be ready to authorize its officers to discuss the application with the applicant before giving a decision, wherever this can usefully be done," [13] it is a common experience that this course is followed less often than it might be. Third, and most important, when local planning authorities refuse to grant permission or grant it subject to conditions they are required to give their reasons for doing so. [14] All too often these so-called reasons are unintelligible.

The Minister repeatedly has urged local authorities to state their reasons clearly and intelligibly, and has issued several circulars to this effect over the years. [15] All have had singularly little effect. By 1957, when the Franks Committee investigated these procedures, it reported, "Fairness requires that those whose individual rights and interests are likely to be adversely affected by the action proposed should know in good time before the enquiry the case which they will have to meet. We are not satisfied that this requirement is fully met." The position was further articulated by the Minister in Circular 9/58:

In planning cases Article 5(9)(a) of the General Development Order, 1950, already requires the planning authority to state its reasons in writing when it decides to refuse an application or to grant permission subject to conditions. It is important that this statement should be full enough to give the applicant adequate understanding of the reasons for the authority's decision. For example, it is not ordinarily sufficient to say merely that the development "would be injurious to amenity" or would "be contrary to the provisions of the Development Plan." In the former case, it should be explained what is the amenity that would be injured; in the latter precisely what provisions in the Plan are involved and how they apply.

So little progress had been achieved in persuading local planning authorities to state their reasons with clarity that the point was again emphasized, this time by the chief inspector of the Ministry of Housing and Local Government, in addressing the Town Planning Institute in 1959: "Nevertheless the reasons given are in a great many cases still sketchy, and where

[13] Ministry of Housing and Local Government Circular 9/58, para. 9 (1958).
[14] Town and Country Planning General Development Order, 1950, art. 5(9).
[15] Ministry of Town and Country Planning Circulars 33 of 1947, 69 of 1949, and Ministry of Housing and Local Government Circular 61 of 1953.

further reasons are given they are often produced for the first time either just before the inquiry or at it." [16] This theme recurs both at the inquiry stage and after.

THE APPEAL

If the applicant desires to appeal from the local planning authority's decision he must do so within the specified time limit. However, the Minister has power to accept late notice of appeal, and, in fact, frequently does so.[17] In 1959 the Minister received 10,657 notices of appeal;[18] this is double the number received in 1953.

The notice of appeal usually is made on a standard form supplied for the purpose, but can be given by letter. It must be accompanied by copies of the original application, relevant plans and drawings, the decision, and any relevant correspondence.[19]

Upon receiving the notice of appeal, the Minister must give both the appellant and the local planning authority an opportunity to be heard by somebody appointed for the purpose if they desire it.[20] Usually the hearing is a public local inquiry conducted under the terms of the Local Government Act of 1933, but sometimes it is private. Alternatively, the Minister may indicate that he feels able to decide the appeal on the basis of the written evidence to be submitted. The consent of both parties is required for the latter procedure to be adopted; if either objects, the matter must proceed to a hearing. In the vast majority of cases where an appeal is pursued there is a public local inquiry. There are no figures as to the number of hearings which took place in 1959, but some estimate may be drawn from the fact that 7,300 appeals were decided by the Minister.

One to two months after submission of the notice of appeal, the appellant and the local planning authority receive notice of the inquiry from the Minister stating the name of the inspector he has appointed to hear it and the date, time, and place at which it will be held. The date of the inquiry usually is about two months after the notice. The site often is the local town hall, a large committee room, or some similar accommodation in the vicinity of the appeal site.

[16] JOURNAL OF THE TOWN PLANNING INSTITUTE, March 1960, p. 86.
[17] Town & Country Planning General Development Order, 1950, art. 11(1).
[18] Report of Ministry of Housing and Local Government, CMD. No. 1927, at 194–195 (1959).
[19] Town and Country Planning General Development Order, art. 11(2).
[20] Town and Country Planning Act, 1947, § 16(2), applying § 15.

PREPARATION FOR THE HEARING

The frequent failure to state clear reasons for decisions has already been emphasized. The Franks Committee urged that "the statutory requirements should, where necessary, be amended to compel . . . planning authorities to give full particulars of their case in good time before the enquiry, so that those affected are better able to prepare and present their case. These particulars should be made available in the form of a written statement." [21] It added: "The statement should be delivered to the applicant with the decision of the local planning authority if that decision is other than unqualified approval. It should explain the reasons for the refusal or qualified grant of planning permission." [22] Although the Franks Committee clearly intended that the local planning authority be required to give the reasons for its decision when the decision was made and that the appellant be notified accordingly, its views were interpreted in a different sense by the government. Writing to local planning authorities about the Franks Committee's recommendations the Ministry said:

When the applicant has notified his intention to appeal, and desires to be heard, it may be that the local planning authority will need to amplify the reasons already given to him for the decision. At this stage it is essential that the applicant should know, as fully as possible, what is the case he has to meet. If, for example, the authority has taken account of any Ministerial statement of policy or of any Departmental circular in coming to its decision that should be explained — with a reference which will enable the applicant to look it up for himself. Indeed, the more clearly that authorities can explain their reasons at the outset the better; but if they do not find it practicable to supply a full statement when giving their decision they must do so in good time before an inquiry. They are also asked to furnish as full a statement as possible where the inquiry is arranged following an appeal against failure to issue a decision within the statutory period.[23]

In the great majority of cases this statement, if produced at all, leaves much to be desired. Rarely does one state the case in terms which a normal and intelligent person can fully understand. Usually it is padded with much that is already known, such as the details of the application and a restatement of the grounds of refusal. The statements, like the original decisions, contain a great deal of meaningless jargon and many muddled,

[21] Report of the Committee on Administrative Tribunals and Enquiries, CMD. No. 218, para. 281 (1957).
[22] *Id*. para. 283
[23] Ministry of Housing and Local Government Circular 9/58, para. 8 (1958).

incoherent phrases. Nor, in the absence of any guidance, is there anything approaching uniformity in the content of these statements. For example, while some of the better statements contain details of what the development plan proposes for the area in question, and set out details of planning decisions which affect the vicinity, both favorable and unfavorable to the appellant, others make no mention of either of these matters.

By far the most serious and persistent complaint about these statements is their extreme tardiness. The inquiry usually is held some four to five months after the date of the planning decision to which it relates. It is by no means uncommon for an appellant to receive the statement, which is supposed to set out the case he has to meet, two weeks before the date of the actual inquiry, as little as one week before the inquiry, or sometimes, not at all. As one inspector noted, in relation to a complaint made to him on this subject in January 1960: "While expressing no opinion on the appellant's claim for costs against the Local Planning Authority I consider that there was no justification for their withholding written observations amplifying the non-explanatory grounds of refusal, both in justice to the appellants and in providing the Minister with information as well." [24]

One feature of the present planning-inquiry machinery is the considerable number of appeals withdrawn before reaching the Minister. Of some 10,600 appeals made in 1959, slightly over 25 per cent were withdrawn before decision. Many were discontinued literally at the inquiry door and some even after the inquiry had opened. Although there are many reasons which account for the large number of appeals withdrawn, a substantial fraction is attributable in large part to the local authority's failure to make its views clear to the appellant in good time. Had a clear and adequate statement been made at the proper time many of these appeals would have been avoided. Although the local planning authority has the power under the General Development Order to require an applicant to furnish further details if it does not fully understand what he seeks to do, the appellant is powerless, at the present time, to compel the local planning authority to state its case more clearly. As a result of the failure to provide clear reasoning, a great deal of time and money is wasted. Many unnecessary appeals clutter up the system, adding to the delay of other cases because the inspector's time often is wasted by late agreements. The chief inspector of the Ministry of Housing and Local Government

[24] Paragraph 69 of inspector's report accompanying a Ministerial Decision Letter of May 16, 1960.

observed in 1959: "Proper thought and clearer exposition in the early stages would almost certainly obviate quite a lot of appeals." [25]

OTHER FORMS OF APPEAL

There are three classes of cases which depart from the general pattern of application and appeal thus far described. If a person desires to ascertain whether a particular activity constitutes development and requires permission, he may ask the local planning authority to determine that question.[26] An adverse answer or failure to give an answer within the two-month period permits the applicant to appeal to the Minister in the manner outlined.

Second, if a party carries out a development without prior consent and the local planning authority believes permission was required, it may serve an enforcement notice.[27] The recipient of the notice is entitled, among other things, to apply for planning permission ex post facto. The application is thereafter treated as any other application for planning permission.

Third, the Minister has the power, as already noted, to "call in" applications of practically every kind for decision by himself. In such cases both the local planning authority and the appellant can ask for a hearing to be held. In practice, the Minister usually issues a statement outlining his tentative view of the matter, the procedure thereafter following the usual lines.

THE INQUIRY

The inquiry is held by an inspector who invariably is a technical officer and a civil servant on the staff of the Ministry of Housing and Local Government. He is usually an architect, engineer, or surveyor, although occasionally he belongs to some other associated technical profession. He is practically never a lawyer, either by training or by qualification.

At the hearing, whether public or private, the appellant and the local planning authority are the only parties who are entitled to be heard as of right.[28] In practice, however, the inspector usually is willing to hear any other parties present who can convince him that, in normal, common-sense terms, they are interested parties. Occupiers and owners of adjoining or nearby properties, representatives of local preservation, protection, or civic societies, or parish councils, or spokesmen for national bodies inter-

[25] *Op. cit. supra* note 16, at 87.
[26] Town and Country Planning Act, 1947, § 17.
[27] Town and Country Planning Act, 1947, § 23. See the paper by J. G. Barr in this volume.
[28] Town and Country Planning Act, 1947, § 15(2).

ested in some principle allegedly involved in the particular case, are frequent third parties.

Appellants and the local planning authorities are entitled to legal representation by a lawyer or any other person of their choice. The appellant may, of course, appear in person. In fact, the appellant has legal counsel in almost all major inquiries, and is represented by a surveyor or land agent in a very large number of cases. In all except the largest inquiries the authorities tend to be represented by their clerk or by a lawyer on the staff of the council, often a specialist in such cases. If the latter is the case, the result usually is highly satisfactory. However, if the local clerk, who may have many other responsibilities, appears for the authority, the effect sometimes is to aggravate a case already confused by the initial failure to give clear reasons for the decision.

The order of procedure at the inquiry follows this general pattern:

(1) The inspector opens the proceedings with a short statement on the purpose of the inquiry and may describe the procedure. He then requests a list of those who wish to be heard.

(2) The appellant, in person or by his representative, makes his opening statement, outlines his case, and calls each of his witnesses in turn. The witnesses are examined, cross-examined, and re-examined in the normal manner.

(3) The local planning authority representative may make an opening statement and call his witnesses, or, alternatively, call his witnesses first and make a statement later. The latter is the more favored of the two methods. The authority's witnesses are examined, cross-examined, and re-examined.

(4) Any interested parties who are to be heard from present their cases. Very frequently they do so merely by making a short statement; sometimes, they appear by counsel and call witnesses, the procedure then being the same as in (2), above.

(5) The appellant makes his closing speech in reply, attempting to summarize and to rebut the points made against him.

(6) The inspector closes the inquiry. Thereafter, he normally visits the site of the proposed development, inviting representatives of all parties concerned to accompany him.

Any consideration of the inquiry must start with the inspector himself. His position was fully studied by the Franks Committee, which was asked to consider and make recommendations on the "working of such administrative procedures as include the holding of an enquiry or hearing by or on behalf of a Minister on an appeal or as the result of objections or representations." [29] The Committee recorded the viewpoints most frequently expressed as follows:

293. First, and most important, it is argued that a Minister is responsible for the final decision and that that decision must often be influenced by considerations of Government policy. The ideal would be for the Minister himself to hold the enquiry and thus hear the evidence at first hand, but since this is clearly out of the question the next best course is for one of his own officers, who can be kept in touch with developments in policy, to perform this function. It is further contended that it may be difficult for the Minister to accept full responsibility for a decision taken in his name if the report on the enquiry, which is an important and sometimes vital part of the advice on which the decision is based, is not made by someone within his Department.

294. The second argument is that, particularly in the case of the Ministry of Housing and Local Government, the number of enquiries is sufficient to justify, and indeed on practical grounds to make essential, a corps of full-time inspectors, if enquiries are to be arranged and completed with reasonable promptitude.

295. Third, it is argued that highly technical considerations frequently arise, particularly in planning enquiries, which make it advisable for the inspector to be a person constantly engaged in this kind of work and therefore a member of the Department concerned.

296. Lastly, it is argued that the establishment of a corps of independent inspectors, particularly if responsibility for it were to be given to the Lord Chancellor — as has been frequently suggested — would foster the impression that the process was judicial. It might thus increase rather than decrease public dissatisfaction, the public being the more likely to expect the final decision to be based solely upon the evidence on the enquiry and the report following the enquiry or indeed to expect the inspector to act as a judge and give a decision himself. If, as an alternative to a corps of inspectors under the Lord Chancellor, independent persons were appointed *ad hoc,* for each enquiry the whole process might be lengthened because of their unfamiliarity with the conduct of enquiries and their inability, through lack of knowledge of departmental policy, to give the Minister the kind of advice which he most needs.[30]

In general, the view of those experienced in these matters has been that a corps of inspectors of some kind would be necessary, and it has been suggested that they should be established under the Lord Chancellor. The Franks Committee summarized the arguments for independent inspectors in this way:

298. First, it is argued that public confidence in the procedure, especially at the enquiry stage, would be increased and that the change would help to

[29] *Supra* note 21, at iii.
[30] *Id*. paras. 293–296.

remove the feeling that the scales are weighted against the individual, particularly where the proposals have been initiated by the very Minister whose inspector is conducting the enquiry.

299. Second, it is argued that the need for the inspector to be conversant with departmental policy has been exaggerated and that it would be equally satisfactory if the considerations of policy thought to be relevant were placed before the inspector in departmental evidence given at the enquiry. As the Minister would continue to make the final decision, policy would, where necessary, prevail.

300. Third, it is pointed out that several Departments employ independent inspectors and find this arrangement satisfactory.

301. Fourth, it is argued that it would be less embarrassing for Departments to give oral evidence before an independent inspector than before a departmental inspector.

302. Finally, it is said that it would be less difficult to publish the report of an independent inspector than of a departmental inspector, since as an independent person he could more freely comment upon the evidence given, and that it would not be so embarrassing for the Minister to give a decision differing from any published recommendations. It is pointed out in this connection that the Ministry of Education, the only Department which invariably publishes inspectors' reports, employs independent inspectors.[31]

It should be added that planning inquiries in Scotland often are held satisfactorily by independent inspectors. The Franks Committee had no hesitation in concluding that inspectors should be placed under the control of a Minister *not* directly concerned with the subject matter of their work. They considered the Lord Chancellor to be the most appropriate person, and accordingly recommended that the inspectors be placed under him. Of this recommendation the Committee said,

Some may say that this would be a change in name only, but we feel no need to argue the point because we are convinced that here the appearance is what matters. This change, by no longer identifying the inspector in the minds of the objectors with the Department of the deciding Minister, would emphasize impartiality at an important stage of the adjudication and thus do much to allay the public misgiving. We see in this no obstacle to the inspectors being kept in close contact with developments of policy in the Departments responsible for the subject-matter of the enquiries.[32]

This recommendation, however, was not accepted by the government. It may be that in so doing the government decided against the weight of informed opinion. Also, the majority of the inspectors concerned favored their transfer to the Lord Chancellor's department. No doubt

[31] *Id*. paras. 298–302.
[32] *Id*. para. 303.

there were many reasons for the decision to reject this recommendation, but one of the most important was the resolute determination of the Lord Chancellor's department not to be made responsible for inspectors.

In describing the inquiry procedure, phrases like "general pattern" have been used. This may seem a loose way of describing procedure governed by rules. However, the fact of the matter is that there are no rules, or rather, no binding rules. The Minister has made some rules for conducting inquiries, but has consistently refused to make them public. These rules are, in fact, so secret that many inspectors have never seen them. As a result, the conduct of the inquiry is largely a matter for the inspectors' discretion.

The absence of any known code of rules, however general, creates one unfortunate feature. This is best described as a climate of opinion characterized by a distinctly casual attitude toward facts and a surprising indifference to the distinction between fact and opinion. Hearsay of the wildest and most unsubstantiated kind frequently is offered as evidence and few if any inspectors demur. In this climate both the appellant and the local authority become somewhat unconcerned with the true facts of the matter under inquiry. This attitude, in turn, shapes the attitude of witnesses. The chief housing and planning inspector summarized widespread criticism of the evidence given at inquiries by planning officers in support of their authorities when he said: "I am often asked what is the position of a planning officer who is required to appear at an appeal inquiry arising from a decision contrary to his advice. Some planning officers feel that their professional integrity requires them to say what they think; others feel that whilst their position is a very difficult one they are appearing as servants of their Council and must put the Council's case to the best of their ability." [33] These witnesses usually are introduced expressly as experts. They retail to the inquiry their full professional qualifications, their length of experience, and any other facts which may increase the apparent value of the technical opinion to the inspector and the Ministry in deciding the case.

The chief inspector's observations are an eloquent reflection on the present procedure which allows inspectors to watch impassively while a qualified professional man gives in evidence opinions in which he does not believe but which are advanced as his own. Even more revealing is the chief inspector's advice to the local authority's witness that "if cross-

[33] See *op. cit. supra* note 16, at 89.

examination becomes insistent on the point [he] can ask the Inspector's protection."

The chief inspector's remarks led to a lively discussion in *The Times* and elsewhere, one position being summarized by Mr. Desmond Heap, who pointed out that

it is the advocate's responsibility to put the local authority's case and the witness's responsibility to go into the witness-box and support that case if he legitimately and conscientiously can. The advocate is not liable to cross-examination but the witness is and it is surely idle (for it makes nonsense of the whole procedure) for a witness, finding himself, as a result of cross-examination, in a spot too hot to hold, to appeal for "the Inspector's protection." What protection can the Inspector rightly, legitimately and properly give in such circumstances? A witness goes into the witness-box for better or worse; evidence which is tendered at an inquiry but which is not allowed to be tested by cross-examination is not to be relied upon and if it is relied upon, then that is something which is neither open, nor fair, nor impartial, both in relation to the conduct of the inquiry itself and in relation to any decision arrived at as a result of the inquiry.[34]

In considering the chief inspector's attitude, which is frequently encountered in inquiries at the present time, the tardiness with which the local authorities produce a statement of their case before the inquiry should be recalled.

If local government witnesses occasionally give unsatisfactory evidence, at least they attend the inquiry. Central government departments often take a hand in the local planning authority's decision, but rarely do their representatives testify at an inquiry. The departments always have been reluctant to do so, the Franks Committee reporting that "Departments are disinclined to adopt a general practice of giving evidence at enquiries." [35] Despite the near-unanimous opposition of the official witnesses who appeared before the Committee, it concluded, "We see no reason why the factual basis for a departmental view should not be explained and its validity tested in cross-examination." It explained its proposals as "designed to broaden the scope of the enquiry sufficiently to give individual objectors and appellants reasonable opportunities for testing the case against them and the evidence for that case; and at the same time to protect official witnesses from questioning on matters for which Parlia-

[34] JOURNAL OF PLANNING AND PROPERTY LAW, June 1960, 384, 386.
[35] *Supra* note 29, at para. 315.

ment is the right forum." [36] The Committee recommended that officials be required to give factual evidence in support of their departments' views if those views were referred to by the local authority in its explanatory written statement or its evidence at the inquiry.[37] The government accepted this recommendation. Nonetheless, despite the fact that the central government departments continue, no doubt rightly, to influence planning decisions on many occasions, very rarely are witnesses from them present at inquiries. No mention is made of their views in the full statement of the case, if any, and so the opportunity to call a witness from them does not arise. Therefore, there remains "the dissatisfaction which arises from the feeling that in many cases the decisive voice is that of an authority which has remained in the background throughout the initial and enquiry stages." [38]

A final cause of current dissatisfaction with the inquiry stage concerns costs. Planning inquiries are not, as the Minister has sometimes hinted, cheap. The magnitude of the issues at stake and the value of consent are so great that appellants would be foolish not to assure full preparation and proper presentation of their cases. Yet, win or lose, unless there has been the most egregious conduct, appellant will receive no award of costs.

The Minister may award costs in his discretion but almost never does. His policy is to do so only when a party is thought to have acted unreasonably or vexatiously. This sounds fair, but is not observed in practice. There are numerous cases of no award of costs being made when one party has acted most unreasonably. The Ministry's advice to local authorities and to applicants and appellants is widely and consistently ignored on many aspects of planning appeals. This situation would change rapidly and much unnecessary nonsense be avoided by even a limited award of costs. It is very difficult not to conclude, with the Franks Committee, that "costs should be awarded more widely than at present." [39]

AFTER THE INQUIRY

"One of the main causes of dissatisfaction . . . is that after the enquiry, when the parties no longer have any further influence upon the course of events, fresh evidence or new opinions may be sought by or placed before the Department of the deciding Minister, and that this new matter

[36] *Id.* para. 316.
[37] *Id.* paras. 317–319.
[38] *Id.* para. 320.
[39] *Id.* para. 322.

may well determine the final decision." [40] This practice was accurately described in *The Times* as "egregious backstairs consultations."

The feeling is widespread that other government departments still tender evidence to the Minister after the inquiry is over. Because their influence in the initial stage need not be stated in the local authority's decision, it may be impossible to call their representative to the inquiry. The problem might be alleviated if the local authority was obliged to state any advice received from government departments. This would enable the appellant to request an appropriate witness to be called if he suspected intrigue. Further, if the decision letter stated clearly the facts found as a result of the inquiry, and the reasons for the decision appeared to flow logically from these facts, any postinquiry influence would become apparent more readily.

The inspectors' reports, which are available to the parties, might be thought to perform this function. Up to a point they are adequate and workmanlike documents. Normally, they contain a full and careful synopsis of the evidence given by all the parties at the inquiry. The reports usually describe and summarize the site and surroundings; the case for the appellants; the case for the council; the case for the interested persons (if any); the inspector's conclusions; and recommendations. Difficulties begin to appear only with the passage itemizing conclusions. Having prepared a careful digest of the evidence presented on both sides and discussed a view of the site, it might be expected that an assessment of the evidence would follow, that some evidence would be rejected, often for stated reasons, while other evidence would be preferred, again possibly with reasons. It might even be expected that a clear picture would result from the evidence accepted. But, as the published examples show, such expectations are largely in vain. Also, the inspectors' recommendations in a great many cases appear eminently sensible, but often it is far from clear which matters were significant in reaching the conclusions. In some cases the connection between any of the evidence and the recommendation is extremely tenuous.

It cannot be that the suggested assessment is impossible or impracticable by reason of the mystique of planning, for the reports rendered in Scotland achieve the desired result admirably. Nor does the absence of such analysis exist because inspectors in England and Wales are incapable of producing it, since even brief acquaintance with inspectors shows that to

[40] *Id.* para. 347.

be quite untrue. Can the reason be that the Ministry, under whose direct control the inspectors come, would rather not have such a digest?

From two months to a year after the inquiry, or an average of six months later, the Minister issues his decision in the form of a letter. Since April 1, 1959, a statute requires him to give reasons for reaching his decision.[41] In the past, reasons were stated in the majority of cases, but often they were, and usually still are, very brief. If he agrees with the inspector's recommendations, he usually says nothing besides that. If he does not accept the inspector's view, more extensive reasons are offered. On the whole, however, they shed little light on the connection between the evidence given at the inquiry and the final decision.

There are some special cases in which the basis of the Minister's view is made reasonably clear. Among these are cases concerned with greenbelts, the employment of modern architectural forms, and development of an alien kind in wholly residential areas.[42]

The standard for the decision letters should perhaps be this: special cases apart, can the practitioner in this field obtain any guidance on how an average case should be prepared from reading the Minister's decision letters in similar cases? The answer now is clearly no. He may well learn the Minister's opinions in such matters. For example, he will soon learn that there is a rooted prejudice against gas stations and, until very recently, against trailers, or that modern architecture is fairly favorably received. What he will find very difficult and often impossible to ascertain is what evidence will carry weight with the Minister in reaching a decision, and what evidence is likely to be regarded as unconvincing or even irrelevant.

If the appellant is largely in the dark about the best way to prepare the appeal, he would seem little better able to judge the chances of his success. While in the special cases, such as those mentioned above, the outcome usually can be fairly well predicted, these constitute less than half of all appeals. As for the remainder, there is but one guide: the Minister has almost consistently, for more than a decade, reversed slightly less than one third of all appeals heard by him. Sample figures are (excluding advertisement appeals):

	Total decisions	Numbers allowed
1957	5,252	1,705
1958	4,930	1,587
1959	5,673	1,736

[41] Tribunals and Inquiries Act, 1958, 6 & 7 Eliz. 2, c. 66, § 12, and STAT. INSTR., 1959, No. 451.

[42] See, for example, H.M.S.O., Selected Planning Appeals (June 1959).

PLANNING APPEALS AND JUDICIAL REVIEW

For all practical purposes, the Minister's decision on a planning appeal is final, with no further appeal available to the High Court, either on matters of fact or law. There are two exceptions. The Town and Country Planning Act of 1959 gives a limited right of appeal to the courts, which must be exercised within six weeks of the Minister's decision. Broadly speaking, the grounds are limited to an allegation that the decision was *ultra vires* or that the proper procedure was not observed.[43] At the time, section 31 was thought by some to have enlarged the right of legal challenge to the Minister's decision. As it has developed, it probably does no more than replace the right to challenge the Minister's action by means of *certiorari* proceedings. The rights conferred by section 31 may, however, come to have greater value. The Franks Committee recommended that "a standard code or codes of procedure should be published and made available to the parties." [44] The Lord Chancellor has now been given power, after consultation with the Council on Tribunals, to make such rules.[45] The proposed rules would be embodied in a statutory instrument which would then be laid before Parliament.[46] If the rules are enacted, any failure to observe them may well give a right of appeal under section 31.

However, from the applicant's point of view, there is little value in this appeal right. He will appeal only when the decision is against him. If his challenge in the courts is successful, his remedy will be to have the decision voided. This will make the refusal of no effect, but the unhappy applicant will be no better off, since he still will not have the affirmative permission sought.

The second exception in which appeal may be had is an even more recent innovation. The recipient of an enforcement notice may apply ex post facto for planning permission to retain the allegedly offending development, such an appeal in most respects being identical with a normal planning appeal. Since August 1960, however, such an appeal from the Minister's decision to the High Court will lie either on a point of law or "by way of case stated." [47] The language of the section may be significant. Clearly, something more than a right to appeal on a point of law is being conferred, or the succeeding words would be otiose. If so, it is difficult to

---

[43] Town and Country Planning Act, 1959, 7 & 8 Eliz. 2, c. 25, §31.

[44] *Supra* note 29, at para. 310.

[45] Town and Country Planning Act, 1959, § 33, amending the Tribunals and Inquiries Act, 1958, by adding § 7a.

[46] *Ibid.*

[47] Caravan Sites and Control of Development Act, 1960, 8 & 9 Eliz. 2, c. 62, § 34.

see how the strictures which the court may pass upon the conduct of such inquiries can fail to be reflected in the conduct of ordinary planning appeals.

Yet here again it would seem that little real benefit will accrue to the appellants. Even if successful, they merely find themselves back at the starting point. There may be some advantage to local authorities in these provisions, however, where they are aggrieved by a decision favorable to an appellant.

There has been, and is, much argument about the proper extent of judicial review of planning appeals, but until the court can do more than merely invalidate a decision, little would seem to be achieved by an appeal. The view finally taken surely must depend upon a conception of the true function and nature of the planning inquiry process itself. There are two classic and strongly contrasting views and these were succinctly described in the Franks Report:

263. According to the first view the entire procedure must be regarded as administrative, in the sense that: — (i) the decisions taken at its culmination have as their purpose the furtherance of the positive processes of government; (ii) provided that the deciding Minister does not overstep the legal limits of his powers, his discretion whether to decide positively or negatively in a particular case and, if positively, whether or not to modify the original proposals, is wholly unfettered; (iii) the Minister is responsible only to Parliament for the decision taken; and finally (iv) in the nature of the subject-matter it is impossible to formulate rules to govern the decision and wholly inappropriate to base it upon precedent.

264. According to the other view the procedure possesses several essential elements of a judicial process, inasmuch as: — (i) special arrangements are provided by statute for the lodging and consideration of objections — a feature not to be found in the general course of administrative activity; and (ii) at the hearing or enquiry two or more parties, taking opposing views of what should be done, dispute the matter before a specially appointed person who, though he does not decide it himself, nevertheless plays an important part in the process of decision. Thus regarded, the enquiry appears to take on something of the nature of a trial and the inspector to assume the guise of a judge. It is further argued that, because of the "judicial" nature of the enquiry, the ensuing decision is or should be "judicial" in the sense that it should be based wholly and directly upon the evidence presented at the enquiry.[48]

Neither of these views has wholly appealed to those concerned with the administration of affairs, to the courts, or to the legislature. The attitude

---

[48] *Supra* note 29, paras. 263, 264.

which the latter has taken stems in large measure from the historical origins of these inquiries, in the procedure of the private bill:

268. In the last century a public authority or an undertaking such as a railway company, wishing to acquire land for its purposes, had always to promote a Private Bill, the procedure for which provides for the lodging of objections and for the hearing of the parties by a Parliamentary Committee. The final decision is, of course, that of Parliament, though the Ministers concerned have an opportunity of influencing that decision by submitting a report or evidence to the Committee and by using the Government's majority on the floor of the House. In the course of time it was decided — because of the extension of governmental responsibilities and the resulting increased need to acquire land for public purposes, and also because of the expense of procedure by Private Bill — to take these matters outside the detailed control of Parliament and to entrust the final decision to a Minister.

269. The intention of the legislature in providing for an enquiry or hearing in certain circumstances appears to have been twofold: to ensure that the interests of the citizens closely affected should be protected by the grant to them of a statutory right to be heard in support of their objections, and to ensure that thereby the Minister should be better informed of the facts of the case.[49]

This brings us to the crux of the matter. The Minister is charged by statute with "securing consistency and continuity in the framing and execution of a national policy in respect of the development and use of land throughout England and Wales." [50] Clearly, he must enjoy wide discretion in the exercise of this power. Yet in granting the citizen a right of appeal, Parliament conferred upon him more than what one distinguished judge has called "legislative permission to fulminate." [51] If the inquiry process is to be an effective compromise between the polar "administrative" and "judicial" viewpoints and is to have any value besides that of a safety valve for angry citizens, then, it is submitted, three important features should be emphasized in the planning decision stage and in the appeal process. First, the Minister's policy should be declared on all important matters (as indeed on limited aspects it now is), and should be characterized by that consistency and continuity which, after all, is enjoined upon the Minister by statute. Second, the application of that policy should rely more explicitly upon clear and recognizable facts, frankly stated and established after a

---

[49] *Id.* paras. 268, 269.

[50] Minister of Town and Country Planning Act, 1943, 6 & 7 Geo. 6, c. 5, § 1.

[51] Per Mr. Justice Henn Collins in Franklin v. Minister of Town and Country Planning, 1 All E.R. 396, at 397 (1947).

proper opportunity to test their validity, and not on preconceived notions and half-perceived theories. Third, and more generally, the whole process should be distinguished by those attributes of openness, fairness, and impartiality for which the Franks Committee so eloquently appealed.[52]

TRENDS AND IMPROVEMENTS

The appeals machinery should be seen in its proper perspective. Planning in England and Wales achieves much of which it justly can be proud. Many hundreds of thousands of decisions are made with remarkably little fuss and difficulty. Indeed, some local planning authorities manage to avoid friction almost entirely, and few are the appeals from their decisions. Only 2 per cent of all decisions are the subject of effective appeals. While this seems small, it is not easy to be sure how satisfactory it is. What percentage of commercial contracts comes to court, it may be asked?

The administration is distinctly good. Many thousands of inquiries are held; usually, they are held after due and timely notice, punctually, in a fairly convenient place, with a well-organized program, before an inspector who is never late or unprepared and who impresses all by his *personal* fairness and patience.

The flaw on the administrative side appears in a limited number of large and protracted inquiries. In these cases the Ministry is uncooperative, makes no attempt to produce a proper program of events until the inquiry has started, and pays scant regard to the expenses incurred by appellants and objectors.

Despite these very real achievements and despite the efforts by inspectors to show appellants every consideration, the average appellant does not feel wholly satisfied with the present situation. Although government spokesmen repeatedly have assured the public that there is really no dissatisfaction and no need for change, the validity of these pronouncements perhaps may be gauged by the responsible and well-informed Franks Committee's having rejected nearly all the conclusions of government witnesses. Almost every one of the Committee's recommendations was made in flat contradiction to the sense of official government evidence, and these recommendations were received with widespread public approval.

Appellants have three main complaints about the whole process. One is delay at every stage. It is common for a year to elapse between the application and the decision on appeal. A second is the lack of *evident* fair-

---

[52] *Supra* note 29, ch. 30, at 89.

ness and openness. They continue to suspect that altogether too much is arranged behind the scenes and actual personal experience on both sides of the inquiry table very strongly suggests that this suspicion is well-founded. Finally, appellants complain about the evident lack of regard for facts. They are often impressed by the time and attention devoted at inquiries (and they suspect in committee and council) to theories, conceptions, and ideas, in comparison with the limited and indifferent attention paid to the facts. This attitude comes, of course, from the top. The Ministry often appears uninterested in the facts of a case and in its background; in turn, this is reflected in the attitude of the inspectors and so finally affects the local planning authority.

Apologists for the status quo sometimes say that these criticisms stem from a desire to see justice done, which, they add, is impossible because planning is founded on policy, not on considerations of justice. Leaving aside some of the surprising implications of this approach, it is a misconception. The affected public wants to be treated fairly and to understand fully what is decided. Most appellants are fair-minded people who, if the procedure is fair and the result is explained and can be understood, will accept the outcome with good grace.

Under the influence of the Franks Report, improvements are taking place. The importance of establishing the essential facts and of relating the decision to them is gradually becoming recognized in the conduct of inquiries. The procedure of the inquiry is becoming less lax; the inspectors are more reluctant to listen to hearsay and unverified or unfounded opinions. And recent statements of the Minister and his senior officials have shown a growing desire to develop an articulated and consistent policy, although it is still very embryonic. The courts as yet have had no opportunity to show how they view these matters in a more liberal climate of opinion.

Other improvements are in prospect or under consideration. A code of rules has been promised, although the promise is an old one, and such rules are at least capable of bringing about some major changes. Efforts to speed up the decision process are being considered in the Ministry. It is unlikely that any major step toward a more consistent policy will be taken until the Ministry's internal organization is changed. At present there is no appeal department, as such; decisions are made by several divisions, each responsible for a geographical area. This arrangement leads to conflicting decisions in different regions.

A provision liberalizing the award of costs is also said to be under consideration; it is to be hoped that some improvement may come out of the review, although it is difficult to guess when it may be expected.

There are at least two further matters in which change would be welcome, but in which there is no sign that it will come. The speed with which decision letters appear has increased slightly, but there has been no noticeable improvement in their quality. The relation between their conclusions and the results of the inquiry they report too often seems to be only one of physical proximity. This lack of apparent connection may well be a conscious act of policy, but it is no less unfortunate for that. Finally, the Franks Committee urged that the inspectors be placed under the control of a Minister not directly concerned with the decision to be made. While that recommendation has not been accepted, it remains a step which would remove misgivings from the minds of appellants. In this, as in so much else, it is often argued that such a change would be only a matter of appearance. It is strange that so many of those concerned with land planning, which attaches so much importance to the visual aspects of our environment, should be indifferent to the fact that throughout the decision and inquiry process it is precisely the appearance of things that matters so much.

CONCLUSION

During the years of operation of the present planning appeal machinery there has been little or no control over the process of decision making by the responsible Ministry. It would be wrong to ignore the great amount of valuable work in creating, organizing, and supervising the new system done by the Ministry. But the role and position of the Ministry often is neither appreciated nor understood. Here, for example, is the view of one professional man:

I have sometimes wondered what would happen if a Judge, having heard the jury return a verdict of "not guilty" on a capital charge, proceeded to pass judgement on these terms: "Mr. X., you have heard the verdict of the jury; however, I do not agree with them, and never intended to do so from the outset of this case; it would seem to me that your actions were contrary to the overall moral intentions of the State and . . . " — an amazed courtroom sees the little black cap appear.

Crazy? Perhaps. But is it not a fact that the Minister of Housing and Local Government is doing this very thing, metaphorically, in passing judgement on certain planning appeals? In the past, I have read of cases where the Minister has not accepted his Inspectors' recommendations: occasionally this has pleased me when I have found that the effect of such decisions may have suited my purpose in the preparation of a particular planning appeal. But when this sort of thing hits one personally between the eyes, the sting promotes a rebellious mood.

I have just received a decision of the Minister which makes it quite clear that he (the Minister) never intended to allow the appeal in question; and his reasons for not accepting the Inspector's recommendations are, in my view, paltry. This was a case in which the "jury" had been fully satisfied that the appellant was "not guilty" of a proposed act of violence to the county development plan or of good planning principles, yet the "Judge" pronounced that the proposed development be "hanged."

A few questions spring to one's mind —

(i) Why should landowners be put to the considerable expense of appeals if the Minister acts as judge in his own cause?

(ii) Why should the taxpayer be called upon to pay the salaries (meagre though they are) of Inspectors, when the Minister has no confidence in his own Inspectors' recommendations?

(iii) Can something be done to rectify this unsatisfactory state of affairs?

(iv) Is the Royal Institution of Chartered Surveyors doing anything about it? [53]

The attitude reflected in this letter and in many similar criticisms of the manner in which appeals are handled, springs in part from a failure to understand the function of the Minister. Nevertheless, it seems unlikely that the public will allow the present situation to continue indefinitely. There is already a noticeable trend toward reform; the inclusion of new, though limited, rights of appeal to the courts in the acts of 1959 and 1960 may be some evidence of current feeling.

If the Minister's decisions are to be subject to some kind of review, the next question would seem to be whether to vest the reviewing power in the political or the judicial field. There are two reasons why the former is unattractive. First, the Minister originally was granted many of his present powers precisely because Parliament was anxious to delegate the work involved in their exercise. Second, although it is often said that Parliament can be relied on to protect the citizen in such cases, this is not true, because "whatever the theoretical validity of this argument, those of us who are Members of Parliament have no hesitation in saying that it

---

[53] Letter by Clifford Dann, published in The Chartered Surveyor, August 1960, p. 104. Reproduced by permission of the Royal Institution of Chartered Surveyors.

bears little relation to reality. Parliament has neither the time nor the knowledge to supervise the Minister and call him to account for his administrative decisions." [54] There would seem to be small point in looking to the political field for help in such detailed matters.

This suggests that a way must be found to obtain effective redress in the courts when individual decisions are not made in accordance with principles that recommend themselves to a general sense of fair dealing. On the other hand, such a remedy must leave adequate freedom to the Minister to form and apply sound land-planning policies in accordance with his statutory duty.

[54] Pamphlet RULE OF LAW, published by Inns of Court Conservative and Unionist Society, p. 20.

FLEXIBILITY AND THE RULE OF LAW IN AMERICAN ZONING ADMINISTRATION

LAWRENCE A. SULLIVAN
MEMBER, MASSACHUSETTS BAR

THE UTOPIAN OBJECTIVE of zoning is to achieve, largely through private initiative rather than public allocation, that harmonious community in which waste and irrationality in the use of urban land are minimized and provision is made for the varied needs of the populace. Prominent among the factors which inhibit a close approach to this ideal are those land-use irrationalities which preceded the enactment of a zoning ordinance and those instabilities occasioned by growth trends and associated social problems which were unforeseen when the ordinance was formulated.

Among the central problems of zoning administration are the manner in which and the institutions through which these stresses are alleviated and the conflicts to which they give rise are resolved. The need is to afford sufficient flexibility and responsiveness to community needs to deal constructively with vicissitudinous situations, yet to assure that zoning restraints are administered pursuant to the rule of law, not unconfined discretion. The rule of law, as the phrase is here used, is an ellipsis intended to suggest the primary values to which policies promulgated and enforced in a democratic society should adhere: that they be rational, and thus capable of articulation at a level of generality removed from the facts to which they apply, rather than merely intuitive and inexplicable; that such policies be reasonable in the sense that they be logically defensible in terms of the context in which they will operate; and that such policies be fair, in the sense that the costs of the social gains sought to be implemented are distributed equitably. All of these, of course, are values protected against extreme intrusions by the due process and equal protection clauses of the federal and state constitutions.[1]

[1] See generally Norman Williams, *Planning Law and Democratic Living*, 20 LAW & CONTEMP. PROB. 317 (1955), which contains an excellent discussion of the questions of social policy which may arise in a planning context. See also Corwin W. Johnson, *Constitutional Law and Community Planning*, 20 LAW & CONTEMP. PROB. 199 (1955), in which the federal and many of the state cases are reviewed.

This paper is an attempt to appraise the extent to which both needed flexibility and conformity to the rule of law have been achieved through existing American institutions for the administration of zoning programs and to offer tentative suggestions for reforms. First, typical problems which exemplify the frictions encountered in zoning administration are delineated. Then the institutions and techniques employed in the United States for dealing with such problems are described and evaluated and institutional alternatives are considered.

THE ADMINISTRATIVE ENVIRONMENT

Zoning is a prospective tool. As traditionally conceived it does not alter existing land allocations[2] directly but merely guides future land-use decisions so as to encourage those which complement one another and to preclude those which conflict. Furthermore, zoning is predicated on the assumption that long-range trends affecting land use may be foreseen by the planner and adequately provided for by the local legislative body. By reason of these characteristics, imperfections are inevitable in any zoning ordinance.

The planner does not begin with a vacant landscape. The comprehensive plan embodied in or implemented by the zoning ordinance must be structured to fit a city in being, inevitably possessed of an ample legacy of land-use irrationalities. The numerous nonconforming uses which prevail, well over a quarter of a century after zoning became common, testify to the continued viability of ancient land-use errors.[3]

More importantly, however much the planner may have refined his predictions, he will discover after a decade or more that he did not foresee all of the growth trends, needs, and developing aspirations of the community. Data from the 1960 census afford statistical confirmation of the increasing rate of change in urban growth patterns. Large cities have decreased in size during the past decade while outlying areas have swelled;[4]

---

[2] Provisions requiring the "amortization" of nonconforming uses over a specified period of time are becoming more common. Ralph Crolly and C. McKim Norton, *Termination of Non-Conforming Uses,* 64 ZONING BULLETIN 1 (Regional Plan Association, Inc., June 1952). Such provisions raise perplexing constitutional issues. See, *e.g.,* City of Los Angeles v. Gage, 127 Cal. App. 2d 442, 274 P.2d 34 (1954).

[3] See Harland Bartholomew, *Non-Conforming Uses Destroy the Neighborhood,* 15 JOURNAL OF LAND AND PUBLIC UTILITIES ECONOMICS 96 (1939).

[4] See U.S. DEPARTMENT OF COMMERCE, BUREAU OF THE CENSUS, PRELIMINARY REPORTS, POPULATION COUNTS FOR STATE, PC (P1)–1 through PC (P1)–50 (Washington, D.C., 1960), which uniformly document the increase in populations of satellite cities and towns and the decrease in populations of central cities. The changing pattern of industrial and

and industry and commerce, as well as commuters, are finding suburban surroundings congenial. Little of this, or of the accompanying social problems, was prefigured in the 1920's and 30's, when existing zoning ordinances were adopted.

Consequently, the most skillfully drafted zoning ordinance will be seriously imperfect, its distortions becoming increasingly disruptive as it is enforced over the course of years. The land-use mistakes which preceded enactment will continue to be bothersome, and the dynamics of community life will rapidly contrive new and unanticipated urban needs and problems.

The difficulties referable to past irrationalities may be exemplified by the problem of the "ill-conforming use." Zoning ordinances typically subdivide the city or town into districts, in each of which specified uses are authorized and building height, bulk, and setback requirements are imposed. Within residential districts small pockets are often found where most of the parcels are devoted to commercial uses which, because they antedated enactment of the zoning ordinance, are permitted to continue; only a few properties actually may be used for legally normative residential purposes. This condition may be the consequence of an artlessly drafted district boundary, a planner's undue optimism about the effect of zoning regulations in inducing owners to amortize nonconforming uses, or the best possible compromise which could be made in view of incongruities existing when the use districts were established. Whatever the cause, such a pocket will be a source of excitation. The residential plots within it, though conforming to legal requirements, are not adapted to their environment. By contrast, the neighboring commercial holdings, though legally nonconforming, impart the basic character of the environment. As might be expected, it is often the ill-conforming parcels — those used for residential purposes — which depreciate and, over the years, are allowed to deteriorate physically. On the other hand, the factually concordant but legally nonconforming commercial properties may prosper. Eventually there will be pressure to permit one or more of the residential lots to be devoted to commercial use.[5]

---

commercial activity can also be confirmed statistically. See, for example, GREATER BOSTON ECONOMIC STUDY COMMITTEE, A REPORT ON DOWNTOWN BOSTON (May 1959), which discloses that in the decade from 1947 to 1957 the City of Boston lost 15,317 industrial jobs, although during the same period there was an increase of 68,364 such jobs in the Boston metropolitan area.

[5] E.g., Coleman v. Board of Appeal of Boston, 281 Mass. 112, 183 N.E. 166 (1932).

A typical problem caused by unforeseen change frequently occurs in connection with district boundaries, particularly where "strip zoning" for commercial use prevails. Many ordinances, following the developmental pattern current in the 1920's and early 1930's, permit commercial uses to the depth of one lot along major thoroughfares, while restricting property fronting on parallel and intersecting streets to residential uses. Increased traffic congestion and extensive use of the supermarket and large shopping center often make the commercial strip inadequate, particularly since it can not accommodate needed ancillary facilities, such as off-street parking areas. As a consequence, demands are pressed to allow residential parcels lying to the rear of commercially zoned land to be devoted to such ancillary uses.[6]

Another recurrent problem is caused by unanticipated changes in housing needs. In many towns and cities, areas close to the business center were developed before the turn of the century with large, single-family, residential structures — the contemporary abodes of business and professional men and their ample families. Often this development was capped in the early decades of this century with formidable, but significantly smaller, three- or four-bedroom homes. Zoning ordinances drafted in the 1920's or 30's frequently restricted such districts to single family residential uses. Today, the older, larger structures — often possessed of a high structural quality and a spacious character absent in more modern buildings, and fit to last another century or more if kept in repair — have but a constricted market for use as single-family dwellings, since they are too large for smaller, servantless families. Pressure is therefore asserted to allow their use as multiple dwellings, an objective often resisted by the owners of newer, smaller residences in the same area.[7]

Also frequent is the difficulty encountered when light industry seeks to move into a suburban area. Land which is now desirable for so-called industrial, research, or executive parks — modern, commercial structures in landscaped settings, devoted largely to "home office," industrial research, or light fabrication facilities — has long been zoned for residential purposes in many suburban towns and partially developed with tract housing. The efforts of developers seeking to free such land for highly productive commercial use and to gain the support of segments of the local population concerned about increasing tax rates, and the stiffening resistance to

---

[6] Compare Pressman v. City of Baltimore, 222 Md. 330, 160 A.2d 379 (1960), with Schoelpple v. Woodbridge Township, 60 N.J. Sup. 147 (1960).

[7] Compare St. Onge v. City of Concord, 95 N.H. 306, 63 A.2d 221 (1949).

change of those living near a proposed industrial site, may result in intense conflict.[8]

Moreover, the conflicts occasioned by growth are not limited to individuals or groups within the same urban neighborhood; they may also have an intersectional axis. Residents of an outlying sector may seek to protect their immediate area against the steady influx of people and industry into the suburbs. Regarding the rural charm of their own community most worthy of preservation, they may seek to channel growth away from themselves into other areas.[9]

These discords, furthermore, give rise to one of the profound social problems of this generation: will the future social organization of the American metropolis involve a methodical segregation of economic classes?

Such is the context in which zoning must operate. In so inconstant an environment a significant degree of flexibility is essential. The errors of the past must be alleviated; the future must be assisted to unfold so as to serve a society which aspires to be both progressive and democratic. To achieve these ends while adhering to the rule of law is the challenge of zoning administration.

THE ADMINISTRATIVE INSTITUTIONS

Over the years problems of the kinds suggested above give rise to efforts to modify the zoning restraints. Ideally, any zoning modification will have a rectifying effect. It will help to amortize mistakes of the past; it will serve to update zoning regulations by keeping them current with new needs; it will reflect communities of interest between municipalities that are part of an interrelated metropolitan area. In addition, any such modification will adhere to the concept of the rule of law; it will emanate from a standard possessing a degree of generality, having a reasonable relation to public ends, and being basically fair in application.

If modification decisions are to approach these ideals, broadly talented individuals must be drawn into the decisional process. Those who make zoning decisions should be literate in the language of the planner. For

[8] For example, the remarkable development of electronics fabrication and research facilities along Route 128, a limited access circumferential highway encircling the Boston metropolitan area, which has added enormously to the productivity and the tax base of the entire area, was not accomplished without recurrent conflicts of this kind.

[9] The myriad planning problems encountered where a metropolitan area is fragmented into a number of municipal corporations are explored in C. M. Haar, *Regionalism and Realism in Land-Use Planning*, 105 U. PA. L. REV. 515 (1957).

example, when considering whether to authorize an industrial promontory which would extend into a commercial district, those who exercise judgment should be able to envision the sequel. When asked to allow parking on a vacant residential parcel to the rear of a new supermarket, the authoritative agency should grasp the consequences of saying no as well as those of saying yes. Another important characteristic of the decision maker is a judicious approach to the exercise of governmental power — an appreciation of the need to preserve the rule of law where community decisions are to be imposed upon individuals. Third, those who decide zoning matters should be sensitive both to generalized community ideals and to specific community attitudes. All zoning decisions are, in a sense, legislative. They entail social choices as well as technical ones. Ideally, an agency making such decisions should apprehend the mores and the purposes of the community and should be qualified both to respond to them and to guide their development.

A satisfactory institutional structure for the resolution of zoning issues would be one which attracted administrators able to deal adequately with the rule-making and adjudicative aspects of their tasks and which provided an administrative environment in which zoning issues might be dealt with constructively. In the following sections institutions currently used to alter zoning constrictions will be described and an effort made to appraise their potential for constructive resolution of the conflicts between zoning goals and the facts of urban life. The grant of variances and special exceptions from zoning ordinances will be considered first. Next, some of the problems of amending existing ordinances will be discussed. Finally, attention will be directed to departures from zoning ordinances which are accomplished by selective nonenforcement.

VARIANCES AND SPECIAL EXCEPTIONS

Any meaningful discussion of zoning variances must demarcate sharply between legal theory and enforcement practices. As will be seen, their relation may be tenuous.

Statutes vary, of course, from state to state. In most jurisdictions, however, enabling laws and local ordinances empower local boards of appeal to vary the application of the local zoning ordinance in certain unusual cases, subject to review first by a trial court and then by an appellate tribunal.

Boards of appeal usually are "citizen" agencies. They sit only occasionally, as the needs of their localities require. Board members, appointed by local executive authority, typically are selected on the basis of political considerations, broad or narrow; they are not necessarily chosen either on the basis of expertise in land-use planning or of any particular professional qualification to perform a quasi-judicial function.[10] At their best, agencies so staffed will represent a fair consensus of current community attitudes toward the land-use questions which come before them. They may fail, however, to perform the higher elements of the legislative function, which are creative rather than merely responsive; and they may fail to bring to their tasks the broad professional perspective either of the planner or of the judge.

Reviewing courts in all states are courts of general jurisdiction. The judges who decide variance cases, therefore, may be expected to be responsive to constitutional values. Seldom, however, will they be specially versed in the planner's discipline; and they may have little chance to acquire an appreciation of relevant attitudes in the communities affected by the cases they decide, or, indeed, even to comprehend that broad social questions may be lurking in a routine zoning case.

While the legal prerequisites for a variance are expressed differently in different jurisdictions, the statutes usually purport to preclude relief unless two essentials are met: first, that enforcement of the ordinance against the applicant would involve a significant degree of hardship upon him and, second, that relief can be accorded without notable interference with the public purposes of the ordinance.[11] Fairly interpreted, the typical statute intends the variance procedure to ameliorate only some of the harshest inequities which may result from zoning regulations and to do even this only where there will be no radiating effects. In practice the variance procedure may be used extensively to achieve much broader objectives. Indeed, it may be used systematically to modify existing zoning restraints in important particulars.

It is not that the courts have consciously adapted the variance procedure to ends which the state legislature did not contemplate. Appellate courts, at least, have quite consistently refused to do this. The use of the variance to accomplish broad-gauged adjustments in the enforcement of zoning ordinances arises, rather, because, in practice, three more or less distinct

[10] See generally John W. Reps, *Discretionary Powers of the Board of Zoning Appeals,* 20 LAW & CONTEMP. PROB. 280 (1955).

[11] *E.g.,* MASS. GEN. LAWS (Ter. Ed.) ch. 40a, § 15(3) (1958); CONN. REV. GEN. STAT. § 8–6 (1958); R.I. GEN. LAWS ch. 342, § 8 (1938). Many state enabling acts are fashioned after the Department of Commerce's model act. U.S. DEPARTMENT OF COMMERCE, STANDARD STATE ZONING ENABLING ACT (Washington, D.C., prelim. ed. 1922; rev. ed. 1926).

layers of variance law have developed: the law announced and enforced by appellate courts; the law applied by trial courts; and the law enforced by local boards of appeal. The point may be illustrated by examining these three types of adjudicative bodies.

A search of the appellate decisions of any given state would probably disclose a series of opinions rigorously applying the standards in the state's enabling law and upsetting variances charitably granted at the local level. The Massachusetts Supreme Judicial Court may be less hospitable to the variance as a means of altering the application of local zoning regulations than the appellate courts of some other states; nevertheless, the Massachusetts cases will serve to illustrate the attitude frequently encountered at the appellate stage.

There are a number of decisions holding irrelevant a showing that land would be worth significantly more if a variance were granted, or even that it is not economically feasible to develop the land for any permitted use insufficient to satisfy the prerequisite of hardship.[12] In addition, the cases emphasize that the hardship relied upon must be uniquely related to the parcel for which relief is sought.[13] In the large, the cases suggest that hardship in the statutory sense is not suffered unless it would be virtually impossible, by reason of physical characteristics of the land[14] or of the pre-existing street and subdivision pattern, to use the parcel in any permissible way.[15]

Decisions dealing with the requirement that relief not derogate from the purposes of the zoning law are fully as severe. The opinion in *Cary v. Board of Appeals of Worcester*[16] is a striking example. A variance had been granted in the court below to allow a residential parcel, having no access to any street except for a right of way over commercial land, to be used for parking in conjunction with the fronting commercial site. The court assumed that hardship was shown and directed its attention to the prerequisite of derogation. The trial court, upon thorough and perceptive analysis, had found that the relief granted would depress neighboring

[12] *E.g.,* Prusik v. Board of Appeal of Boston, 262 Mass. 451, 160 N.E. 312 (1928); Phillips v. Board of Appeals of Springfield, 286 Mass. 469, 190 N.E. 610 (1934). Cases from other jurisdictions are collected in E. C. YOKLEY, ZONING LAW AND PRACTICE, § 139 (Charlottesville, 2d ed. 1953). The Massachusetts statute was amended in 1958 to minimize the severity of the judicial test by authorizing relief in instances of substantial hardship, "financial or otherwise." The extent to which this language may have changed the law is not as yet clear.

[13] *E.g.,* Brackett v. Board of Appeal of Boston, 311 Mass. 52, 39 N.E.2d 956 (1942).

[14] *E.g.,* Kairis v. Board of Appeal of Cambridge, 337 Mass. 528, 150 N.E.2d 278 (1958).

[15] *Cf.* Cary v. Board of Appeals of Worcester, 340 Mass. 748, 166 N.E.2d 690 (1960).

[16] *Id.*

residential property values to some extent, but, on balance, would be in the public interest because it would help to alleviate a severe traffic congestion problem centering at the locus. Since preservation of property values and relief of traffic congestion are both public purposes specifically mentioned in the Massachusetts enabling statute, the basis for a variance would seem to have been made out unless the reviewing court were to re-evaluate the facts or reappraise the weight to be accorded to each factor. Nevertheless, the court reversed, though it accepted the findings below and did not question the trial court's appraisal of their relative significance. It held that since derogation from one zoning purpose was established by the finding that the values of adjacent properties would be adversely affected, a variance was precluded as a matter of law. In substance, it ruled that a variance might not be granted if there is significant derogation in respect of any statutory purpose, regardless of any countervailing advantage in respect to other zoning ends. This would seem to be a most limited view of the situations in which a variance lawfully may be granted.

These decisions are indicative of the law applied at the appellate level, although emphasis may vary from state to state. If, however, one were to search the trial court decisions from which no appeals had been taken, he might conclude that the law applied was noticeably different. A substantial number of trial court decisions seem to accord the boards of appeal a somewhat wider range of choice. And if, in turn, one were to examine the decisions by local boards of appeal which had never been judicially reviewed he would almost certainly conclude that relief had been granted in a large number of cases which, if appealed, would likely have been reversed.[17] Time and again, heedless of the admonitions of appellate courts, these local agencies grant variances in a variety of situations where rational application of the rules enunciated at the appellate level would forbid such relief.[18] Such variances, moreover, usually are not supported by opinions other than very brief statements descriptive of the situs and the nature of the petition, and conclusionary findings, paraphrasing the statute, to the effect that hardship uniquely affecting the situs has been shown and that relief can be granted without derogating from the purposes of the zoning regulations.

[17] The literature confirms that there is great "leakage" through loose standards in board of appeal decisions. See Reps, *Discretionary Powers of the Board of Zoning Appeals, supra* note 10, at 281–282; *Administration of Zoning Variances in 20 Cities*, 30 PUBLIC MANAGEMENTS 70 (1948).

[18] See note 17, *supra*. See also Hugh R. Pomeroy, *Losing the Effectiveness of Zoning through Leakage*, Planning and Civic Comment, Oct. 1941, p. 8,

Thus it appears that the three layers of variance law are informed by different considerations and vary significantly in their impact. The differences, moreover, mirror the institutional distinctions which characterize the agencies involved.

The layer of theory, expressed in the statutes and applied with some consistency by appellate tribunals, is a logical, reasoned construct, faithful to zoning abstractions. At this level high priority is given to the need for uniform application of the zoning ordinance. It is recognized that zoning entails the imposition of restraints which may be severe in particular situations, but it is affirmed that such restraints must be suffered if the public purposes of the ordinance are to be achieved. Casual amelioration of the legislative decision, it is insisted, would cause the collapse of the entire legislative structure. But the appellate decisions often speak as if in an ideal world — a world in which planning errors are never committed and unforeseen changes never occur. Appellate judges at times seem to value too lightly the need for flexibility in the administration of a program prospective in its operation and predicated on long range predictions. Also, they appear unresponsive to community attitudes which zoning administration properly could reflect.

It seems unfortunate that judges are not more keenly aware of the limits of the planning art and of the severity of the pinch which zoning constrictions may impose upon individual landholders because of such limits. For example, judges have so often asserted that "mere financial hardship" is not sufficient to warrant a variance that they may have lost all empathy for the human condition to which their words refer.[19] It is also unfortunate that judges fail at times to perceive the validity of distinctions predicated on a thoughtful evaluation of planning considerations. For example, the conviction implicit in the *Cary* decision, that collisions between competing planning considerations should not be resolved administratively seems unduly rigid. Finally, it is unfortunate that judges fail to grasp the social implications in some variance cases — for example, that different considerations may be relevant to the question of

[19] See note 12, *supra*. The problem of financial hardship is a vexing one. Certainly a variance should not be granted if the evidence merely shows, for example, that petitioner could derive greater income from the land if afforded, through a variance, a monopolistic franchise to conduct business in a residential district, and that petitioner, because of unique personal problems, is in dire need of additional income. On the other hand, if the impact of zoning restraints precludes anything other than an economically marginal use of a particular plot, thus reducing the income it produces to the vanishing point, conceptions of fairness, if not the demands of the constitution (compare Nectow v. City of Cambridge, 277 U.S. 183 (1928)), would seem to suggest the propriety of relief.

whether a variance for multiple housing should be permitted where the petition is filed by a Negro who has just acquired property a block beyond the prior bounds of the Negro neighborhood than are involved in the question whether such a petition should be allowed when filed by a white owner three or four blocks removed from a Negro neighborhood.

At the trial court level the rigor of statutory logic is tempered by a more sympathetic evaluation of the incongruities implicit in particular situations, but the difference is one of degree. Here too, decisions are often made by judges who find the conceptions of the planner difficult to manipulate and who may avoid hard choices by insistence upon inflexible administration of the restraints embodied in the ordinance.

Law at the local administrative level pays less heed — at times, very little heed — to favored juridical values such as treating in a similar manner all persons similarly situated, and great heed to the pinch upon individual landholders resulting from the inadequacies of particular applications of the planning art. Members of boards of appeal, moreover, eager to do equity in the cases immediately before them, may fail to appraise the impact of particular decisions on an over-all enforcement program.[20] With respect to larger social issues, as with respect to many others, the performance of boards of appeal is often difficult to evaluate because of the paucity of words with which such boards have expressed themselves.

A lawyer is likely to be offended by the thought of local agencies ignoring precedents of appellate courts much as he might be offended by the prospect of a jury bringing in a verdict of manslaughter in a case where, on the instructions and the evidence, rationality insists that the defendant is either guilty of murder or innocent of crime. On the other hand, he may recognize that judge-made rules are not always sufficiently refined to point a sound result in all situations, particularly in a field where a degree of flexibility is manifestly essential. Indeed, he may concede that any decision-making agency should have a broader spectrum of responses available to it than an appellate court. However, he may still be troubled, since the law applied by boards which consistently ignore legal standards can be little more than undisciplined, *ad hoc* justice; such justice, in its zeal to treat the widow more kindly than the professional developer, may impede effective, consistent enforcement of an important community program.

In summary, the institutions which presently constitute the variance procedure are inadequate. At no level are the need for flexibility and the

[20] See notes 17 and 18, *supra.*

demands of the rule of law brought into a balanced conjugation. At the lowest level of decision the former value is emphasized to the near exclusion of the latter; but it is often emphasized in an overly charitable context, without sufficient regard, either at the technical level or at the level of policy, for planning considerations which alone can render a zoning program reasonable and advantageous. At review levels the emphasis is reversed by an overcompensatory reaction; here planning considerations which point to the need for flexibility may be inadequately perceived. Further, aside from the inadequacies at each level of decision, the over-all structure is defective in that the standards which govern any individual case may be made to turn upon a near fortuity — whether the case is of sufficient moment for any party to seek judicial review.

Special exceptions or special-use permits granted by boards of appeal are similar to variances in adding a degree of flexibility. The ordinances may authorize specified uses, which would not otherwise be permissible, when conditions particularized by the local legislative body have been met. Usually, the enabling statute authorizes a board of appeal, which must determine whether the conditions set forth in the ordinance are fulfilled, to impose such further conditions in granting an exception as it may deem appropriate.[21]

Exceptions are most frequently provided to enable more particularized control of uses which are not frequent and which may present unique problems, such as hospitals, cemeteries, or public utility structures. However, the special exception technique is beginning to be used somewhat more broadly and its potential as a tool for added flexibility, even within the existing institutional framework, has not as yet been fully explored. Thus exception permits might constitute a successful way to deal with uneconomically large, old dwellings in single family districts. An exception for multiple dwelling use in such a district could be provided, for example, on a showing that a building exceeded specified age and floor space minima. Moreover, a permit could be conditioned on board approval of plans for structural changes in order to ensure compatibility with the general character of the neighborhood. Conceivably, the special exception could be directed toward palliating the most severe effects of segregation

---

[21] *E.g.,* Mass. Gen. Laws (Ter. Ed.) ch. 40a, § 5 (1962); R.I. Gen. Laws ch. 342, § 8(c) (1938). There is considerable confusion in the cases between a variance and an exception, but the distinction, in principle, is clear. See, *e.g.,* Mitchell Land Co. v. Planning & Zoning Board of Appeals, 140 Conn. 527, 102 A.2d 316 (1953); Lough v. Zoning Board, 74 R.I. 366, 60 A.2d 839 (1948).

in private housing; thus, exceptions for higher orders of multiple occupancy than otherwise permitted might be authorized if the structure was to be made available to members of a group which was discriminated against.

Again, in a residential-use district specifying a minimum lot size, exceptions might be authorized for groups of houses on smaller parcels, provided that sufficient contiguous land to offset the reduced lot size were preserved as open space or devoted to communal facilities, such as a swimming pool or play area. In this manner over-all density standards could be maintained while giving developers greater flexibility to experiment with arrangements other than the game-board configuration which, with monotonous consistency, now typifies residential tracts.[22] Similarly, exceptions for low-density apartment structures, or for low-density executive, industrial, or research parks, could be authorized within more narrowly restricted suburban areas, conditioned upon the establishment of adequate buffer areas to protect residential developments against severe incursions.

As may be seen, the special exception facilitates greater flexibility without offense to the values adhering in the rule of law. In theory, however, exceptions do not facilitate departures from the normal application of zoning restraints except to the extent that the desirability of specific types of variations may be foreseen at the time the ordinance is enacted.

While decisions on exceptions are not as numerous as those dealing with variances, it nevertheless appears that boards of appeal may use the device (just as the variance is used) to achieve modifications of a more comprehensive scope than the language either of enabling statutes or of local ordinances seems to envision. Thus, the conflict which pervades so many zoning problems, between the need for flexibility and the imperative that the police power be exercised only pursuant to the rule of law, is also latent in the administration of special exception provisions.

Whatever one's view of the extent of flexibility needed in zoning administration, it is patent that the administration of variance and special exception procedures is inadequate under existing institutions. Discriminations may be rampant in individual cities and towns and standards may vary markedly from municipality to municipality within the same metropolitan area. Certainly the situation has reached the point where extensive reform is in order.

[22] See Eli Goldston and James H. Scheuer, *Zoning of Planned Residential Developments*, 73 HARV. L. REV. 241 (1959).

One solution might be to require that all variances and exceptions be reviewed by a professionally staffed state zoning commission having authority to reverse or revise decisions of boards of appeal.[23]

Perhaps responsiveness to change and implementation of the skills of the planner might be enhanced without compromise of the rule of law if the scope of the special exception technique were broadened. For example, statutes could be drafted to enable regional planning boards, after notice and hearing, to promulgate the conditions for the grant of exceptions, pursuant to guiding general policies established by the state legislature. There would be no affront to the rule of law if purposes were established by statute and an expert agency were authorized, through rule-making procedures, to promulgate more specific rules which would have general applicability, but which could be altered and modified from time to time as needs were more clearly perceived.

Conjunctively or alternatively, less confining legislative standards for variances than those now typically imposed could be enacted[24] and the authority to grant variances could be conferred on specialized courts (or commissions) having metropolitan, territorial jurisdiction and subject only to a limited, discretionary review by the highest appellate court.[25] The judges of a specialized court could be expected to achieve greater success in synthesizing local attitudes, planning desiderata, and sensitivity to the demands, in a planning context, of the rule of law. As judges, they should have a finer appreciation of legal values than do local administrators. In view of their specialization they could become more broadly familiar with planning concepts than typical appeal board members or typical judges. And as their work within territorial jurisdictions progressed, they could build up a background of information about local aspirations and pressing social problems, not merely in one town, but in all related areas. Such an agency, moreover, could be given jurisdiction

---

[23] See the critical discussion of the existing situation in Illinois and the suggestions for reform in Richard F. Babcock, *The Unhappy State of Zoning Administration in Illinois,* 26 U. CHI. L. REV. 509 (1959).

[24] If decisions respecting variances were made by a responsible agency, the enabling statute, without risk to the substantial achievement of zoning objectives, could invest the agency with sufficient authority to evaluate such criteria as hardship and the impact of the proposed change on planning desiderata, such as the preservation of property values, the relief of congestion, and the like, and to reach a decision in the public interest. So long as standards for decision were expressed with a reasonable degree of definiteness, the rule of law would be preserved.

[25] A court would seem the preferable agency, in view of the criteria for the ideal institution. Local constitutional provisions would have to be consulted regarding whether a court could exercise the functions here referred to.

in other zoning cases, such as petitions by a city to enjoin alleged violations or cases which challenge the validity of an ordinance. The resulting improvement in zoning administration might be significant.

Changes and adjustments in institutions for enforcing public policies cannot save a democratic community from its own inadequacies. Effective zoning enforcement never will be accomplished unless all local officials and affected members of the community understand and support the program. Nevertheless, important public purposes should be expressed through the most effective governmental agencies devisable. In the field of zoning the evidence is persuasive that this has not yet been done.

AMENDMENT OF ZONING REGULATIONS

The second technique to be considered is that of amending the existing zoning ordinance to meet problems which become apparent after enactment of the original ordinance. This procedure is more complicated than the variance or exception procedure. As a practical matter, since it involves municipal legislative action, it may be available only where municipal officials perceive initially the need for the change or become convinced of its desirability on the urging of interested individuals.

Many problems relating to zoning amendments may arise in cases typically classified under the rubric "spot zoning." While many of these actually have a broader significance, the spot-zoning concept affords a convenient focus for their discussion.

In the literature and in the cases spot zoning is an opprobrious term. The courts uniformly have held an arbitrary change in the zoning classification of a small area — commonly called spot zoning — violating due process, equal protection, or both, and invalid.[26] While it is difficult to quarrel with the rule as thus stated, a reading of the decisions indicates that the principle may be applied at times in such a way as to inhibit the implementation of carefully conceived, reasonable public policies.

Here again, many of the difficulties seem to result from a difference in focus between the planner and the judge. The judge is bound to be con-

[26] See, *e.g.,* Eden v. Town Planning & Zoning Commission, 139 Conn. 59, 89 A.2d 746 (1952); Penning v. Owens, 340 Mich. 355, 65 N.W.2d 821 (1954). A variety of "tests" have been posed by the courts in various contexts to determine the validity of an amendment, the implication seeming at times to be that an amendment will be judged more severely than an original enactment: Does the amendment conform to the comprehensive plan embodied in or underlying the original ordinance? (Jefferson County v. Tunnel, 261 Wis. 39, 51 N.W.2d 518 (1952)). Have conditions in the neighborhood changed since the original ordinance was enacted? (Polk v. Axton, 306 Ky. 498. 208 S.W.2d 497 (1948)). However phrased, the test is essentially one of reasonableness.

cerned about legislative favoritism, the possibility that a large number of landholders may be unfairly treated by a zoning change favoring a few, or that a small number of landholders may be unfairly treated by a zoning change having a disproportionately adverse effect upon them. However, he may fail to see the rational relation between a given change and pertinent planning considerations. By contrast, the legislative draftsman, in focusing on a specific planning objective, may fail to recognize that his solution may distribute the costs of a particular social gain in an arbitrary manner.

At the level of constitutional doctrine, the solution ought to entail an evaluation of the relation of any given change affecting a small area to a reasonable planning program. Suppose, for example, that a suburban town's zoning ordinance, enacted in the 1920's, established a commercial district at the center and placed all outlying land, much of it then undeveloped, in a residential district. Suppose further that those outlying areas which had been developed prior to the enactment are served by occasional "corner stores" which are nonconforming commercial uses. Suppose finally that as open land is developed for housing it appears to the members of the local planning board that three small, widely separated plots, convenient to new residential tracts, should be rezoned to permit small neighborhood stores, similar to those operating elsewhere as nonconforming uses, and that, after careful consideration, an amendment is enacted by the town council to accomplish this result.

Focusing solely on the scope of the change — the fact that a few sites in an extensive residential area were singled out for what might be deemed favorable treatment, and that immediately adjacent residential properties were in a sense singled out for what might be deemed unfavorable treatment — the conclusion that the amendment was unfair and hence unlawful might be invited. If, however, one were to focus on the purpose of the change — that is, the correction of what is now reasonably regarded as an earlier planning error, so as to afford commercial facilities convenient for all — a contrary conclusion would be reached. True, only a few properties are affected, and there may be a distinct gain for the individual parcels to be zoned for commercial use and a degree of hardship imposed on immediately adjacent residential properties. But so long as the choice of parcels to be rezoned is made on the basis of which sites feasible for commercial use will afford maximum convenience to all residential neighborhoods, the distinctions would appear to be no more arbitrary than the distinctions drawn between adjacent parcels located on different sides of any boundary between use districts; differences in treatment are warranted, since they arise out of a reasonable method for achieving reasonable public ends.

Certainly there is no compelling basis for elevating to the level of a constitutional imperative the zoning practice of establishing homogeneous use districts.[27] This is still the dominant zoning technique, but its universal desirability is subject to question.[28] Good planning may call for a balance between complementary uses within a district, as well as for a balance between different use districts within a city or town. At least upon an appraisal of pertinent planning considerations, the local legislature reasonably could so conclude.

While the language of some cases suggests hostility even to a rezoning such as that hypothesized above,[29] most courts, it appears, would accept the analysis here suggested. Few courts today would regard the size of the area affected by a zoning regulation as being determinative of the legality of the regulation.[30] Where a zoning change directly affects only a small area there may be reason to pause and question; there is certainly not, on this basis alone, reason to strike down.

The types of cases which cause greater difficulty may be illustrated by modifying somewhat the facts hypothesized above. Suppose, for example, that the amendment, instead of establishing commercial plots at various convenient points throughout the residential district, established only one new commercial site. Suppose, also, that the impetus for this change came from a developer who held an option to purchase the land in question and wished to use it for an outlying shopping center. Suppose, finally, that the vote of the planning board recommending the change and the vote of the council enacting the amendment each contained a "whereas" clause disclosing that the change was approved because the proposed shopping center would produce needed new tax revenues.

It would now be more difficult to justify the change in terms of traditional planning objectives. Some courts, seizing upon the fiscal goal,[31]

[27] But compare Rockhill v. Chesterfield Township, 23 N.J. 117, 128 A.2d 473 (1956).

[28] As the art of planning strives to become a science numerous new zoning tools and techniques are being developed. See, for example, M. F. Waring, *Performance Standards in Industrial Zoning,* American Society of Planning Officials [1952] PLANNING 161.

[29] See, *e.g.,* Clifton Hills Realty Co. v. Cincinnati, 60 Ohio App. 443, 21 N.E.2d 993 (1938); Orr v. Hopeville Realty Investments, 211 Ga. 235, 85 S.E.2d 20 (1954).

[30] See, *e.g.,* Huff v. Board of Zoning Appeals, 214 Md. 48, 122 A.2d 83 (1957); Bartram v. Zoning Commission, 136 Conn. 89, 68 A.2d 308 (1949); Keller v. Council Bluffs, 246 Iowa 202, 66 N.W.2d 113 (1954).

[31] Compare Beach v. Planning and Zoning Commission of Milford, 141 Conn. 79, 102 A.2d 814 (1954).

on the fact that the source of the idea of providing a shopping center in the residential district was a developer, and on the fact that the particular site selected would accommodate the developer,[32] would rule that the amendment was unlawful spot zoning. The soundness of such a result, however, would be questionable.

First, to consider municipal fiscal considerations irrelevant to municipal planning would be to accept an unduly narrow view of the public welfare. As ever increasing demands for services are made upon local government, problems respecting the municipal fisc will be among the most urgent and vexing faced by the nation as a whole.[33] Such problems are public in nature, and zoning decisions predicated in part, or even primarily, on fiscal objectives can hardly be said to rest on irrelevancies.[34]

With regard to fiscal objectives, the really important question is not whether they exist (which they do) and are implemented through zoning (which they are), but the social consequence of the specific policies which proceed from them. Courts have approved zoning which excludes from large suburban areas all development other than expensive, and hence high revenue producing, housing; since an extensive area is affected, no question of spot zoning is thought to exist. A suburban town may procure the tax revenues needed for excellent community facilities in this way, but, retrogressively, only for families which can afford expensive housing. If, by contrast, a suburban community makes the more democratic choice of heterogeneity in housing and then, by zoning a small sector for a high tax producing, low service cost industrial structure, seeks to obtain sufficient revenues for adequate community facilities and ameliorate the severity of progressive taxation on homeowners (the necessary consequence of heterogeneous housing), it may, anomalously, be faced with a constitutional barrier.

Second, the fact that an amendment is first suggested by an investor rather than by a municipal planning agency is hardly a sufficient basis for holding it illegal. Any planning decision is in essence a legislative decision. Any such decision which undergoes the careful scrutiny of the planning board, which must approach it from the wide prospective of over-all planning considerations, and of the city or town council, where all

---

[32] See County Commission v. Merryman, 222 Md. 617, 159 A.2d 854 (1960).

[33] See Peter Drucker, *Three Unforeseen Jobs for the Coming Administration,* Harper's Magazine, July 1960, p. 46.

[34] There is some recognition in the case law that zoning decisions may properly be informed by municipal fiscal considerations. See, *e.g.,* Ward v. Township of Montgomery, 28 N.J. 529, 147 A.2d 248 (1959).

divergent interests in the municipality may be represented, must be presumed, albeit not conclusively, to implement a public planning end. Zoning legislation originally sponsored by a private interest should be no more suspect than any other legislation so sponsored. Indeed, zoning theory presupposes a nice balance between the exercise of public authority and the expression of private initiative, and it is to be expected that the private decision-maker frequently will wish to be heard in the legislative forum.[35]

Neither should an amendment be invalidated on the sole ground that the decision as to the particular land to be rezoned was not made on the basis of an appraisal by a public planning agency of all land in the municipality.[36] Here again, the presupposition that most land-use decisions will be privately made is pertinent. Where the municipality concludes that it would be in the public interest for a particular type of development to be undertaken, it must apply the stimulus where the desired response will be forthcoming. A community seeking construction of a shopping center in an outlying area could hardly implement its plan by rezoning a parcel theoretically ideal for the purpose but devoted by the owner to another use which he has no intention of changing. Nor does there seem any constitutional compulsion for the municipality to canvass the owners of all suitable potentially available land and make the choice from among those who agree to be considered. Certainly democratic decision making need not follow so rigid a procedure before it can qualify as other than arbitrary.

Many of the anomalies hidden in the complexities of spot-zoning decisions have their genesis in the all too frequent failure of the courts to grasp what the planner is about. Judges may not understand fully either the objectives of the planner or his tools. When his performance is humdrum, as when he divides a city or town into homogeneous use districts, he is tolerated. But let him turn his arts to the alleviation of the momentous social problems which surround him, let him exercise a measure of creativity in devising techniques to cope with these problems, and he may be met with judicial suspicion or even hostility. For example, among the problems which have caught the interest and imagination of planners is that of stimulating residential neighborhoods in which large and small structures are intermixed in a harmonious architectural relationship[37] and in which varied housing accommodations will attract a cross-section of

---

[35] See Pitman v. Medford, 321 Mass. 618, 45 N.W.2d 973 (1942).

[36] See Pressman v. City of Baltimore, *supra* note 6.

[37] See, *e.g.,* Arthur C. Holden, *Zoning . . . An Impediment to Good Design?* Progressive Architecture, Nov. 1946, p. 94.

cultural and economic groups.[38] But should zoning provisions be adjusted in small areas to accommodate such experimentation, judicial resistance, implemented by the spot-zoning concept, might well be encountered.

The demands of the rule of law are essentially the same when applied to zoning amendments as when applied to other police power legislation. It is now widely accepted that the police power may validly be exercised for the development of a well balanced and economically healthy community. Accordingly, reasonable programs to implement such an objective are valid exercises of governmental power.[39]

The question whether an amendment challenged as spot zoning is legal must turn upon whether it is reasonable, both as a choice of means and in particular applications. To pass upon reasonableness, the court must consult the planner's teaching: the critical question of reasonableness must first be evaluated from the vantage point of the planner.

This would conform to the traditional approach where social or economic legislation is involved. The avoidance of labor unrest, for example, may be viewed as a reasonable end for the exercise of police power. In passing upon the constitutionality of legislation adopting a particular means for its achievement, the court must begin by evaluating its reasonableness from the perspective of the labor economist. The constitutional question — whether the legislature could reasonably have regarded the means selected as appropriate to the achievement of the end sought [40] — can only be answered after the socioeconomic question has been explored. In the same fashion, when experimental zoning changes are put to the constitutional test, the court should confer with the planner. It cannot perform its function without understanding what the planner has to say. This does not imply judicial abnegation; it calls, rather, for more meaningful judicial involvement in the decisional process. The courts should participate fully, but in their accustomed role. In this way flexibility in planning administration could be facilitated while adequately preserving the rule of law.

Furthermore, if courts were to accord the planner the same deference which they have accorded other social scientists, greater creativity and responsibility among planners could be anticipated. In the present atmosphere, pretense and rationalization at the planning level are not unusual; planners expend considerable energy in fitting new conceptions into

[38] See, e.g., Plans for a Cooperative "Balanced Community," The American City, Feb. 1947, p. 86.
[39] See, e.g., Berman v. Parker, 348 U.S. 26 (1954).
[40] Compare N.L.R.B. v. Jones & Laughlin Steel Corp., 301 U.S. 1 (1937).

categories which have already passed muster before the courts. If reassured that their work product would be fairly judged on the basis of its intrinsic rationality, planners could devote themselves more fully to refining their own discipline in a rational way, and to communicating to the rest of us what it is they are about.

A more traditional judicial approach to planning problems, moreover, would do more than invite creativity among planning board staffs; it would also encourage the potential creativity of private developers in meeting the emerging needs of metropolitan areas. Developmental and construction activity, carried on so long by the relatively small investor, increasingly is becoming a field in which large capital aggregates, employing outstanding professional planners, are deployed. The talents of privately engaged planners must, of course, be made to subserve public ends. Private developmental proposals must be tested in the light of the public interest, but they should be tested without hostility.

As applied to the range of problems grouped under spot zoning, the approach here suggested would facilitate the development of new commercial land-use patterns such as the executive, research, and industrial parks which are springing up in suburban areas, and thus, perhaps, provide the revenue balance which is needed to reduce the pressure for suburban housing homogeneity. Furthermore, such an approach would help to accommodate experimentation in suburban areas with such residential devices as row housing, cooperative garden apartments, residential parks consisting of high-density clusters of homes adjacent to extensive open areas, and economically and architecturally balanced neighborhoods. In so doing, it might render the suburbs more accessible to lower-income groups and might assist in solving problems generated by tightening mortgage credit and increasing scarcity of prime land as core cities continue to dissolve into their suburbs.

The public planning agency should, of course, take vigorous part in evaluating and in refining any zoning amendment intended to permit novel uses in a small section of a town or city. It should exercise and express a judgment on whether a private proposal can be integrated into over-all planning goals and should suggest any conditions to the proposal which seem essential to the achievement of public objectives. For example, a local planning board, having studied a developer's proposal for a research park and having found it in conformity with over-all planning objectives, might attach provisions assuring an attractively landscaped buffer zone between the park and nearby single-family residences, thereby minimizing the impact of the change on the few landholders most adversely affected.

It cannot be assumed, however, that a local planning agency will antici-pate all of a community's needs or presage all reasonable means of meeting them. Whether the "comprehensive plan" to which a zoning amendment must conform is conceived of as the master plan of the planning board, as the plan emanating from the zoning ordinance itself, or as the entire complex of planning and related policies currently in effect in the mu-nicipality,[41] it must be a dynamic program, viable enough to amalgamate new aspects, by whomever conceived, which, upon honest appraisal, appear to serve public ends.

In the coming decades every municipality would do well to evaluate with care any serious developmental proposal in which private capital is ready to invest. And courts, invited to strike down an experimental zoning amendment following such evaluation, should proceed with caution. The court should satisfy itself that the decision is in substance, as well as form, a public decision — that it is made on the basis of a reasoned appraisal of planning considerations. But no judge should subject a municipal planning decision to the test of his own policy convictions, or worse, condemn it because he is not well enough informed to appraise it knowledgeably. Review of the reasonableness of legislative decisions should proceed from adequate comprehension both of the policy considerations and of the technical considerations which condition them.

There is a limit, of course, to the argument that small sectors may be treated uniquely so long as the local planning board and the local legis-lative body express approval. If a given zoning restraint is unnecessary as to Tom, then it is also unnecessary as to Dick and Harry if, with respect to all relevant considerations, each of the trio is similarly situated. Whether derived from the constitutional requirements of due process or, in terms of judicial treatment in this context, the substantively identical demands of the equal protection requirement, the reasonableness requirement entails an imperative that arbitrary distinctions not be drawn.[42] And it is the unique and vital role of the courts to be sure that this aspect of the rule of law is observed.

A distinction between the treatment of one parcel and the treatment of another would be arbitrary if the end sought to be achieved by it were

---

[41] See the comprehensive discussion in C. M. Haar, *In Accordance with a Comprehensive Plan*, 68 HARV. L. REV. 1154 (1955) of the meanings which courts have accorded to the statutory phrase "in accordance with a comprehensive plan."

[42] Compare State v. Northwestern Preparatory School, 228 Minn. 363, 37 N.W.2d 370 (1949).

grossly disproportioned to the burdens it imposed. The proposition can be conveniently illustrated as applied to restraints pertaining to architectural style. On the one hand, it would not seem arbitrary to limit those living in a small sector having historical interest to architectural patterns conforming to the historical tradition, though allowing nearby residents greater freedom.[43] By contrast, it would seem arbitrary to subject a few lots within a residential tract to more severe setback restrictions on the ground that occasional spatial divergencies add to visual interest. It is no longer defensible to assert that police power may not be exercised for ends having aesthetic overtones; such restraints may be imposed when it could reasonably be concluded that the community will be enriched to a commensurate degree. But it would be arbitrary in the context of planning considerations, and hence in the constitutional sense, to purchase elements of minor aesthetic moment at an inflated cost in diminished freedom. It has been held, in other connections, that a valid goal does not warrant the choice of a disproportionately discriminatory means.[44] The same principle should be applicable here.

Differences in treatment may also be arbitrary because they distribute the costs of social gain in a manner which falls short of minimum standards of fairness. An instance may be drawn with respect to zoning restraints aimed at reducing traffic congestion. It would seem reasonable to require all retail establishments in a traffic-generating commercial sector to provide off-street parking for their patrons.[45] The traffic problems in central areas and some outlying points are gargantuan; certainly restraints aimed at their alleviation are as closely connected with public safety and welfare as any other zoning regulations. On the other hand, a requirement that a single parcel within such a commercial sector be devoted to parking and to no other use would seem an unfair burden on one landholder for the benefit of the community as a whole.[46]

It may seem difficult to require a court to distinguish between these hypotheticals. That such distinctions are indeed difficult is evidenced by the fact that courts have frequently refused to make them. Many have announced that zoning for aesthetic ends is invalid.[47] Some courts have concluded that zoning may not be used to require off-street parking

[43] See Opinion of the Justices, 333 Mass. 773, 128 N.E.2d 557 (1955).

[44] Compare Dean Milk Co. v. Madison, 340 U.S. 349 (1950).

[45] Compare Town of Islip v. Summers Coal & Lumber Co., 257 N.Y. 167, 177 N.E. 409 (1931). But see Denver v. Denver Buick, Inc., 141 Colo. 121, 347 P.2d 919 (1959).

[46] See Vernon Park Realty v. Mount Vernon, 307 N.Y. 493, 121 N.E.2d 517 (1954).

[47] A collection of the numerous cases is found in Clinton Rodda, *The Accomplishment of Aesthetic Purposes Under the Police Power*, 27 So. CAL. L. REV. 149 (1954).

facilities.[48] They should have ruled instead that restraints reasonably imposed to achieve commensurate advances in the economic, social, or physical environment for wholesome living are unobjectionable. The critical matter is whether a particular regulation is reasonable in all of its ramifications, an issue which cannot be resolved merely by looking at the realm of living which the regulation purports to affect.

In summary, the lesson drawn from experience with spot-zoning problems is not that the rule of law precludes needed flexibility in the amendment process; it is, rather, that the values relevant to land-use planning are varied, that relevant differences may exist between one plot and other similar ones which would be difficult to articulate except by reference to planning conceptions, and that the constitutional barriers which might frustrate the achievement of reasonable planning goals through appropriate means ought to be erected most hesitantly.

Here, as well as with respect to other zoning questions, the conclusion might be ventured that the law could develop more constructively if jurisdiction to pass in the first instance upon the validity of zoning amendments were conferred upon specialized courts. Courts of general jurisdiction have articulated abstract constitutional values with clarity; they have taught the planners the ultimate meanings of our constitutional traditions.[49] However, such courts have erred not infrequently, for they have not always learned as well as they have taught. They have sometimes failed to appreciate the full range of considerations relevant to a planning context and have viewed meaningful, rational distinctions as the expressions of caprice. By contrast, the judges of specialized courts might conjoin the jurist's sensitivity to constitutional imperatives with a perceptive eye for differences — germane to the planner and hence to the public — between one land-use situation and another. And their decisions, articulating their premises in the accustomed judicial fashion, would doubtless be accorded a broad measure of respect when subject to appellate review.

Does the spot-zoning doctrine have an inversion? If, as the cases suggest, a use district may be too small to be reasonable, may a district be unreasonable for being too large? If invalidity may result from a preference accorded to a group too few in number, may it also result from a preference conferred upon too numerous a group? These thematic inquiries

---

[48] See Denver v. Denver Buick, Inc., *supra* note 45.
[49] The planner's concern for constitutional values is expressed in Roland B. Greeley, *A City Planner Looks at Zoning Laws*, 34 B.U.L. REV. 337 (1956).

may focus consideration of the amendments, becoming ever more frequent in suburban towns, which have the effect of insulating the enacting locality from the larger metropolitan community of which it is a part. Such amendments are of great concern, for an analysis of their validity and treatment by the courts gives insight into the failure of existing institutions to come to grips with the remarkable intensification of urbanization in this nation. Change and growth have given rise to land-use problems of a new magnitude; but there has been no adequate response either through modifications in existing institutions or the creation of new institutions for adjusting to change of such scope.

The basic purpose of the enactments in question is to preserve the land-use status quo — to defend the enacting town against demands upon its resources to accommodate the forces of the urban revolution. Whether the community is one of large luxurious homes, with extensive areas of open space, or semirural, with residential "farms" and extensive wooded land and meadows devoted to grazing, the effort is to preserve its character. The techniques used are varied. Perhaps the dominant one is a very large minimum lot size requirement. Minimum floor space or cubic content requirements also have come into prominence recently. Classification of speculative development as a business use; subdivision control regulations requiring that a "need" be shown for new subdivisions; minimum building cost requirements; exclusion of residential uses in "agricultural" districts; exclusion of all industry; exclusion of churches; and exclusion of private (including church) schools are among the other techniques which have been attempted or suggested.[50]

Such devices may preserve communities possessed of a rural character. In the process, residential homogeneity, with resulting economic, class, and, at times, racial or religious segregation in housing can be effectively accomplished.[51] Worse still, the consequent trend toward the segregation of economic groups into separate, fiscally independent municipalities within each metropolitan area leads to retrogression in the support of important public facilities — most notably, educational institutions. Indeed, if the current exclusionary trend were to progress to its perfection, it would produce a metropolis in which each economic class would live an

[50] See the discussion *ibid*.

[51] A related problem concerns the exclusion by municipalities of nonresidents from municipal parks and other recreational facilities. Two legislators from the Bronx in New York City recently charged that such exclusions practiced by suburban Westchester communities were aimed at keeping out Negroes and Puerto Ricans who resided in New York City. See *Westchester Bias in Parks Charged*, New York Times, July 20, 1960, p. 31, col. 1.

insulated existence, providing for itself, through its separate municipal government, the educational institutions and other public facilities for which it had the ability to pay. The professional and executive class, for example, would occupy suburbia, living a dream life of liberal language and preclusive policy. Private education would be rejected as divisive and the costs of a superlative public educational establishment for this group, but no others, would be equitably shared by the occupants of expensive houses through real estate tax levies. But the unassimilated, the uneducated, and the impoverished, unencountered by suburbanites except through the windows of a passing train, would be caught in the city slums; and the real estate tax revenues from the properties they occupied would barely cover the costs of the overcrowded and understaffed school facilities allotted to them.[52]

The cases in which status quo zoning has been challenged rarely have faced up to the social implications of exclusionary ordinances. The courts have not fully considered whether an ordinance can be viewed as reasonable where its manifest effect and implicit purpose is to maintain a municipal island dedicated to the simplicities of the past in the midst of a burgeoning metropolis, where the complexities of the present and future demand expression. They have not, for example, explored the distinctions which might be drawn between status quo zoning in an isolated country town and status quo zoning by a town on the fringe of an expanding city.

What is worse, the courts have not adequately distinguished between a policy of excluding or decelerating all growth of every kind and one calculated to permit growth but to maintain residential homogeneity. The opinions have focused primarily upon the particular zoning technique used: does a minimum floor space or a large minimum lot size requirement serve to advance a reasonable public purpose, or is it manifestly arbitrary? The opinions indicate that the courts will not question legislative motives[53] and, further, that they generally will not find irrational legislative decisions which differ only quantitatively from concededly valid ones.[54]

---

[52] The social problems of economically segregated housing are perceptively discussed in Williams, *Planning Law and Democratic Living, supra* note 1.

[53] See, *e.g.,* Duffcon Concrete Products v. Borough of Cresskill, 1 N.J. 509, 64 A.2d 347 (1949) (total exclusion of industry); Valley View Village, Inc. v. Proffett, 221 F.2d 412 (6th Circ., 1955) (entire town residential); Lionshead Lake, Inc. v. Township of Wayne, 10 N.J. 165, 89 A.2d 693 (1952), *appeal dismissed,* 344 U.S. 919 (1953) (large minimum floor space requirement throughout largely undeveloped suburban town).

[54] See Fischer v. Bedminister Township, 11 N.J. 194, 93 A.2d 378 (1952) (five-acre minimum lot size); Flora Realty & Investment Co. v. Ladue, 263 Mo. 1025, 246 S.W.2d 771 (1952), *appeal dismissed,* 344 U.S. 802 (1952) (three-acre minimum lot size).

But judicial analysis even in these terms has not been highly refined. For example, a lot size requirement associated with height and setback requirements may have a direct effect on structural density, and hence upon access to light and air and upon traffic generation; as to such a requirement it may be meaningful to say the question is one of a little more or a little less, and that this is a choice for the legislature, not for the court. But standing alone, a minimum floor space requirement is directly related to nothing but construction costs; unless associated with correlated occupancy requirements, such a requirement is difficult to defend as a health measure aimed at precluding overcrowded structures. Nevertheless, the recent decisions uphold these devices indiscriminately.[55]

In applying a standard of reasonableness, courts are accustomed to insist that a zoning restraint, to be valid, must implement a comprehensive plan; a restraint standing alone, unrelated to any over-all program for the public welfare, is felt to be arbitrary.[56] Seldom, however, have courts postulated the essential attributes of the comprehensive plan. Though the reasonableness of a particular restraint depends on its relation to such a "plan" — and thus in logic should depend upon the reasonableness of the plan itself — courts have been quite content to assume the reasonableness of any zoning program which is "comprehensive" in the sense that it covers the entire municipality, wholly without inquiry as to whether it is "planned" in any meaningful sense.

Must courts accept so narrow a view of their review function? Could a court not impose upon the plan itself at least a minimal qualitative test?

Picture a town covering a large area, mostly undeveloped, lying on the fringe of a burgeoning metropolitan area. Suppose the town amends its traditional zoning ordinance to provide for a single, townwide zone in which all commercial development is forbidden and all residential development other than large homes on spacious lots is foreclosed. Might a court not conclude that such a plan is so out of tune with the developmental needs of the metropolitan area as a whole as to be unreasonable?

These questions are not intended to be entirely rhetorical. The most that courts could accomplish in coping with exclusionary efforts would be to palliate the most obtrusive sectionalism of individual municipalities.

[55] The problems here alluded to are discussed and the cases analyzed in C. M. Haar, *Zoning for Minimum Standards: The Wayne Township Case*, 66 HARV. L. REV. 1051 (1953); Val Nolan, Jr., and Frank E. Horack, Jr., *How Small a House? — Zoning for Minimum Space Requirements*, 67 HARV. L. REV. 967 (1954). See also Haar, *Regionalism and Realism in Land-Use Planning, supra* note 9.

[56] See Haar, *In Accordance with a Comprehensive Plan, supra* note 41, and the cases there discussed.

And perhaps even this is too much to expect, given the limitations of judicial inquiry.[57] In the end, any effective resolution of the dilemmas generated by fractionalized metropolitan areas demands legislative action.

Such legislative action might take a variety of forms. The most drastic response would be to deprive municipalities of zoning power and confer it on a metropolitan agency, professional or representative. Such a change might be accomplished in conjunction with a comprehensive reform of metropolitan governmental institutions; land-use planning, after all, is but one aspect of the complex of problems associated with the Balkanized metropolis; others also cry for attention.

A politically more feasible alternative might be to augment the work of regional planning bodies by requiring the master plan for each municipality within a metropolitan region to conform to the regional plan, and local zoning ordinances to conform in turn to the master plan for the municipality. The municipal plan might even be made subject to review by the regional planning commission. This would facilitate decisions at the metropolitan level on matters of metropolitan concern, leaving each municipality free to pass upon matters of only local interest. For example, the regional plan, focusing on the needs and resources of the entire metropolitan area, could, in general terms, propose for each city and town a proportion of anticipated residential growth in various economic categories and a proportion of commercial and industrial development. Each municipality could, in turn, undertake the detailed planning necessary to accommodate the anticipated growth and implement such planning through its zoning ordinance.

If regional planning is deemed not to have progressed sufficiently to warrant a solution of this kind, state legislatures at least could reverse those judicial decisions indicating that what occurs beyond a municipal border need not be considered in passing upon the validity of a municipal zoning ordinance and could help to educate municipal officials to a more metropolitan point of view by requiring that each municipality's plan take due account of planning programs in neighboring municipalities.

The most pernicious effect of exclusionary zoning in a segmented metropolitan area — retrogressive local taxation which limits the members of each economic class to the community facilities for which they can

---

[57] Courts have consistently refused to strike down ordinances on the ground that their restraints did not correlate with those of adjacent municipalities. See, *e.g.,* Town of Surfside v. Skyline Terrace Corp., 120 So.2d 20 (Fla. 1960); Bonaldi v. Board of Appeals of New Haven, Conn. 153 A.2d 429 (1960). The cases through 1957 are discussed in Haar, *Regionalism and Realism in Land-Use Planning, supra* note 9.

afford to pay on a per capita basis — might be attacked by fiscal reform rather than by zoning reform. The problem could be relieved, for example, if a greater portion of the revenues needed for vital community services, such as education, were provided through grants-in-aid from funds obtained through progressive taxation at the state or federal level.

Whatever the ultimate solutions, this much, at least, is clear: Complex land-use problems can no longer be handled in the near anarchy of unfettered autonomy granted to a multiplicity of uncoordinated city-states within every metropolitan area. The evidence is ever more ample that metropolitan problems — of which land use is the most pervasive — can be solved only through institutions which serve the needs of the metropolitan area. Such problems will only be intensified if each municipality continues to seek its own ends, through its own local institutions, at the expense of neighboring communities.

MODIFICATION BY SELECTIVE NONENFORCEMENT

Selective nonenforcement, often discussed by sociologists but too seldom considered by lawyers, deals with law not as expressed in statutes or in the opinions of judicial or quasi-judicial tribunals, but with law as expressed by the activities of local officials.

In many cities and towns a significant number of zoning ordinance violations are tolerated.[58] No enforcement action is even initiated to redress them. In some instances such nonenforcement is by default, resulting from any number of causes, such as inadequate resources, to do what concededly ought to be done. In other instances, however, such nonenforcement may be a more or less deliberately adopted instrument of policy.

Local officials frequently may refrain from enforcing certain zoning restraints in order to cope with the strains generated by zoning imperfections. For example, because local officials are sensitive to the land-use economics entailed, a family owning and occupying a large, old, single-family structure in a single-family suburban district may be granted a building permit to construct a new kitchen on the second floor and a new bath on the first and may thereafter be permitted to rent out one of the floors to a second family without interference. Similarly, if local

---

[58] There is, of course, no source of statistics on nonenforcement of zoning ordinances; the instances will not be tabulated in the annual report of the board of selectmen or of the building department. Observation and inquiry, nevertheless, will confirm that the incidence of nonenforcement is significant.

authorities sense pressure on the tax base, a nurseryman located in a residential and agricultural district in which products may be sold at retail only at the farm upon which they were grown may be allowed without hindrance to establish a complete retail garden center with extensive store and parking facilities, though he actually grows himself only a small range of plants.

Zoning modifications of this kind may be viewed as informal variances — variances in which *ad hoc* standards such as those often adopted by boards of appeal are applied by the executive branch and in which there may be no corrective whatever. The use of this technique is, of course, subject to all of the criticisms which have been made in respect of loose standards utilized by boards of appeal. Worse still, it may give rise to public disrespect for and misunderstanding of the objectives of zoning and may invite either corruption or the appearance of corruption. Such a practice, therefore, may render all enforcement efforts difficult and may cause some enforcement efforts to appear grossly unfair. Any landholder who is forced to observe the letter of an ordinance while others are permitted to violate it with impunity will be justifiably resentful.

Selective nonenforcement may also have the effect of intensifying important social problems which arise in association with zoning administration. Thus, officials siding with those who favor segregated neighborhoods may tolerate illegal multiple occupancies in Negro sections only in order to reduce the pressure to expand Negro occupancy into white neighborhoods; or officials may permit nonconforming, quasi-nuisance commercial uses, such as junkyards, to expand in slum areas, even though the rules against expansion of nonconforming uses are enforced in other neighborhoods.

It is true, of course, that officials empowered to prosecute must be vested with some measure of discretion. A city attorney, for example, might advise against bringing a given enforcement proceeding on the ground that the applicability of the ordinance to the facts in question is doubtful and that a precedent should first be established in a related but clearer case. Conceivably there might be rare situations where extralegal considerations might appropriately enter. But in cases where an ordinance clearly is being violated there is no justification for utilizing nonenforcement as a conscious instrument for the achievement either of goals which are within the ambit of planning considerations, such as additional revenue, or of goals, such as segregation of races, which are without the ambit of democratic government. Planning decisions should be made and effectuated through duly constituted processes, not on the basis of the private exercise of an unreviewable executive discretion.

There are a few cases in which individuals against whom enforcement proceedings have been initiated have sought to defend on the ground that the ordinance has not been enforced against others, and hence that the enforcement proceeding was discriminatory. Courts, so sensitive to discriminations in other respects, have uniformly rejected such defenses, ruling that a municipality is not estopped to enforce the law because municipal officials have failed to do so in other instances.[59]

This is perhaps the inevitable answer to the specific problem posed by the cases. A particular building inspector and particular members of a board of selectmen are incumbent in office for only a relatively short period. Human limitations being what they are, it is inevitable that there may be occasions where, due to inadvertence, mistake, the demands of duties deemed more pressing, or deliberate nonfeasance a particular aspect of a municipal legislative program may not be rigorously enforced. It would be a stifling doctrine if such defaults were to preclude later enforcement.

The remedy, then, should not be to spread the error evenly by a judicial refusal to enforce the ordinance in instances where the authorities pay it heed. The redress should be to correct the error by requiring that the authorities enforce it where they have refrained from doing so. Perhaps in a proceeding to enjoin alleged violations of a zoning ordinance, a court, upon a claim that the ordinance is being enforced in a discriminatory manner, could explore the issue (allowing other interested parties to intervene) and, if the charge were proved, either issue a mandatory injunction directing enforcement or issue a decree conditioning relief against the defendant upon the initiation by municipal officials of an over-all enforcement program.

It is of the essence in zoning administration that, within their areas of applicability, restraints be enforced uniformly; a plan from which exceptions are available without standards is no plan at all. For this reason, and because one cannot presume that officials administering such ordinances typically will be men of large stature and outlook, it is particularly difficult properly to temper the justice of zoning laws with equity. One must rely on institutions, such as those described above, designed to provide equitable adjustments in an orderly way subject to regular procedures and standards of general application.

[59] The cases are collected in YOKLEY, ZONING LAW AND PRACTICE, *supra* note 12, § 109.

CONCLUSION

Zoning, both in theory and in practice, is predicated on the assumption that classical economic theory is essentially sound as applied to the allocation of urban land. It presupposes that the highest social good will be achieved and democratic values will be maintained if such allocations are made predominantly in the private sector of the economy, subject to minimal restraints calculated to assure congruence. If these fundamental assumptions are to be vindicated, institutional changes, some of considerable magnitude, are in order. It is important that the institutions through which zoning operates be efficient and effective at the technical level; it is vital that they be made to reflect social policies consistent with democratic traditions and that they not be used to subserve divisive and retrogressive ends; it is essential that they operate within the limits imposed by the rule of law.

Since World War II the question has recurred at all levels of government whether the democratic system is capable of reflexive analysis and can be made to respond adequately to urgent, new needs — whether it possesses processes through which existing institutions can be modified and new ones created which will be sufficiently responsive to sudden revisions of politically relevant forces in the distribution of populations, power, and wealth.

It is not inappropriate to ask broad questions in respect to relatively narrow aspects of the process of democratic government; certainly the basic presuppositions that underlie zoning practices are being tested, just as are other facets of government, at this time when the capacity of democratic government to initiate and execute needed institutional changes has yet to be proved.

An analysis of zoning administration in these terms is at once discouraging and encouraging. There is no question that local government, at least in this area, is guilty of the charges often leveled at the government of the nation: it has not been sufficiently inventive; it has offered little real leadership; its response to change has been inadequate. Yet, a review of existing problems and of possibilities for solving them reveals how little modification is necessary in the assumptions of zoning theory (let alone in the basic precepts of democratic society) to accommodate in much larger measure the vast readjustments in the urban structure. Better administrators are needed; but surely they can be found. A more effective institutional structure is essential but substantial gains might be made within the tradition and framework of administrative and judicial organization. Neither traditional constitutional notions nor traditional suspicion of broad governmental discretions need preclude flexibility, so long as constitutional concepts are intelligently applied and discretions granted are intelligently controlled. When the possibilities for administrative improvements are considered, it seems a particular irony that so little use has yet been made of available planning tools for the one public purpose that should engender little pause: to maximize the diversity, efficiency, and interest of the urban environment, rather than to waste it or reduce it to mediocrity.

ENFORCEMENT OF
PLANNING CONTROLS
IN ENGLAND AND WALES

J. G. BARR
SOLICITOR AND PARLIAMENTARY OFFICER
TO THE LONDON COUNTY COUNCIL

ALL PLANNING CONTROLS ultimately have the same object — the maintenance or the improvement of amenity, using that word in its broadest sense. Whether the desire be to secure architecture of good taste, to preserve trees and woodlands, to protect residential areas from industry, to reduce a city's working population in order to secure proper population densities and reasonable traveling conditions between home and place of work, or to preserve buildings of beauty, the ultimate goal is amenity. Its attainment requires that planning controls be capable of effective enforcement. The grant of planning permissions with elaborate conditions is pointless unless those conditions can be enforced, and it is vain to encourage good development of land adjacent to some offensive use unless means are provided for removal of the offensive use to a site where it can do no harm.

The local planning authority may attain many of these objects by the purchase of land; the subsequent redevelopment then can be controlled not only by the use of planning powers but by the powers of ownership as well. The discussion in this paper, however, will be limited to the methods of enforcing planning controls provided by Part III of the Town and Country Planning Act of 1947.

ENFORCEMENT ACTION: SECTIONS 23 AND 24

The substantive provisions of the 1947 act for controlling development were based on some forty years of practical experience of town and country planning in England and, in the main, have proved most successful. The enforcement procedure contained in sections 23 and 24, however, was not based on practical experience and has provided a notable exception to the act's general success.

Town planning legislation had its birth in Great Britain in the act of 1909. Previously, the owner of any freehold could deal with it as he wished, provided that he committed no common-law nuisance, refrained from infringing his neighbors' rights of light and way, observed any restrictive covenants to which his land might be subject, and obtained the license or consent of some public authority when necessary, as, for example, before building over a sewer or in front of a building line, or before operating a statutory offensive trade.

The act of 1909, and its 1919, 1925, and 1932 successors, were based on the principle that the planning authorities should make detailed planning schemes, prescribing the purposes for which each parcel of land in their areas could be used. The planning authority was to have the power, after notice, to remove, pull down, or alter any building or other work which contravened the operative scheme. In 1932 the power of enforcement was extended to "uses" contrary to the approved scheme.

Because only a handful of schemes were ever made operative, there was little or no practical experience of the enforcement powers contained in those early acts. Their sanction was that any development carried out between the date of passage of the resolution to prepare a scheme and the date the scheme became operative without an "interim development permission" could be stopped or removed without compensation when the scheme finally became operative. While this was an effective deterrent against unauthorized development involving capital outlay, it was no deterrent at all when the unauthorized use involved little or no capital outlay or the development consisted simply of a change in the use of existing buildings or land to some purpose which would produce a handsome profit.

The Town and Country Planning (Interim Development) Act of 1943 added two things. First, it brought all land within planning control; previously, only land covered by resolutions of the planning authorities had been controlled and there were many big gaps. Second, it gave new powers of enforcement when development was carried out without permission. The enforcement procedure contained in that act never was really tested — it was effective during wartime, and the immediate aftermath of the war, and such development as took place during its operation either was directly connected with the war effort or was largely housing carried out by public authorities, to which the bulk of the national building effort was directed in the years immediately following the war.

Consequently, the bill for the act of 1947 was prepared with the benefit of effective experience as to what would produce workable control of development generally, but with little or no practical experience of how enforcement action should work. Certainly there was no experience at all of the ingenuity which has since been displayed by those who have sought, too often successfully, to avoid the controls of the act.

Out of that lack of experience were born the enforcement provisions in sections 23 and 24 of the 1947 act. Seldom can the enforcement provisions of an important statute have produced so much litigation, difficulty, or delay.

The act's scheme for control of development is simple. Before any building, engineering, mining, or other operation may be carried out in, on, over, or under any land, or before any material change may be made in the use of any buildings or land, planning permission must be obtained, unless the development falls within certain prescribed exemptions, such as repair and maintenance or agriculture. If permission is not obtained, the planning authority may, within four years from the development, take enforcement action under section 23 to secure the removal or the alteration of the building or the discontinuance of the unauthorized use.

Formal action is initiated by resolution of the planning authority (usually of the authority's planning committee acting under delegated powers), to serve an enforcement notice on the owner and on the occupier of the land. It is here that the first substantial delay can occur. The name and address of the occupier usually is easy to ascertain, although not always, as was found when enforcement notices were to be served on a multitude of peripatetic stallholders, each occupying a small part of a bombed site in London on Sundays for an unauthorized market. But finding the correct name and address of the "owner," as defined by the act, may take considerable time. "Owner" is defined as "a person, other than a mortgagee not in possession, who, whether in his own right or as trustee or agent for any other person, is entitled to receive the rack rent of the land or, where the land is not let at a rack rent, would be so entitled if it were so let." While the act empowers the planning authority to require the occupier of land and any person who directly or indirectly receives the rent in respect of land to state in writing the nature of his interest and the name and address of any other person known to him as having an interest therein, the town council is not empowered to obtain information of the rents received or paid by the various interested parties. Even when such information can be had it is not always easy to decide which one of the several rents is the rack rent. Since an enforcement notice not served on the "owner" is invalid and useless, the fullest inquiries as to ownership must be made before it is served. The act makes provision for impersonal service by fixing the notice on the land when the name and address of the "owner" cannot be ascertained after reasonable inquiry, but that machinery cannot be used until the planning authority makes the inquiries permitted by the act. Notwithstanding the planning authorities' power to demand information from occupiers and others and the penalty of a small fine for refusal, an occupier does not readily supply information about his immediate landlord when he knows that the purpose of the inquiry is to put him out of business.

There is no comprehensive registration of land interests in England. Although in London and in some other cities compulsory registration of land has existed for many years (and a local authority can obtain from the register such information as it is empowered to obtain from an owner), such registration is compulsory only on transfers made after the introduction of the registration system, and it is remarkable how much property remains unregistered, even in London. Leases for less than 21 years are in any event not registerable; and there may be many sublease interests standing between the freeholder and the occupier, any one of which may be the "owner" as defined by the statute.

After service of notice personally or impersonally, the developer has an opportunity for large-scale delaying tactics. Section 23 empowers him to challenge the merits of the enforcement notice by application to the planning authority for planning permission for the development; he can do this even if his application has been refused previously. If he fails before the planning authority he can appeal to the Minister of Housing and Local Government and some months will elapse before the appeal can be heard and the decision issued. But section 23 also empowers the developer to appeal to the magistrates court from the terms of the enforcement notice. If he loses there, he has a further right of appeal to quarter sessions. Moreover, he can elect to follow one or the other of those two courses, or both at the same time. To avoid confusion, the magistrates may well adjourn the appeal to them until the decision of the appeal to the Minister is made, producing another substantial delay. If he so wishes, he can also introduce the matter to the High Court at a suitable stage (which may be delayed until proceedings for penalties have been instituted for failure to comply with the enforcement notice) either by appealing on a point of law from the magistrates court or quarter sessions, or by seeking a declaration that the whole process, including the Minister's decision, has been invalid because, as he claims, he has existing-use rights.

Months, and sometimes years, can elapse between the time when the planning authority first directed enforcement action and the date on which it may take effective action against disobedience of the enforcement notice.

In addition to the delays which an unauthorized developer desirous of continuing his development for as long as possible may interpose, the section has proved to be full of technical rocks on which many enforcement notices have foundered. The courts have always construed provisions of this kind, restricting the owner's common-law rights of user, in the strictest manner. The attitude of the courts to enforcement procedure is well illustrated by the following quotations:

> It was . . . contended that the Act was highly technical and, as it encroached on private rights, the court must insist on strict and rigid adherence to formalities. This, as a general proposition, commands assent and not the less because disregard of an enforcement notice is an offence involving sufficiently serious penal consequences. — Lord Simonds in *East Riding County Council v. Park Estate, Bridlington,* [1956] 3 Weekly L.R. 312 at 316–317.

> It is no doubt true that notices which may have penal results, and which are served pursuant to legislation which has the effect of curtailing ordinary proprietary rights, should be strictly construed, and the court should be careful to see that they are adequate documents having regard to the terms of the legislation. — Lord Justice Jenkins in *Francis v. Yiewsley and West Drayton U.D.C.,* [1957] 3 Weekly L.R. 919 at 925.

While the draftsman of an enforcement notice must approach his task with all the skill and particularity of the draftsman of a criminal indictment, he now must do so with the added knowledge that the act and the subsidiary orders made under it may have made it impossible for any valid enforcement notice at all to be drafted. Such a situation occurred in *Cater v. Essex County Council,* [1959] 2 All E.R. 213, where an enforcement notice which recited that "development consisting of a material change of use has been carried out on the land . . . without the grant of permission required . . . under Part 3 of the Act, the said land being used for the purpose of a caravan [trailer] site" was held to be a nullity, because under the Town and Country Planning General Development Order of 1950 general permission was given for the "use of any land for any purpose on not more than 28 days in total in any calendar year, and the erection or placing of movable structures on the land for the purposes of that use." In his judgment in that case, Mr. Justice Donovan said:

I feel bound, and with the like reluctance, to agree. The construction which this Court is now putting on the words "permission required in that behalf under this Part of this Act," viz., that such permission is given inter alia by the Town and Country Planning General Development Order, 1950, granting twenty-eight days' permission, will make the enforcement of planning control even more difficult than it is already, and perhaps in a large number of cases impossible. For that reason I have sought a construction of the words which would avoid the result which I do not think Parliament could ever have intended. In this search I have failed. — 2 All E.R. at 218.

This particular damage to the cause of enforcement was repaired with speed by the last-minute inclusion of what is now section 38 of the Town and Country Planning Act of 1959, which was on its way through Parliament when the decision was given.

In considering the enforcement action provisions, not everything should be placed on the debit side. The existence of the threat of proceedings normally has been sufficient to stop unauthorized development which would involve heavy capital outlay, or which would in the end be likely to involve the developer in substantial expense without the opportunity to make a worthwhile profit in the meantime. But where the developer is faced with relatively little or no capital expenditure, or with expenditure which can be expected to be recouped within a short period of time, the procedure has proved to be no deterrent at all. Major troubles have been experienced with unauthorized trailer sites and (particularly in London) with drinking clubs of an unsavory character. The end of a long enforcement chase too often has meant that, when the notice has taken effect at last and the planning authority is in a position to take proceedings for penalties, the trailers have been moved to the next field, or the club has been moved down from the first floor to the basement and the chase has had to start all over again.

While trailers are used extensively for vacations and touring, they are also used for living in all the year round. A recent survey has shown about 150,000 people living in some 60,000 trailers as distinct from those just taking vacations in them, of which some 10,000 are stationed on sites which appear to have been established in contravention of planning control. Many of the sites lack the facilities for decent living conditions. Many vacation trailer sites have been established in the wrong places and with inadequate facilities. A lot of money has been and is being made by the owners of these sites.

The government sought a remedy in the Caravan Sites and Control of Development Bill. In introducing it to the House of Commons, the

Minister explained the reasons why special legislation for trailer sites was needed: to assure that they do not become established in the wrong places and to secure an improvement in living conditions on the sites. The bill indirectly makes it an offense to establish a trailer site without planning permission, unless it comes within one of the exemptions, such as a site of five or more acres used for not more than 28 days in the year as a trailer site and by not more than three trailers at a time, and land used by a traveling showman who is at the time in the course of traveling for the purpose of his business.

The act bars any occupier of land from allowing any part of the land to be used as a trailer site unless he obtains a license so authorizing. Violation makes him liable to maximum fines of £100 for the first offense and £250 for a second or subsequent offense. Of course, he will not get his site license unless either he has first obtained planning permission, or the site already has existing use rights the continuance of which the planning authority is not prepared to stop by the payment of compensation.

Another part of the act seeks to improve the general enforcement provisions. In introducing it the Minister said, "The difficulties about the present enforcement procedure in Part III of the Town and Country Planning Act, 1947, are by now fairly notorious. They have been troubling the Courts for some time. They have been criticised by lawyers as severely as by the planning authorities. The whole issue has been brought into special prominence by the caravan problem but it is by no means confined to caravans." No one could accuse the Minister of overstating his case.

The major change effected is the removal of the duality of appeal formerly available, substituting a direct right of appeal to the Minister from all points of an enforcement notice. He will pass not only on the planning merits but also on issues of fact and law presently dealt with by the magistrates courts. Provision is made for a right of appeal to the High Court on points of law, and the Minister, on his own initiative, will be able to state a case for the opinion of the High Court.

The change can only be welcome to planning authorities: Anything which will simplify procedure and cut out delay must be welcome. The proposal has not been without criticism, however, largely on the ground that the initial argument, involving points of law, will be before a lay inspector of the Minister, not a court of law. This means that legal submissions will have to be reported by the inspector to the Minister and, in practice, adjudicated by members of the Ministry's legal department who will not have heard the argument. Criticism has also been directed at the power given the Minister to state a case for the opinion of the High Court on his own motion, which might result in the parties to an appeal arguing before the High Court, at considerable expense to themselves, some point of law which a member of the legal department of the Ministry may think worthy of the High Court's judgment. Nonetheless, it is difficult to perceive a practicable alternative if the present duality of procedure is to be eliminated. Planning merits, which depend upon planning policy, can be dealt with only by the Minister and by no one else.

Other substantial changes of the act are to make the landowner who has failed to comply with an enforcement notice requiring something other than the discontinuance of a particular use liable for penalties (previously the planning authority's only remedy was to enter upon the land, carry out the work, and recover the cost); a provision that if, after an enforcement notice has been served, planning permission legalizing the use is given, the notice shall cease to have effect; a doubling of the penalty from £50 to £100 for failure to comply with an enforcement notice requiring the discontinuance of the use of land; and, most important of all, a provision that once an enforcement notice has taken effect compliance with it shall not have the effect of discharging it: a notice registered against the land will remain in full force, and it will not be necessary to start the machinery all over again on a future breach.

One source of past difficulty also is removed by authorizing entry upon land to persons authorized by the Minister or a planning authority to ascertain whether there actually has been compliance with any notice or order under Part III of the act, including an enforcement notice.

It is the hope of planning authorities that the new enforcement code will assist in removing some of the worst procedural difficulties which have led in the past to disheartening delays and which too often have left those who secure compliance with planning controls feeling that they have been engaged in a game of snakes and ladders, where it is always snakes and never a ladder. It will not remove the need for planning authorities to serve notices both on "owners" and occupiers, nor will it remove the need for the most careful accuracy in the drafting of the notices themselves. The case law which has been built up on that subject is not superseded. It will not disturb the principle that to develop land without planning permission is to commit no offense against the Town and Country Planning Acts, notwithstanding that that development may in itself be unlawful. But if the development is by the unauthorized provision of trailers, which has been the greatest single source of difficulty, or by the institution of a use forbidden by an operative enforcement notice, then proceedings for penalties will be available.

What further improvements in the procedure could be suggested? While action could be speeded if enforcement notices had to be served only on the occupiers and not on the "owners," it is unlikely that Parliament would agree to such a proposal because its operation could affect adversely the owner's proprietary rights without opportunity to be heard. Nor is it feasible to suggest that, as a general proposition, development without prior planning permission should be a punishable offense. Often, arguments in particular cases turn on mixed issues of law and of fact as to whether planning permission is necessary at all, or whether the development complained of is not in law the continuance of an existing use. Again, there is always the possibility that if planning permission were sought after proceedings for penalties had been commenced it would be granted either by the planning authority or by the Minister on appeal, and the courts would be most reluctant to deal with a prosecution until it had been ascertained whether the offense was simply technical (as it would be if permission were subsequently granted), or real (as it would be if permission were refused). To make such a system work, it would be necessary first to compile an all-embracing Domesday Book of existing uses and permitted uses — not only an impossible task but effectively throwing away the flexible pattern of the 1947 act and substituting for it the rigidity of the detailed planning schemes of the prewar legislation, whose unworkability is already proved.

It would seem that a general system of enforcement designed to cover all types of cases and all kinds of development, from the trivial to the serious, where the points in issue may or may not have far-reaching effects on property values, must necessarily be so wrapped around with safeguards as to obviate the speed which a particular undesirable breach of planning control may seem to require. But the prescription for trailers embodied in the act may point to a method of dealing with any particular class of development which may become a serious problem. Drinking clubs of bad character have become such a problem in recent years, particularly in London, that the government has announced that it is considering legislation to deal with it. Under present law a drinking club requires no license and can be opened after registration simply by payment of a nominal fee and completion of certain forms. If the pattern of the trailer legislation were followed, making it an offense for a drinking club to be commenced without some form of selective registration — such registration not being granted until either a valid planning permission or a certificate of existing-use rights was produced to the registration authority — the town planning difficulties now experienced with these clubs would largely disappear, although many other difficulties not related to town planning would remain to be dealt with. But if these two classes of cases, trailers and clubs, could be dealt with on the same basic pattern, the resulting reduction in the number of cases requiring enforcement action would enable the planning authorities to devote greater attention to the remaining cases. In London and other big cities temporary difficulties have been caused by the misuse of derelict bombed sites, but their cure lies in the value of the sites, which encourages proper redevelopment by their owners now that the postwar building restrictions have been removed. Such sites apart, trailers and drinking clubs have been and are the two classes of development which have had the most obvious and harmful effect on amenities. In most other cases no serious harm is done if a relatively long period of time must elapse between the start and finish of enforcement action.

AGREEMENTS REGULATING THE DEVELOPMENT OR USE OF LAND: SECTION 25

Section 14 authorizes the planning authority to attach conditions to a planning permission, including conditions regulating the use of any land under the control of the applicant (whether or not it is land in respect of which the application for the permission was made) or requiring particular works on any such land. Any conditions properly so imposed can be enforced later by action under sections 23 and 24.

But in dealing with the redevelopment of sites in big cities, circumstances sometimes arise which cannot be met effectively by the attachment of conditions to section 14 planning permissions. It may happen, for instance, that the applicant owns two neighboring parcels of land: one he proposes to develop right away, but he is not presently "in control" of the other, which is subject to existing leases. In a recent case, the owner in possession of a parcel of residential property on the edge of a commercial zone wished to redevelop it as commercial property and was willing to agree to redevelop into residential property, a few years later, an adjoining commercial parcel located in a residential zone, which he owned subject to existing leases. Because he was not "in control" of the second parcel at the time of his application, its future redevelopment could not be controlled by attaching conditions to the permission to redevelop the first parcel, but an alternate means of dealing with the matter was found under section 25. This section empowers the planning authority, with the approval of the Minister, to enter into agreements restricting or regulating the development or use of land, either permanently or for a limited period. An agreement under this section is expressly made enforceable by the planning authority against any successor in title of the other party to the agreement as if the planning authority possessed adjacent land and the agreement had been made for its benefit. The burden of such an agreement therefore will run with the land in the same way as a restrictive covenant, enforceable in equity against successive owners of the land under the rule in *Tulk v. Moxhay,* 2 Phillips 774, 41 Eng. Rep. 1143 (1848).

However, the provisions of section 25 are not broad enough to allow imposition of an obligation to carry out a positive act so as to bind successive owners of the land, and for that reason it has severe practical limitations. As a matter of policy, the Minister will not grant approval to such agreements if their object can be obtained by attaching proper conditions to the planning permission.

REMOVAL OF NONCONFORMING USES AND BUILDINGS: SECTIONS 26 AND 27

Against the backdrop of the history of English cities and villages, planning is an innovation. The hearts of the big cities have developed through centuries without its aid and without its control. The development plan for a great city may show areas zoned for residential, commercial, or industrial development, but an inspection of the ground will show nonconforming uses which have existed for many years and which have existing-use rights. An old residential building in a commercial or industrial zone will soon bring itself into line: the greater value of a commercial or industrial use will ensure redevelopment, producing new uses which will conform to the zoning. But the reverse is not true; on redevelopment, existing-use rights will entitle the owner to rebuild and to retain his nonconforming use unless compensation is paid by the planning authority.

While financial restrictions are a substantial limiting factor, it may not be practicable for one reason or another to wait for redevelopment before putting an end to a nonconforming use. Enforcement action is not available, since the use itself is lawful; so sections 26 and 27 empower the planning authority to make an order requiring discontinuance of a particular land use or continuance subject to new conditions, or alteration or removal of buildings or works. The order has no effect until it is confirmed by the Minister, who, before doing so, is required to give a hearing to any owner, occupier or other person affected by the order; notice of such hearing must be given to them by the planning authority. If the Minister confirms the order the continuance or renewal of the forbidden use renders the offender liable to penalties and, if any buildings or works are not removed in compliance with the order, the planning authority may enter and do so.

The planning authority must pay compensation to the owner for damage suffered by any interest in the land. If the owner is able to show that the land in its existing state subject to the restrictions of the order is no longer capable of reasonably beneficial use and that it cannot be rendered capable of such use by development for which permission is available, he may take steps under section 19 to require the planning authority to purchase his interest in the land.

The obligation to compensate limits severely the use which planning authorities can make of these provisions. To stop a nonconforming use by invoking them means incurring a substantial bill for compensation without the acquisition of any interest in the property. The London County Council annually allocates something like half a million pounds from its budget for the removal of nonconforming uses; the great bulk of this money is not spent on implementing sections 26 and 27, but on the purchase by agreement of nonconforming uses, whose sites can then be used for housing, education, or open spaces. The financial burden of these provisions means that only very exceptionally are they used.

In these sections lies the only remedy for dealing with the large number of trailer sites protected by existing-use rights but located in the wrong places. It is said that throughout the country as a whole over 2,000 sites, accommodating at present some 10,000 residential trailers, enjoy such rights, amounting to about one sixth of all the residential trailers in the country. The expensive process available under these sections remains the only way of getting rid of them.

PRESERVATION OF TREES AND WOODLANDS: SECTION 28

Under section 28 a planning authority, by means of orders confirmed by the Minister after consideration of objections by interested parties, can secure the prohibition of cutting down, topping, lopping, or willfully destroying trees without its consent. The standard tree preservation order exempts from its operation the removal of trees which are dead or dying, dangerous or a nuisance, or which must be removed, for example, to permit an electricity board to construct mains transmission and other lines.

The procedure for such orders is detailed and laborious, often requiring the service of many hundreds of notices when the trees are in a garden shared by the occupiers of large blocks of flats, but great use has been made of it not only in the countryside but in the big cities. In the County of London nearly 200 orders have been made and confirmed in the past twelve years covering a large variety and number of trees. Some orders have dealt with as few as ten trees, others have dealt with hundreds.

BUILDINGS OF SPECIAL ARCHITECTURAL OR HISTORIC INTEREST: SECTIONS 30 AND 31

Ancient monuments like Stonehenge and Crown properties like the Tower of London have long been preserved by machinery outside the planning acts. So, too, have the great cathedrals and churches, while provision has been made by the National Trust and by financial grants-in-aid for the preservation of many historic houses. In addition to these show-pieces of history and of architecture, there are throughout the length and breadth of the country thousands of buildings and structures of special architectural or historic interest, some of which must be preserved at all costs and many others of which should be preserved for as long as possible.

The principle of preservation and the machinery for it was included in the act of 1932, but the current provisions of the act of 1947 are much more elaborate and all-embracing, and no longer depend solely upon the interest or initiative of the planning authority for their operation.

Section 30 charges the Minister with the duty of compiling, and from time to time amending, a list of buildings and structures of special architectural and historic interest. Relevant parts of the list, compiled with the aid of architectural, antiquarian, and similar interests, are deposited with the planning authorities and local authorities to whose areas they relate. The entries in the list are registered as local land charges and notice given to the owners and occupiers affected. So long as a building remains on the list it may not be demolished, altered, or extended in any way which would seriously affect its character unless at least two months' notice has been given to the planning authority, which must furnish a copy to the Minister. The execution of works in breach of this provision is a punishable offense and the planning authority also is empowered to require the building to be restored to its former state.

The planning authority has two months from the notice of the intended demolition to decide whether to let the building go or whether to make a building preservation order under section 29; but it is not necessary to wait until such notice is received before making an order. The order can be made at any time, but has no effect until confirmed by the Minister. A building preservation order may require the planning authority's consent for the execution of works specified in the order; enable the planning authority to require the restoration of the building to its former state where any such works have been executed in contravention of the order; and provide for compensation by the planning authority for loss caused by a refusal of consent or by the grant of conditional consent.

"Listed" buildings are divided into different categories. Obviously, some are much more worthy of preservation than others, and when the owner wants to demolish and gives notice under section 30, the planning authority has to consider urgently whether the building's merits outweigh the cost of compensation to keep it in being. Budgetary considerations mean that, where the owner is intent upon demolition, only the most important buildings can be preserved by this machinery.

It will be noted that the powers of a building preservation order are wholly negative in form. The owner is prevented from demolishing or altering the building, but he cannot be forced to maintain it. It is remarkable how rapidly a building on a site where redevelopment rights are valuable can "decay" to a point beyond preservation, demolition then becoming an urgent necessity.

If the owner does not share a desire to preserve it, positive action to ensure the continued existence of a building can be taken only if the planning authority is prepared to purchase the building either by agreement or under section 41 by means of a compulsory purchase order made by the planning authority or local authority, and confirmed by the Minister (or, if the Minister of Works decides to intervene, a compulsory purchase order made by him). The owner can contest the confirmation of such an order, not only on its merits before the normal form of ministerial inquiry, but also on appeal to a magistrates court and thereafter to quarter sessions, on the ground that he is taking all reasonable steps for the proper preservation of the building. If the court so finds, an order staying the compulsory purchase proceedings must be made.

CONTROL OF ADVERTISEMENTS: SECTIONS 31 AND 32

One of the greatest causes of damage to amenity with which the act of 1947 had to contend was the indiscriminate display of commercial advertisements. Sections 31 and 32 did not set out to provide a complete code of control; rather, they provided for the detailed code restricting and regulating the display of advertisements to be written as regulations by the

Minister. The Town and Country Planning (Control of Advertisements) Regulations of 1948, as subsequently amended, are still in force. They have provided a meticulous, workable, and uniform code facilitating removal of offending advertisements from scenic spots and from inappropriate places in urban areas within a relatively short time after becoming effective.

"Advertisement," as defined in the act and in the regulations, is considerably broader than the everyday usage of the word. It includes, for example, a doctor's professional nameplate and the frame or boarding on which an advertisement is displayed as well as the advertisement itself; but by careful drafting of the classes of advertisement which may be displayed without the consent of the planning authority, the maximum freedom and the minimum of inconvenience resulted. Normal professional nameplates, "House for Sale" notices of a normal design, advertisements on public transportation, in newspapers, handbills, and election posters are examples of advertising exempted by the regulations from control.

All new advertisements which are not exempt must receive the planning authority's express consent. In deciding whether to grant its consent, the planning authority must consider those factors laid down in the regulations, including amenity, which covers not only the general characteristics of a locality but also its historic or cultural features. No condition can be attached to a consent if its operation would amount to censorship by the planning authority of the subject matter of the advertisement.

The procedure for applications for express consent is akin to that of applications for planning permission. An appeal lies to the Minister from refusal or conditional assent, but the Minister is not required to hear the parties if he is satisfied that he is sufficiently informed to decide the appeal without a hearing.

Advertisements in existence when the regulations came into force (August 1, 1948) lived on for a period of grace — three years for advertisements which were being displayed on January 7, 1947, the date on which the bill for the act was published, and one year for advertisements displayed after that date. When the grace period expired, the existing advertisements became subject to challenge, that is, the planning authority could require the owners of the advertisements to apply for express consent for their retention as though they were new advertisements, and the planning authority could either grant consent, refuse it, or impose conditions. Appeal to the Minister was available, but if the refusal or conditions were upheld the advertisement had to be removed or altered without payment of any compensation; an exception in the case of advertisements displayed on and after January 1, 1947, was that the owner could recover the reasonable cost incurred in removing or altering them. No "existing-use rights" were recognized for compensation purposes.

The act and the regulations empower the Minister to declare areas of special control where the beauty of the countryside or the special features of a part of the town require special protection. The practical effect of such declarations is that commercial advertising of the normal kind disappears altogether in those areas.

The controls of advertising contained in these regulations are meticulous and have worked with a minimum of complaint. The regulations were drafted within the twelve months following the passage of the act and bear all the marks of careful and well-considered subsidiary legislation. The contrast between their success and the failure of the code for enforcement action contained in sections 23 and 24 makes it regrettable that these sections were not also left the subject of subsidiary legislation, worked out and drafted at leisure after the heat of the parliamentary battle on the bill had cooled.

POWER TO REQUIRE PROPER MAINTENANCE OF WASTELAND: SECTION 33

The planning authority has power to require by notice the owners and occupiers of any garden, vacant site, or other open land to take the steps specified in the notice to abate any injury of the amenity of the area within the allotted time. The machinery of sections 23 and 24 is applied by regulation to secure enforcement.

Little use has been made of this power. The burden of establishing "serious injury" to amenity is very substantial. Some light has recently been thrown on the limitations of this section by the Court of Appeal in *Stephens v. Cuckfield R.D.C.* (*The Times,* London, June 3, 1960), holding that vacant land within the curtilage of premises used for car-breaking, which caused a serious injury to amenities, could not be dealt with "as open land" under this section. Presumably, direct enforcement action under sections 23 and 24 was unavailable in this case and proceedings under section 33 were tried unsuccessfully as an alternative to the process under sections 26 and 27, involving compensation.

Regulation and Taking of
Property under Planning Laws

REGULATION AND PURCHASE:
TWO GOVERNMENTAL WAYS
TO ATTAIN PLANNED LAND USE

DAVID W. CRAIG
CITY SOLICITOR, PITTSBURGH, PENNSYLVANIA

To REVIEW the landscape behind us, the traditional nature of eminent domain should be compared with the accepted meaning of the police power.

The exercise of eminent domain has traditionally involved the taking of property for a public use; compensation is paid to the owner. The police power, as ordinarily understood in relation to private property, has involved a suppression or limitation applied to the property in the owner's hands, in order to protect the public health, safety, morals, or general welfare against dangers arising, or likely to arise, from the misemployment of the property; compensation is not paid to the owner.[1]

Thus, with respect to ownership, the police power leaves the title to the property unchanged, but eminent domain changes it. The police power does not re-employ the property in the hands of another owner, but restricts it in the hands of its present owner. With respect to goal, eminent domain has been aimed at converting property to use by the public for a public purpose. Thus the goal of eminent domain has ordinarily been closely centered upon the particular property itself. The goal of the police power, on the other hand, usually involves persons or things external to the property; often there is an intention to protect outsiders from the property itself or from a particular use of the property.

THE ISSUE HYPOTHESIZED

A state supreme court has pointed out:

Police power controls the use of property by the owner, for the public good, its use otherwise being harmful, while eminent domain and taxation take property for public use.[2]

[1] 18 AM. JUR. *Eminent Domain* § 11 (1938).
[2] White's Appeal, 287 Pa. 259, 264, 134 A. 409 (1926).

One rule of thumb has been that property is taken by eminent domain because of the usefulness of the property in the hands of the public, but property is regulated by the police power because of its harmfulness in the hands of the owner.[3]

Although discussions of the relationship of the police power to property have ordinarily used negative terms for the purpose of underscoring the harmfulness of the property or its use, the positive side of the same coin should not be overlooked. As indicated by the court opinion quoted above, police power regulation is positive in the ultimate; that is, it suppresses a negative threat in order to seek the "public good." Therefore, to characterize the police power as simply negative in nature and eminent domain as wholly positive in nature would be a misleading oversimplification.

Overlapping in the two concepts has continued for many years. Sometimes a single governmental action can be directed not only to devoting property to use by the public, but also toward eliminating a dangerous aspect of that same property. For example, private title at a dangerous railroad crossing may be appropriated, to close the crossing, so that the former dangers of the crossing are eliminated. This matter is accomplished by eminent domain, even though the ultimate result is familiar to the police power.[4]

Similarly, the degree of suppression by the police power can be so great as to deprive the owner of the property as fully, in a practical sense, as if ownership were taken away from him. The classic illustration has been the situation in which private houses, located in the path of an advancing fire, are demolished in order to create a firebreak which will halt the fire.[5] Only the police power is involved. The land does not become the base for any public activity or structure; thus the land and its title are not devoted to any public use.

However, the old distinctions are becoming less workable. The interdependency of property prompts the use of the police power to eliminate a structure from the path of a conflagration. Similarly, in securing greenbelts, we are prompted to eliminate a parcel from the path of development by eminent domain. Thus public purchase is now used to take a property out of circulation, as well as for the conventional purpose of recirculating it for the public. In recent years, particularly in its application

---

[3] ERNST FREUND, THE POLICE POWER, PUBLIC POLICY AND CONSTITUTIONAL RIGHTS 546, 547 (Chicago, 1904), quoted in C. M. HAAR, LAND-USE PLANNING 544 (Boston, 1959).

[4] See McKeon v. N.Y., N.H. & H. RR., 75 Conn. 343, 53 A. 656 (1902), aff'd. 189 U.S. 508 (1903).

[5] Bowditch v. Boston, 101 U.S. 16 (1879).

to planned land-use control, eminent domain goals have been broadened from "public use" to a wider concept of "public purpose," [6] thus minimizing the importance of the public's mere title in the taken property and emphasizing the purpose, possibly negative, for which the title has been taken.

Thus, in terms of goal, eminent domain and police power regulation are becoming less distinguishable in the field of land-use control. In terms of title, distinctions between the two methods become less significant when we see both methods used to achieve purposes which may involve, in either case, comprehensive limitation or direction of use. If title is composed of a bundle of rights, then the rights which are the components of title may be modified by regulation nearly as extensively as by purchase.

In the past regulation and purchase were distinguished by examining purpose and title. By such means, we were able to identify whether we were dealing with regulation or with purchase, and we therefore knew when compensation had to be paid. Now, however, if the purposes of regulation and purchase become indistinguishable in the field of land-use control, and if their respective effects on title are blended, then guides to the necessity of compensation are weakened or lost.

Thus we may hypothesize an issue, to be tested by examining particular situations. The issue is: Is the line of demarcation between regulation and purchase now being made unusably vague by a tendency to employ regulation and purchase for like goals in the control of land use?

If this question is answered affirmatively, then we will know that we lack certainty in the tests we have been using to determine whether or not compensation should be paid. We may be thus alerted to examine whether or not our employment of regulation has pushed past some constitutional definition of that concept. We could be brought to feel that some degree of purchase should be used more widely.

REGULATION AT PRESENT

In the United States, the nationwide standard governing the reasonableness and fairness of particular exercises of the police power is embodied in the Fourteenth Amendment to the Constitution of the United States, which reads, in part:

No State shall . . . deprive any person of life, liberty, or property, without due process of law; nor deny to any person within its jurisdiction the equal protection of the laws.

[6] Schneider v. District of Columbia, 117 F. Supp. 705, 716 (1953).

As applied to the validity of regulation, this constitutional provision is said to require "substantive due process."

The meaning of substantive due process is defined as a requirement that there must be a reasonable relation between the restriction imposed on property and the purpose of the restriction.[7] Where a given restriction is arbitrary and unreasonable, without connection to the public health, safety, morals, or welfare, the protection of the due process clause can be invoked.[8]

This view, that due process questions involve a balancing of the factual nature of the restriction against the factual nature of its purpose, is derived from decisions of the United States Supreme Court. In *Nebbia v. New York,* that Court stated:

> And the guaranty of due process, as has often been held, demands only that the law shall not be unreasonable, arbitrary or capricious, and that the means selected shall have a real and substantial relation to the object sought to be attained.

In addition, it is clear that the reasonableness of the means and purposes must be weighed in the light of the surrounding circumstances. The *Nebbia* case adds:

> A regulation valid for one sort of business, or in given circumstances, may be invalid for another sort, or for the same business under other circumstances, because the reasonableness of each regulation depends upon the relevant facts.[9]

An exercise of the police power must be in reference to "the particular situation and needs of the community." [10]

Hence, in weighing the validity of any regulation, we examine its two-sided effect, in its actual environment, by use of the following balance:

Does it, by its	Is it, in its
NATURE have a	DEGREE of restriction,
NECESSARY relation to	REASONABLE in its effects upon
POLICE POWER needs?	PRIVATE PROPERTY?
Protection of Public	Regulation of Individuals

The Factual Environment

---

[7] SUM. PA. JUR. *Constitutional Law* § 219.5 (1955).
[8] 12 AM. JUR. *Constitutional Law* § 684 (1938).
[9] 291 U.S. 502, 525 (1934).
[10] New Mexico v. Denver and R. G. R. Company, 203 U.S. 38, 55 (1906).

The Fourteenth Amendment also contains the "equal protection" clause, which embodies the basic concept of fairness and uniformity of application of a law to like situations. Similar guarantees of reasonableness and equality are also contained in the constitutions of the states themselves.

A survey of the application of police power regulation to land-use controls might well begin with those regulations which impose a set of rules uniformly throughout the jurisdiction.

In the American pattern, two types of such jurisdiction-wide rules are building codes and housing codes. Building codes govern the method and materials used for the erection of structures, primarily for fire prevention and structural safety reasons. The so-called housing codes govern the construction, size, and amenity of dwellings, primarily for the protection of the health of those who reside in them.

The older, traditional type of building code and housing code was a specification code; that is, it spelled out specifically the construction technique, the type of material, or the devices and methods by which standards were to be achieved. Such codes have the virtue of certainty in interpretation and application, but they often lag behind modern developments in techniques and materials.

Less certain in interpretation, but more flexible, is the performance type of building or housing code. Although performance codes must still specify some matters with particularity, they attempt primarily to describe the required standard in terms of the result which must be achieved; in other words, they describe a given noise level in decibels, or a degree of fire resistance, rather than a specific kind of noiseproofing material or a specific kind of fireproofing material.

The general validity of building and housing codes is well established. However, in all such regulation, because elasticity is not a desirable quality in a uniform yardstick, considerable tension is experienced between the need, on the one hand, for certainty and predictability in order to make uniformity of application easier and, on the other hand, the desirability of flexibility in order to permit the yardstick to conform, like a tape measure, to situations of various shapes.

Unlike present-day jurisdiction-wide building codes, zoning regulations are geographically delimited. Fundamentally, they involve the division of the regulated jurisdiction into districts or zones, and the description of allowable uses and structures, as well as the spacing and bulk of structures, for each class of zone.

Although building and housing laws may be adopted directly by either state governments or local governments, zoning regulations as such are ordinarily enacted at the local county or municipal level, pursuant to general enabling laws adopted by the respective states. Until after World War II, many of the state enabling acts were similar in that they were based upon a common parent, the Standard State Zoning Enabling Act promulgated at the instance of the federal Department of Commerce in the 1920's for voluntary adoption by states.[11] This model thus formed the mold for the first or second round of state enabling acts adopted in the United States. However, now that the earlier enabling acts have begun to be replaced in many states, the third round shows a much more variegated pattern, primarily because no widely accepted national model is currently available.

However, the continued use of the standard zoning enabling act pattern by many states, and the continued influence of its concepts and wording, even in those states which have turned to new statutes, permit the standard act to be regarded as a sample of the statutory foundations of zoning. The kind of requirements permitted in states which follow the standard act may be listed as follows:

1. Height, number of stories, and size of buildings and other structures.
2. Percentage of lot which may be occupied.
3. Size of yards, courts, and other open spaces.
4. Density of population.
5. Location and use of buildings, structures, and land.[12]

The police power purposes of zoning — that is, its relation to the protection of the public health, safety, morals, and general welfare — are spelled out, by those laws which are based upon the standard act, in a specific listing, as follows:[13]

1. To lessen street congestion.
2. To secure safety from fire, panic, and other dangers.
3. To promote health.
4. To promote the general welfare.
5. To provide adequate light and air.
6. To prevent the overcrowding of land.
7. To avoid undue concentration of population.
8. To facilitate the adequate provision of transportation, water, sewerage, school, parks, and other public requirements.

[11] David Craig, Pennsylvania Building and Zoning Laws 149 (Pittsburgh, 1951).
[12] New York Village Law, § 175, 63 McKinney's Consol. Laws § 175 (Brooklyn, Supp. 1959).
[13] New York Village Law, § 177, id. § 177.

9. To conserve the value of buildings.

10. To encourage the most appropriate use of land throughout the municipality.

Local regulations, to be valid, must be directed toward one or more of the purposes thus enumerated by state law. Also, as noted above, substantive due process, for constitutional validity, requires that the nature of a regulation be related to its purpose. Hence a listing of purposes can be said to be a generalized listing of the kinds of regulation in terms of results. In other words, by rough analogy to the two types of building codes described above, the first of the two preceding lists constitutes a collection of specifications and the latter list constitutes a set of performance standards.[14]

The pressure for flexible performance codes in the building code field has proved to be a little-noticed harbinger[15] of a similar pressure for flexibility in zoning. Flexible zoning means particularized zoning. And particularized zoning is one more step further away from jurisdiction-wide regulations and one step closer to the particularized approach of eminent domain.

Since the early days of zoning laws, the state enabling statutes have generally provided for the granting of "variances" administratively whenever the unique characteristics of a particular parcel of land would render it unusable under the applicable district regulations. Thus the variance power has served as an escape valve built into zoning ordinances, in order to relieve the pressure of unconstitutionality arising from a confiscatory effect of the regulation in a particular situation. The variance was not designed as part of the productive machinery of the zoning ordinance, but rather as a piece of emergency equipment. Among the zoning idealists, it was accorded only a grudging place in the zoning scheme.

The "special use" or "special exception," on the other hand, has been a device provided by the enabling acts as part of the regular operating machinery of zoning ordinances. Briefly, the special exception is a use (or

[14] It is interesting to note that population density is stated both as a requirement type and as a goal.

[15] There has been too little exchange of experience between those concerned with building and housing codes and those who develop zoning ordinances. In most cities building codes are enforced by a building inspector or unit within a safety department. Housing codes have usually been in the province of public health departments. Although the routine administrative aspects of zoning codes may often be in the hands of the building code enforcer, zoning administration in depth and zoning revision have ordinarily been the concerns of two independent boards, the planning commissions and the boards of adjustment or appeal.

departure in area or bulk) allowable by administrative action, but only when the proposal meets standards and criteria expressly written into the particular zoning ordinance by the enacting body.

In recent years, constraint has been felt in trying to fit the district-by-district zoning girdle to the municipality because of zoning's mass-of-lots approach, which tends to assume that each lot in a district is an interchangeable unit. The tendency to make extensive use of the administrative exception approach has increased.[16] Extreme departures from the districting approach of zoning have been rebuffed by the courts, under the concepts prescribed by the conventional type of enabling law. In one case, the court disapproved a zoning ordinance which denominated the entire township as residential and agricultural, but also provided, pursuant to general standards, that administrative permission from the planning board and governing body could be obtained to establish, without reference to zones, neighborhood business, shopping centers, service stations, restaurants, light industrial uses, and so on. This approach was held to be the "negation of zoning," because it "overrides the basic concept of use zoning by districts." [17]

Nevertheless, the unwillingness of local government and developers to be confined within zoned classifications has continued to mount. Repeatedly the conventional approach, districting in advance, has loomed as an obstacle to a seemingly desirable shopping center development or industrial park. In large cities as well as small communities, the response of the governing body has often been to rezone in order to accommodate a desired development, or to foster all sorts of administrative exceptions.

One could justifiably suppose that zoning by districts has been unsatisfactory primarily because of the lack of a comprehensive prestudy and preplanning foundation in the original determination of the zoning ordinance map. Fast-running development has apparently landed upon many communities before they were aware of their need of long-range land-use planning. The tendency to substitute free-style flexibility for long-range planning has been met with qualms by planners and by lawyers.

Final judgments, however, are not easy. Zoning area and bulk specifications on a mass-of-lots basis have proved to be architecturally confining and, in many instances, wasteful and detrimental. It is easy to write a zoning requirement which regulates bulk by geometric specifications, but a sound wedding of structure to site and function often demands the op-

---

[16] Philip P. Green, *Are "Special Use" Procedures in Trouble?* 12 ZONING DIGEST 73 (1960).
[17] Rockhill v. Chesterfield Township, 23 N.J. 117, 128 A.2d 473 (1957).

portunity to select from alternatives too numerous to be easily itemized in advance.

It is easy to see that particularized zoning, dealing with each site separately, is more likely to be employed for some of the purposes ordinarily served by eminent domain. In this respect, particularized zoning acquires some of the characteristics of subdivision control.

From the community-wide nature of building codes and housing codes to the zoning ordinance, a community-wide collection of zones is one step, and then it is yet another step to the level of regulating the development of particular sites by specific examination and advance administrative approval of each site. Subdivision control is the most common legal tool for such site-by-site control of development.

Subdivision control grows out of antecedents different from those which underlie zoning. American municipalities, as well as states, have long had considerable power over the development of public road and highway patterns. In addition to the power to establish a public way by purchase, it followed that local governing bodies should also regulate the private establishment of future public ways by having the power to accept or reject dedications of land and to prescribe standards to be met before a proposed way could become part of the public highway pattern. From these powers, long and frequently used, there developed the necessity of regulating, under preapproval methods, the layout of subdivisions of land, involving new subcommunity street systems and new lot patterns adjacent to existing streets.

In zoning, there was at least a hope that the governing body could list, in advance, the variety of uses which might be thought to make up a given use-district classification, but variations in topography, ownership, and the purpose of subdivisions made it difficult for the governing body in advance to provide, across the entire community, an exact overlay of the ideally required street and lot pattern in three dimensions. Therefore, subdivision control developed as a means of regulating the growth of particular sites by the device of prohibiting the subdivision of land until the plan of such subdivision was approved and, ordinarily, recorded. Subdivision control presents an example of the challenge of regulating individualized designs under general rules because the requirement of equal protection continues to demand an advance statement of standards, theoretically uniform as to like situations.

The kinship of subdivision control with eminent domain powers is suggested by several clues. First, as mentioned above, the historical background of subdivision control was originally linked to government's power to purchase streets and other public areas. A second basis of kinship involves the requiring of public improvements. With the increase of intensive development in suburban areas, local governing bodies slowly and painfully learned that many subdividers were reaping profits out of the added value presented by the suggested inevitability of city streets, sewers, and other utilities, even though the subdivider-developer did not supply those improvements to his purchasers. In many situations, after the subdivider had sold his lots and gone on to find greener pastures, the municipality was left with a new residential community wallowing in the mud of unpaved streets and suffering in the filth of its own cesspools and septic tanks.

After many such lessons, subdivision control laws were enlarged to impose upon the subdivider a function which previously had been performed by the municipality's own capital purchase powers; the subdivision control laws came to require the subdivider to install improved streets meeting community standards and to install adequate trunk sewers, street lighting, and other facilities before his plan of subdivision could be authorized.

Even though government's power to require developers thus to bring their site improvements up to the present standard is established, some controversy exists as to government's power to require a developer today to install improvements which will meet a standard not existent but foreseeable in the future. The clearest example of this issue has been provided by the capped sewer cases. Some municipalities, where no trunk sewers exist, have required that the developer install adequate on-site sewage disposal facilities, and have also required that the developer install a trunk sewer system in the site and then merely cap it shut so that it will be in readiness when a future day brings trunk sewers to the locale.[18] Of course, if the market permits, the costs of the improvements are ultimately (and logically) paid by the developer's customers. Subdivision control regulation has given a foretaste of the tendency to use regulation in matters formerly related to government's purchase power.

Experience in guiding the familiar residential subdivision, in which a single developer erects dwelling after dwelling upon lot after lot, has provided us with primary education in large-scale development. However, much of the residential subdivisions of the past have been uniform de-

---

[18] See Saxony Construction Company Appeal, 178 Pa. Super. Ct. 132, 113 A.2d 342 (1955).

velopments, in that they consisted of an aggregation of roughly similar dwellings upon roughly equal lots. Such fungible production was able to live fairly comfortably with zoning ordinances which prescribed regulations on a mass-of-lots basis.

Then there came developers who, crowded here and there by unusual topographical features, asked for permission to lay out some subminimum size lots on the basis that the same subdivision would also contain some oversize lots, so that the total population density result would be equivalent to that sought by the zoning ordinance. Other developers saw the desirability of setting aside some of their rough land for common use in the subdivision as a park or similar public site, provided that their dwelling lots could be smaller than the minimum allowed by the zoning ordinance, arguing again that the basic population density standard would not be violated. But, all too often, the zoning ordinance, with its compound eye, could visualize only an aggregation of like lots.

Urban redevelopers began to experience similar encounters with zoning ordinances. They found fault with extremely compartmented use classifications in zoning ordinances.

Today a number of private and public developers and redevelopers in large cities are putting forth imaginative schemes for mixing residential types, for employing a variety of area relationships, and for including compatible commercial and other nonresidential uses in an entire large-scale development.[19] Suddenly, while zoning is yet a new thing in many rural and suburban areas, traditional zoning has become senile-appearing in large cities. Strangely enough, the zoning ordinance, once eagerly sought by planners, has now become a villainous obstacle to many plans of the planners.

To break away from the geometrically repetitive shackles of conventional zoning, those who wrestle with zoning ordinances have sought to legalize a flexible approach to the large-scale unit by inventing legal or architectural fictions or by distorting variance procedures far beyond their legitimate scope, but the better approach has been to write new special exception provisions into zoning ordinances to allow "planned unit developments."[20]

The typical nature of a planned unit development can be illustrated by the following sample definition of a planned residential unit development:

[19] C. M. Haar, *Emerging Legal Aspects of Zoning,* speech to American Institute of Planners, [1954] PLANNING 138.

[20] Eli Goldston and James H. Scheuer, *Zoning of Planned Residential Developments,* 73 HARV. L. REV. 241, 251 (1959).

A planned residential unit development is a large-scale development to be constructed by a single owner or a group of owners acting jointly, involving a related group of residences and associated uses, planned as an entity and therefore susceptible of development and regulation as one complex land-use unit, rather than as a mere aggregation of individual buildings located on separate unrelated lots.

Fundamentally, the goal in this situation is to punch a hole in the zoning map, and then, pursuant to a new set of standards, to insert a planned unit development in that hole.

Until now, attempts to meet this new challenge have overlooked the possibility of utilizing subdivision control powers and techniques in the planned unit development situation, which is fundamentally analogous to subdivision development in that an entire composite unit is regulated at one time.

Some subdivision control enabling statutes provide for the regulation of subdivision of land for the purpose of "improvement" or "building development" as well as for the purpose of sale.[21] Once the necessary hole has been punched in the zoning map by special exception or by rezoning, then regulation of the development as an "improvement subdivision" becomes possible. The nature of an improvement subdivision, and its use in relation to a planned development, can be illustrated by a sample law provision, as follows:

A planned residential unit development shall be approved as, and based upon, an improvement subdivision pursuant to Code Section 0001, such subdivision for improvement which divides a tract by streets, building groups, and other features rather than by ownership lot lines, being distinguished from subdivision for sale.

Hence, in some American jurisdictions, the challenge of the planned unit development can bring zoning regulation and subdivision regulation together in a marriage long overdue. Thus new habits of development turn the direction of regulation.

Zoning ordinances have been readily distinguishable from the specific approach of eminent domain because zoning ordinances are theoretically devised "in accordance with a comprehensive plan." [22] The basic theory has been that zoning is truly a set of rules prepared in advance, to cover all the standard classifications of lots and uses, not something devised on a case-to-case basis. However, if zoning techniques in large cities move

---

[21] OHIO REV. CODE ANN. § 711.001(b) (1953); PA. STAT. ANN. tit. 53, § 22769 (1957); WISC. STAT. ANN. § 236.02(7) (1957).

[22] C. M. Haar, *In Accordance with a Comprehensive Plan,* 68 HARV. L. REV. 1154.

closer to the techniques used for the regulation of mass subdivisions, and if the zoning approach becomes more particularized as cities show signs of becoming connected clumps of renewal areas, then the localized thrust of planning regulation at a named corner or a certain neighborhood assumes a tailormade air formerly attributable only to compulsory purchase techniques.

PURCHASE AT PRESENT

Most textbooks and legal encyclopedias contrast the power of eminent domain with the police power, implying that the two powers are mutually exclusive.[23]

From the federal standpoint, however, eminent domain has been classified as a subordinate implement of the police power. The United States Supreme Court has, on occasion, outlined the police power and then stated that "the power of eminent domain is merely the means to the end." [24] Thus it is suggested that regulation and eminent domain are each merely methods by which the police power is exercised, rather than each being separate basic powers in themselves.

This difference in point of view can partially be explained by reference to a difference in constitutional expression as between the states and the federal government.[25] Most state constitutions refer to the power of eminent domain as a separate entity and expressly mention the payment of compensation as incident to its exercise. The federal Constitution, on the other hand, does not set forth any specific grant of eminent domain power. The Fifth Amendment has not been construed as such.[26] Therefore it was necessary that the federal courts consider eminent domain to be a power ancillary in nature, necessary for the execution of express powers.[27]

In any event, in this comparative study, it is convenient to use terms which clothe eminent domain with status as a separate power. Treated as such, we think of eminent domain fundamentally as the power of government to compel the purchase of property for a public use.

At times "public use" has meant merely use by public bodies.[28] Modern

---

[23] 29 C.J.S. *Eminent Domain* § 6 (1941).

[24] Berman v. Parker, 348 U.S. 26, 33 (1954).

[25] Technically the federal government can be said to have no police power (except possibly with respect to the District of Columbia) in the sense of the true police power which is a residuary power of the states. See Annot., *Illustrations of exercise by Congress of power analogous to police power exercised by state legislatures,* 99 L. Ed. 40 (1955).

[26] United States v. Carmack, 329 U.S. 230, 241–242 (1946).

[27] United States v. Gettysburg Electric Railway, 160 U.S. 668 (1896).

[28] Philip Nichols, Jr., *The Meaning of Public Use in the Law of Eminent Domain,* 20 B.U.L. Rev. 615 (1940).

use of eminent domain, however, particularly as applied to land-use control in contexts such as urban redevelopment, suggests that "public use" means something like "public purpose." Thus the traditional employment of eminent domain displays it as a power easily distinguishable from the police power, but modern developments seem to equate the purpose of eminent domain with the purpose of police power regulation; hence our problem.

Compulsory purchase of sites for public buildings such as courthouses, and for public structures such as highways and bridges, is universally familiar. The land-taking activities of ancillary public bodies, such as school districts and public utilities, have also been common.[29] Although these everyday uses of eminent domain may seem to be routine, they often markedly influence the land development pattern and pressures over a wide area, and thus are important far beyond the boundaries of the property immediately purchased. For example, the far-reaching effects of the federal interstate highway system upon thousands of municipalities has been long recognized. The problem of determining just compensation is always present, but there is little problem concerning the purpose of such purchases. They are clearly for public use and occupation, and therefore do not intersect with police power regulation.

In an area more specifically identified with land-use planning, eminent domain has been an important tool in establishing publicly sponsored housing. Because public acquisition of land for such purposes involves compensation and the money to pay it, the federal government, empowered to act only fiscally in this field, was enabled to enter the field with the Housing Act of 1937, which provided federal aid toward the development of low-cost housing by local authorities in place of slums.[30] Largely in response, housing authority laws were adopted by the states to provide for public corporations able to finance and operate low-rent housing projects. Although debate over the public benefits of such functions has now somewhat subsided, public housing unquestionably represented a broader concept of public use, in that the resulting product was one usually accomplished by private business. However, some states sought to augment the public housing thrust by the adoption of statutes which authorized limited-dividend housing companies to be formed by private

---

[29] In some places, the lack of cooperation of such bodies with land planning has been notorious. Indeed, in some states, public utilities or school districts are exempted from land-use controls, such as zoning, by state law or local ordinance.

[30] Act of Sept. 1, 1937, c. 896, 50 Stat. 888, 42 U.S.C. §§ 1401–35.

interests, with the power to use eminent domain for regulated private housing projects.[31]

Although the private housing companies, as permitted by states such as New York and Pennsylvania, were not widely accepted or used, these enabling laws nevertheless represented one further step. Traditionally, eminent domain had been exercised by government to acquire land to be occupied by the government, or by public utilities to obtain land to be occupied by the utility; however, the advent of public housing laws involved the acquisition of land by government for the establishment of individual homes on the property. Then private housing companies were given the benefit of eminent domain for the same purpose. Thus, in a broad sense, the programs proceeded from acquisition by the public for public occupancy to acquisition by the public for private occupancy, and then to acquisition by private agencies for private occupancy. Nevertheless the exercise of these powers, particularly in their slum clearance aspects, has been so clearly related to the public good that their legality and legitimacy as uses of eminent domain has been generally accepted.

The next step came in the adoption by the states of urban redevelopment laws, which permitted government or government corporations to take private land found to be blighted, in order that the land could be reassembled and redeveloped, by private purchasers as well as by government.[32] This widened use of eminent domain was given impetus by the Federal Housing Act of 1949, which provides federal financial aid to subsidize the difference between the land acquisition and preparation cost and the resale value of the land as sold to the private redeveloper.[33]

The earlier uses of eminent domain, even though they involved private occupants, had the title to the land, after acquisition, continue in the governmental body or the public utility. Urban redevelopment, however, ordinarily involves resale of the land so that the taken land winds up in purely private ownership. Although this ownership result has been particularly impressive and significant to the man on the street, it has not replaced purpose as the salient legal factor. The courts generally have appreciated that resale into private ownership could nevertheless serve a public purpose. They have continued to review urban redevelopment actions from the standpoint of whether or not they will serve a public purpose.

[31] Pennsylvania Limited Dividend Housing Company Law, PA. STAT. ANN. tit. 35, §§ 1601–22 (1949).

[32] PA. STAT. ANN. tit. 35, §§ 1701–47 (1949).

[33] Act of July 15, 1949, c. 338, 63 Stat. 413, 42 U.S.C. §§ 1441–83.

In urban redevelopment, the public purpose has depended upon the nature of the pre-existing condition which is to be eliminated. A public purpose is served if the redevelopment removes a condition identifiable as a slum or a blighted area or a substandard or insanitary area. Therefore the courts have exercised review to make sure that blight did exist.[34]

Further extensions of eminent domain horizons in the redevelopment area have centered around a widening and liberalizing of the concept of the pre-existing evil. From the requirement that redevelopment eliminate an existing slum, the concept moved to the necessity for the removal of an incipient slum. It was further recognized that blighted areas may not be limited to intensely built-up properties, but could include areas predominantly open, vacant, or unimproved.[35] Another step was recognition that redevelopment may not involve a total exercise of eminent domain over the entire afflicted area. This recognition was a corollary of the Federal Housing Act of 1954, which introduced the concept of "urban renewal," which embraces rehabilitation without rebuilding as well as redevelopment through rebuilding.[36]

State redevelopment laws were amended to reflect this view, by recognizing that

certain blighted areas, or portions thereof, may require total acquisition, clearance and disposition, subject to continuing controls as provided in this act, since the prevailing condition of decay may make impracticable the reclamation of the area by rehabilitation, and that other blighted areas, or portions thereof, through the means provided in this act, may be susceptible to rehabilitation or a combination of clearance and disposition and rehabilitation in such manner that the conditions and evils hereinbefore enumerated may be eliminated or remedied.[37]

If some properties in the renewal area are to be rehabilitated without being acquired, how can such rehabilitation be compelled without regulation? Thus, the modern concept of urban renewal suggests a teamwork combination of regulation with purchase.

In 1923, the Missouri Supreme Court approved a Kansas City ordinance which established a building line along a boulevard, restricted the use of property near it, and provided for the payment of compensation for damages resulting from such restrictions and for assessment in respect to

[34] Bristol Redevelopment and Housing Authority v. Denton, 198 Va. 171, 93 S.E.2d 288 (1956).

[35] Oliver v. City of Clairton, 374 Pa. 333, 98 A.2d 47 (1953).

[36] Act of Aug. 2, 1954, c. 649, 68 Stat. 626, 42 U.S.C. § 1460.

[37] PA. STAT. ANN. tit. 35, § 1702 (Supp. 1959).

benefits derived from it.[38] Like restrictions, with provision for compensation, had been approved in a number of decisions.[39] However, governments in the United States, generally speaking, have not adopted approaches which involve the payment of compensation to owners of property limited by governmental development restrictions. Many zoning cases have involved provable losses of market value of property, resulting from the zoning classification; the courts have universally concluded that such loss of potential value does not impair the validity of the zoning classification and is not compensable.[40] Floating value, and the manner in which it may be brought down to earth by development restrictions, has been given little legal recognition in the United States.

However, recognition of the increasing rate of population expansion has prompted a growing awareness of the need to prescribe areas within which future development shall not take place. The wasteful, leapfrogging selection of land for development, which has been the visible characteristic of urban sprawl, has prompted a clamor for governmental intervention under laws which would permit the purchase of development rights so that an owner could be left with his property in its present state of use and yet be compensated for a legal inability to develop it for a more intensive use or for the erection of structures.[41]

ILLUSTRATIONS OF THE LINE BETWEEN

The oversimplification fallacy involved in painting regulation as negative and purchase as positive is not the only misleading generality to be avoided. In comparing the regulatory power with the purchase power, another generality to eschew is the view that eminent domain is necessarily more versatile than police power regulation.

There are some situations in which police power regulation can, in a sense, go further than eminent domain. For example, whenever the public purpose test of eminent domain is viewed more narrowly than the public welfare test of the police power, then police power regulation will be afforded a wider scope. At one point, the justices of Massachusetts overthrew a localized redevelopment statute, overruling such an exercise of eminent domain on the ground that:

[38] *In re* Kansas City Ordinance No. 39946 (Kansas City v. Liebi), 298 Mo. 569, 252 S.W. 404 (1923).

[39] Annot., *Power to establish building line along street,* 28 A.L.R. 314 (1924).

[40] Pincus v. Power, 376 Pa. 175, 101 A.2d 914 (1954).

[41] Whyte, *Urban Sprawl,* Fortune, January 1958. Proper treatment of such legal machinery for the creation of greenbelts is left to other sections of this book; see the papers of Messrs, Hart, Heap, and Sullivan.

there is no suggestion that the area is now a slum. There is only an apprehension lest it become one. There would seem to be other means, perhaps through building and zoning regulations, of preventing that result.[42]

Thus, in the view of some courts, compulsory purchase may be used to renew slum areas and blighted areas, but the public's buying power may not be used to turn over to a private redeveloper an area which is not yet blighted. In such a view, the wider reach must be left to police power regulation.

Of course, police power regulation, even though it may be used across a wider front, must nevertheless be used in a less intense manner. For example, regulation cannot treat a blighted area as intensely as eminent domain can; regulation cannot be used to transfer the premises to a new owner for the purpose of preservation or restoration. Thus, despite the danger of generalities, when the breadth of "public purpose" is not the issue, the degree of intensity with which government deals with property becomes important in describing the line between regulation and purchase.

Mr. Justice Holmes stated this proposition of degree resoundingly, but not very hopefully, in one of the classic United States Supreme Court decisions on the point, where his opinion for the majority stated:

> Government hardly could go on if, to some extent, values incident to property could not be diminished without paying for every such change in the general law. As long recognized, some values are enjoyed under an implied limitation and must yield to the police power. But obviously the implied limitation must have its limits, or the contract and due process clauses are gone. One fact for consideration in determining such limits is the extent of the diminution. When it reaches a certain magnitude, in most if not in all cases there must be an exercise of eminent domain and compensation to sustain the act.[43]

By that decision, the United States Supreme Court invalidated a Pennsylvania statute which prohibited the underground mining of anthracite coal so as to cause the subsidence of private or public buildings, rights of way, and streets. More specifically, the decision affirmed the right of the mining company to mine the coal under a private dwelling, where mining rights and the right to surface support had been reserved in the coal company by prior conveyance. Because the right to mine coal has the status of a specific estate in land under Pennsylvania law, a conveyance or reservation of that estate could not be nullified by a police power regulation. By way of dictum, the court suggested that, even where a

---

[42] *In re* Opinions of the Justices, 332 Mass. 769, 783, 126 N.E.2d 795, 803 (1955).
[43] Pennsylvania Coal Company v. Mahon, 260 U.S. 393, 413 (1922).

public street is involved, the government would be obliged to acquire the right of support by purchase, just as it would have to pay for use of the surface itself.

The majority decision was matched by an equally resounding dissenting opinion of Mr. Justice Brandeis, who characterized the majority as resting upon the assumption that police power exercise in such a situation must be justified by "an average reciprocity of advantage as between the restricted person and the rest of the community." The dissent argued that such a test, suitable as between classes of property owners, was not pertinent where the regulation is intended to protect the general public from danger. The dissenting opinion pointed out that the police power, without granting any reciprocal advantage, had been allowed to prohibit an owner from using his oil tanks, his brickyard, his livery stable, his billiard parlor, his oleomargarine factory, and his brewery.[44]

Mr. Justice Brandeis' dissent at least succeeded in demonstrating that it is not easy to apply Mr. Justice Holmes' statement that "the general rule at least is, that while property may be regulated to a certain extent, if regulation goes too far, it will be recognized as a taking." [45]

Land planners assume that one of the effectuation tools of their planning will be some means to hold land in relative nonuse for varying periods of time. The power to designate land for nonuse, at least in the sense of prohibiting structural development, is essential if the timing and programming of development are to be controlled. It is also essential for the preservation of buffer areas, open areas, and greenbelts. It may be useful for the purpose of reserving land for future acquisition by the public.

As might be expected, regulation gets into trouble when it is used so closely alongside purchase that the contrast is readily apparent. For this reason, the use of regulation to reserve private land in nonuse, without compensation, so that the land will be available in undeveloped condition for a later acquisition by the public, has run into constitutional trouble.

Constitutional disapproval has been the fate of a statute which purported to authorize the designation of private land for future public parks so that a municipality could within three years thereafter purchase the land without paying compensation for any improvements meanwhile erected

---

[44] Oil tanks — Pierce Oil Corp. v. Hope, 248 U.S. 498 (1919); Brickyard — Hadacheck v. Sebastian, 239 U.S. 394 (1915); Livery stable — Reinman v. Little Rock, 237 U.S. 171 (1915); Billiard parlor — Murphy v. California, 225 U.S. 623 (1912); Oleomargarine factory — Powell v. Pennsylvania, 127 U.S. 678 (1888); Brewery — Mugler v. Kansas, 123 U.S. 623 (1887).

[45] Pennsylvania Coal Company v. Mahon, *supra* note 43, at 415.

on it.[46] Generally speaking, the courts have frowned upon such use of regulation to discourage the use of substantial sites for the purpose of aiding future public acquisition of them for parks or other public purposes. Similarly, courts have nullified statutes which provide for public mapping of future streets across private property and negate compensation for private improvements erected within the future street area.[47]

Of lesser degree are the "location" ordinances, authorized by some states, which permit a municipality to designate strips for possible future widening alongside existing streets and negate compensation for improvements placed by private owners within the designated possible widening strips. From experience, one may note that many municipal councils are loath to press this power to its fullest extent; when an owner protests that the designation of possible widening is pinching his use of his property (as the designated line may do with particular stringency if it is used as the beginning point for measuring front-yard zoning requirements), the municipality often proceeds to the actual taking and payment or else abandons the designated widening location.

Perhaps those municipalities lack confidence in such police power regulations because of the older line of "building line" cases which required compensation.[48] It may be that they find no comfort in the United States Supreme Court decision of *Gorieb v. Fox*,[49] which approved a building line as part of a comprehensive zoning scheme, although not as a device to minimize future cost of public acquisition.

It is noteworthy that front-yard setbacks imposed as part of a zoning scheme are usually dissociated in terms from the possible future acquisition of the front-yard area for street-widening purposes. Although a by-product of such zoning requirements certainly could be the later acquisition of land for street widening at less cost, zoning ordinance front-yard requirements are usually supported upon health, safety, and welfare goals other than minimizing public acquisition costs.

Residential zoning is another device which can be, and has been, used as a disguised method of holding off the development of land so that it

[46] Miller v. City of Beaver Falls, 368 Pa. 189, 82 A.2d 34 (1951).

[47] Forster v. Scott, 136 N.Y. 577, 32 N.E. 976 (1893).

[48] Listed in the annotations in 28 A.L.R. 314 (1924), 44 A.L.R. 1377 (1926), and 53 A.L.R. 1222 (1928). The last-cited annotation hopelessly confuses the Pennsylvania cases by incorrectly concluding that White's Appeal, 287 Pa. 259 (1926), invalidated building lines per se. The Pennsylvania cases have approved setback requirements unless they are vague and discriminatory, as in White's Appeal, *supra*, or deemed to be excessive in degree, as in Schmaltz v. Buckingham Twp., 389 Pa. 295, 132 A.2d 233 (1957).

[49] 274 U.S. 603 (1927).

might later be acquired by local government for public purposes without paying for costly improvements. A certain municipality plans to locate a small park on a specific parcel but lacks funds to make the purchase now. Hence it has zoned that acreage for residential use only. Because the property consists of a narrow ribbon of land bounded on one side by a high-speed highway and on the other side by a railroad, the municipality's water-pumping station, and a large river, it is attractively situated as a potential industrial development unit, but its single-family residential classification successfully keeps it unused.

Thus the municipality's zoning powers are used to accomplish reservation for future acquisition without displaying the obvious legal weaknesses attached to other methods. Of course, where property is actually unusable for any and all of the purposes permitted in the particular zoning district, its classification may be held to be confiscatory and invalid, but such litigation would involve an uphill fight against the presumptions which favor the municipality. In any event, such indirect enforcement of a reservation for future acquisition seems to be equivalent to the acquisition of an option right without compensation.

More frequently, residential zoning is used as a device to accomplish control of the timing and programming of development. Where the topography is such that land preparation costs would warrant only an income-producing use, stringent single-family residential zoning may delay development, particularly if high minimum lot area per family requirements are included. As might be expected, such residential zoning is not ordinarily used with an admitted desire to retard all development. Occasionally, however, the proponents of such a classification will admit that its low-density requirements are designed to slow the pace of development until more intensive municipal facilities are available, at which time the ordinance may be liberalized by amendment.

A more forthright means of holding against structural development is farm zoning. As reported by an open-space advocate, the farmers of Santa Clara County, California, established exclusive agricultural zones in order to prevent mass development from sprawling into farmlands.[50]

The most common and perhaps the most wasteful means of obtaining nonuse, in the sense of low-density results, is by so-called acreage zoning. Currently painted by mass developers as a villainous scheme, "acreage zoning" is simply an overdrawn term referring to the establishment of relatively high minimum lot areas per family in residential districts. Of

[50] Whyte, *supra* note 41.

course, lot areas of one acre or more may be permanently compatible with particular neighborhoods and their peculiar limitations of public facilities; the use of minimum lot area requirements for such neighborhoods is more readily acceptable than their use as part of an attempt to affect the timing of development.

For the most part, court decisions dealing with the validity of such area requirements have assumed that they were established as bulwarks against immediate police power purpose problems and have not troubled themselves with the development-timing aspects of such regulations. A one-acre minimum has been approved for some time in New England as well as in New York.[51] More recently a one-acre minimum was approved in Pennsylvania by a court equally divided.[52] Two-acre minimums have also been approved, in New York.[53] And some minimum lot areas still higher have been upheld elsewhere.[54]

In the face of increasing pressures for more efficient use of land, if not for its more intensive use, minimum lot area requirements will probably decrease in importance as a means of achieving temporary or permanent nonuse by regulation. Although a minimum lot area requirement may suppress structural development by permitting only one structure on each acre, thereby leaving most of the land unbuilt upon, it is obvious that such a regulation also ultimately would result in at least one structure on every acre; thus it attains a scattered and spattered pattern of development over a wide area, rather than a concentrated, economical, easy-to-service community development bordered by open green belt. This wasteful aspect of acreage zoning may drive it into the discard.

Just on the other side of the line in the nonuse area is the purchase approach which, in the United States, is embodied in the attempts of a few states to purchase development rights. Of course, any development-right purchase scheme is founded upon the assumption that development

---

[51] Simons v. Town of Needham, 311 Mass. 560, 42 N.E.2d 516 (1942); Village of Westbury v. Foster, 193 Misc. 47, 83 N.Y.S.2d 148 (1948).

[52] Bilbar Construction Co. v. Easttown Twp. Zoning Board of Adjustment, 393 Pa. 62, 141 A.2d 851 (1958). A key precedent in this decision was *Berman v. Parker, supra* note 24, and its broad definition of the public welfare aspects. Thus, it is interesting to note, the language of the United States Supreme Court in an urban redevelopment purchase case has affected judicial views as to police power regulation matters.

[53] Dilliard v. Village of North Hills, 276 App. Div. 969, 94 N.Y.S.2d 715 (1950); Franmor Realty Corp. v. Village of Old Westbury, 280 App. Div. 945, 116 N.Y.S.2d 68 (1952), *affirmed* 121 N.Y.S.2d 95 (1953).

[54] Flora Realty v. City of LaDue, 263 Mo. 1025, 246 S.W.2d 771 (1951), *appeal dismissed* 344 U.S. 802 (1952) — 3 acres; Fischer v. Bedminster Township, 21 N.J. Super. 81, 90 A.2d 757 (1952) — 5 acres.

rights can be acquired for a cost less than that of buying the entire land outright. In some areas, this assumption has met trouble. The state of Wisconsin has made some provision for the purchase of development rights, but it is reported that juries in eminent domain cases there have been requiring their government to pay for development rights the full market value of the entire title to the land, even though the basic title to the land and its continued use for agricultural purposes remains with the farmer.[55]

Nevertheless, it is not hard to argue that development-rights purchase is preferable to the use of regulation for pacing development and providing buffers and greenbelts. Uncompensated reservation of land may have confiscatory effects. Overstringent residential zoning may be dishonest. The use of exclusive agricultural zoning is more straightforward, but all such zoning ordinances are subject to repeal or amendment when the pressures for intensive development become too strong to resist. Low-density zoning is wasteful as well as being an oblique approach to the problem.

Generally speaking, the American states might well look toward developing, in their legislative armory against the population explosion, workable systems for the purchase of development rights, Of course it must be expected that such methods will have to face questions like those which have been put with respect to the Uthwatt Report, as when it was asked by the

Speculative Builders:
If the Treasury owns Development Rights,
Does it mean we'll be offered suburban sites, or SHOT,
                The Report of Uthwatt? [56]

Urban redevelopment has been the most common and most effective tool for accomplishing the reuse of land in the United States. In 1954, new strength was given to the legal underpinnings of urban redevelopment by the unanimous decision of the United States Supreme Court in *Berman v. Parker.* The Court decided that the existence of individual unblighted buildings in the redevelopment area should not be permitted to frustrate redevelopment intended to overhaul and redesign an entire area. The Court tended to treat the "public purpose" basis of eminent domain as substantially equivalent to the police power, equating public

---

[55] Whyte, *supra* note 41.

[56] F. J. Osborn, *The Report of Uthwatt,* 53 MUNICIPAL JOURNAL 783 (1945), CAN MAN PLAN? AND OTHER VERSES 107 (London, 1959).

purpose with the public welfare. A much quoted portion of the opinion reads as follows:

> The concept of the public welfare is broad and inclusive . . . The values it represents are spiritual as well as physical, aesthetic as well as monetary. It is within the power of the legislature to determine that the community should be beautiful as well as healthy, spacious as well as clean, well-balanced as well as carefully patrolled.[57]

With such a foundation, urban redevelopment is likely to remain the chief tool by which government accomplishes large-scale reuse of land.

Small-scale reuse of land, on the other hand, is being attempted by some zoning experiments. This regulatory approach is exemplified by the nonconforming use elimination provisions which may be found in an increasing number of big city zoning ordinances. The nonconforming use or structure, a use or structure which lawfully existed in its location before the adoption of a zoning regulation prohibiting that type of use or structure in that location, has ordinarily been permitted to continue indefinitely. From the start, however, there have been attempts to confine nonconforming uses as much as possible. Many zoning ordinances prohibit expansion and enlargement of nonconforming uses. Conversion of a nonconforming use into a different type of nonconforming use has also been regulated. Repairs and alterations of nonconforming use structures have been limited to those required for safety. Most zoning ordinances have attempted to prevent the resumption of nonconforming uses after they have been discontinued or abandoned. Of course, the ordinances have generally forbidden the replacement of buildings designed for nonconforming uses.

Zoners had hoped that nonconforming uses, thus circumscribed, would ultimately wither away and disappear. This hope has been found to be unjustified. Nonconforming uses and buildings have not disappeared or substantially decreased; instead they have generally become solidly entrenched and strengthened, sometimes because of the monopolistic advantage afforded them by the zoning ordinance itself, which, for example, fences competitors away from the commercial nonconforming use.[58]

Therefore, in the more recent history of zoning, regulatory power to eliminate nonconforming uses has been sought. In general, regulations which require the immediate cessation of a nonconforming use without

---

[57] *Supra* note 24.

[58] Note, 9 U. Chi. L. Rev. 477 (1940); Grant v. Mayor and City Council of Baltimore, 212 Md. 301, 303, 129 A.2d 363 (1957).

compensation have been held to be unconstitutional,[59] except where the existing use was immediately abatable as a nuisance.[60] Requiring the elimination of nonconforming uses and structures after allowing them a period of depreciation remains as a potential approach, however.

In five of the states, zoning enabling statutes expressly authorize one or more classes of municipal government or counties to adopt regulations providing for the elimination of nonconforming uses after an amortization or grace period.[61] The statutes of a few other states, however, prohibit regulation which would require the removal of nonconforming uses, thus giving them statutory recognition as vested rights. Interestingly, the decisions upholding the validity of such nonconforming-use elimination provisions have tended to come from states where the enabling acts do not expressly mention such regulations one way or the other.

As might be expected, the leadership in the adoption of such regulations lies with the larger cities. The best-known big-city zoning ordinance provisions of this type are those found in the zoning codes of Chicago, Denver, Los Angeles, and San Francisco. As indicated below, provisions in Baltimore and Buffalo have been considered in the courts. A few smaller cities have also enacted such provisions.[62]

A majority of the court decisions on the subject have approved these so-called amortization requirements, at least wherever the financial impact upon the nonconforming-use holder has seemed minor in relation to the public benefit. Approval of the required removal of open-land uses such as junkyards and repair yards has been given by the courts of Kansas and Washington, in cases involving one and two year periods.[63] On the other hand, the required removal of a junkyard after a one-year period was invalidated in Ohio and in Texas, although the Texas decision was expressly confined to the particular facts of the case.[64] The required termination of a nonconforming use in a conforming structure, a plumbing business office in a residence, was upheld in *City of Los Angeles v.*

[59] Jones v. Los Angeles, 211 Cal. 304, 295 P. 14 (Sup. Ct. 1930).

[60] Hadacheck v. Sebastian, 239 U.S. 394 (1915).

[61] 5 COLO. REV. STAT. § 106-2-19 (1954); 20 GA. CODE ANN. tit. 69, § § 69–835 (1935); KAN. GEN. STAT. § 19–2930 (1959); PA. STAT. ANN. tit. 16, § 2033; 2 UTAH CODE ANN. § 17-27-18 (1953).

[62] An example is the city of Clairton, a satellite of Pittsburgh, whose requirement was involved in Pittsburgh Outdoor Advertising Company v. Clairton, 390 Pa. 1, 133 A.2d 542 (1958), a judicial procedure decision.

[63] Spurgeon v. Board of Commissioners of Shawnee County, 181 Kan. 1008, 317 P.2d 798 (1957); City of Seattle v. Martin, 154 Wash. Dec. 663, 342 P.2d 602 (1959).

[64] City of Akron v. Chapman, 160 Ohio St. 382, 116 N.E.2d 697 (1953); City of Corpus Christi v. Allen, 152 Tex. 137, 254 S.W.2d 759 (1953).

Gage.[65] Two less impressive decisions, of rather long standing, have upheld the compulsory removal of a grocery and drugstore business after a one-year waiting period.[66]

With respect to the required removal of nonconforming structures, the decisions indicate that nonbuilding structures, such as billboards, may be subject to removal after periods of about five years. A Maryland decision approved such a requirement in Baltimore, despite the absence of express enabling law authority for it,[67] but the New Jersey courts held that enabling law authority would be necessary.[68] In Iowa, however, the required removal of nonconforming billboards has been held to amount to a taking of property without just compensation.[69]

The extent to which reuse can validly be accomplished by such elimination provisions was analyzed in an important New York decision in 1958, *Harbison v. City of Buffalo.*[70] In that case, a majority of the New York Court of Appeals established a rule of reason for testing the validity of a given removal requirement. The case was remanded to the lower court (whose original decision had invalidated the regulation) with instructions to consider, in each case, (1) the nature of the surroundings, (2) the existing improvements, and (3) the feasibility of moving the business, if any. The majority opinion indicated strongly that the required cessation of nonconforming uses on land or in conforming buildings would be readily supported, but indicated that elimination of substantial structures would be more likely to be questionable. Indeed, after the case was remanded the lower court held that the financial impact of the regulation in that particular case, because of the value of structures in the junkyard there involved, was so stringent as to cause the application of the requirement in that instance to be unconstitutional.

The required removal, after a period, of substantial buildings has been upheld in a decision involving a gasoline service station after a ten-year period.[71] However, a California decision, even after the decision in *Los Angeles v. Gage,*[72] refused to permit the compulsory cessation of a planing

[65] 127 Cal. App. 2d 442, 274 P.2d 34 (1954).

[66] State *ex rel.* Dema Realty Co. v. McDonald, 168 La. 172, 121 So. 613 (1929), *cert. denied* 280 U.S. 556 (1939); State *ex rel.* Dema Realty Co. v. Jacoby, 168 La. 752, 123 So. 315 (1929).

[67] Grant v. Mayor and City Council of Baltimore, 212 Md. 301, 129 A.2d 363 (1957).

[68] United Advertising Corp. v. Raritan, 11 N.J. 144, 93 A.2d 362 (1952).

[69] Stover McCray System v. City of Des Moines, 247 Iowa 1313, 78 N.W.2d 843 (1956).

[70] 4 N.Y.2d 533, 152 N.E.2d 42 (1958).

[71] Standard Oil Company v. Tallahassee, 183 F.2d 410 (5th Cir. 1950).

[72] City of Las Mesta v. Tweed & Gambrell Planing Mill, 146 Cal. App. 2d 762, 304 P.2d 803 (1956); City of Los Angeles v. Gage, *supra* note 65.

mill erected originally in an area zoned industrial and subsequently zoned residential.

Thus, a general survey of decisions involving nonconforming use removal provisions indicates that such requirements will be upheld with respect to open-land uses and with respect to the removal of nonconforming uses in buildings which are themselves conforming and hence adaptable to permitted uses. The trend also indicates that the required removal of nonconforming billboards after a few years will also be approved.[73] As respects substantial buildings, however, it is likely that the required elimination of such structures by zoning will prove to be either not constitutional or not feasible. Because the decisions indicate that the length of the depreciation period in relation to the value of the structure will be an important factor, requirements for the compulsory elimination of nonconforming structures would have to involve inordinately long amortization periods. A requirement that a reinforced-steel building be removed fifty years hence is a requirement with little utility. Such a long removal period does not measure up well against the feeling that the vision of city planning seldom extends further than twenty or twenty-five years. Therefore, as respects the required reuse of particular properties, it appears that resort to compulsory purchase must be had at the point of dealing with substantial enclosed structures. Legislation authorizing this use of eminent domain has been adopted in Michigan.[74]

In urban renewal projects, the workings of police power regulation and eminent domain can be seen at their closest conjunction. Formerly, urban redevelopment concentrated on demolition and rebuilding from the ground up, but now renewal programs, with their rehabilitation and conservation techniques, involve the use of regulations such as housing codes, building codes, and sanitary codes, applied within the renewal area to properties not taken by eminent domain. Indeed, the renewal area presents a plain need for special regulation, more comprehensive and pointed at higher standards than the regulations which are enforced generally throughout the city. For example, in a renewal area, the structural nature and arrangement of the retained commercial uses must be

---

[73] Regulation and relocation of billboards may also involve the view that billboards constitute an excessive use of the public's easement over the public ways. In the future, some use may be made of the novel view, recently voiced, that billboards constitute an unlawful interference with a right to a line of sight uninterrupted by structures which have no function other than the interruption of sight. Howard Gossage, *How to Look at Billboards*, Harper's Magazine, Feb. 1960.

[74] MICH. STAT. ANN, § 5.2933(1) (1958).

brought up to, or held at, the relatively high standard of commercial construction which will be introduced into the area by redevelopment; however, ordinary building codes, sanitary codes, and fire-prevention codes regulate only for hazard prevention rather than for efficiency, and housing codes, although often more intense, do not deal with commercial uses at all.

In the renewal area, many properties are purchased and rearranged or rebuilt in a businesslike fashion, to obtain a standard of efficiency and economy markedly higher than the minimal standards enforced by regulatory codes. If some buildings and properties within the renewal area are to be left in private hands, the need to subject them to equally high standards is obvious. Of course, the renewal process could involve public acquisition of all properties within the renewal area, but such an indiscriminate approach is unnecessarily expensive and may well involve needless hardship.

For these reasons, present-day renewal plans contain rehabilitation requirements broader in scope and more rigorous than the requirements contained in general codes. A simple illustration of such a renewal plan requirement, applied to commercial uses, is as follows:

> G. Architectural Treatment of Commercial Properties.
>   1. Upper story windows shall be glazed or uniformly painted, and where glazed, are to be backed with shades, blinds or curtains in colors to be approved by the Authority. Signs shall not be painted on windows, except as provided in paragraph G-4 below.[75]

If such special requirements are adopted, they must be enforced by some means. Of course, if widespread public participation has been enlisted in a renewal area, the support of local businessmen's organizations may prompt voluntary cooperation with commercial standards, but in other instances, voluntary acceptance will not be forthcoming.

Special regulations can be enforced by the usual police power sanctions, or by including them in the urban renewal plan, using eminent domain in a supporting role. Police power sanctions can be used for the special requirements only if such requirements are adopted as part of city ordinances so drawn that the special requirements will be applicable only in

---

[75] This example is modeled upon a requirement of the Urban Redevelopment Authority of Pittsburgh in the GENERAL NEIGHBORHOOD RENEWAL PLAN, EAST LIBERTY, Redevelopment Area No. 10, Project No. Penna. R-18.

certain parts of the city, such as urban renewal areas. An example would
be the zoned housing code advocated by Dr. E. R. Krumbiegel of
Milwaukee. However, the validity of such zoned regulations has not yet
been clearly adjudicated.[76]

The remaining approaches involve eminent domain, at least indirectly.
The use of eminent domain powers in this situation is exemplified by
an urban renewal plan provision developed by the Urban Redevelopment
Authority of the City of Pittsburgh, which reads as follows:

Standards and Controls — Rehabilitation: The rehabilitation of existing structures, residential or non-residential, designated to be retained is to be accomplished by a combination of voluntary action on the part of individuals,
voluntary neighborhood action, building code and housing code enforcement,
and by exercise of eminent domain powers to acquire, where necessary for
the effectuation of the Plan, those properties which fail to meet the applicable
requirements of the Plan. In those cases where the owner is either unwilling
or unable to rehabilitate his structure, the Authority will acquire title to the
property and resell it, subject to its being rehabilitated by the new owner.[77]

Thus, where a property is designated for retention and rehabilitation
rather than for acquisition, the owner has an option as to whether or not
he will meet the special renewal area standards. If he does not or cannot,
his property may be purchased like the other properties in the area. Thus,
the presence of the eminent domain power creates the possibility of the
two choices; if the property owner chooses the course of compliance with
the special requirement, then the indirect effect of the compulsory purchase power is to be thanked.

The usual twin legal problems of reasonableness and equality must be
considered.

The reasonableness of the special requirement, and the legality of using
eminent domain powers in aid of it, will probably stand or fall together.
In other words, if the special requirement standard is an appropriate one
in its context, then the employment of eminent domain to attain it
directly or indirectly should be legitimate. The underlying legal assumption in the whole renewal field is that police power types of goals supply
the needed "public purpose." For example, in upholding the use of
eminent domain for slum clearance, a state court has said:

[76] Joseph Guandolo, *Housing Codes in Urban Renewal,* 25 GEO. WASH. L. REV. 1, 42–
48 (1956).
[77] Urban Redevelopment Authority of the City of Pittsburgh, Item C-2-a (vii) in GEN-
ERAL NEIGHBORHOOD RENEWAL PLAN, EAST LIBERTY, *supra* note 75.

What we now decide is that when the power of eminent domain is thus called into play as a handmaiden to the police power and in order to make its proper use effective, it is necessarily for a public use.[78]

Thus the use of eminent domain as a "handmaiden" to attain a rehabilitation standard should be valid, provided that the required standard itself would be considered reasonable as part of a police power regulation in this context. However, consideration of the context leads to the real issue: Is the use of a more stringent class of requirements in the renewal area justified by that special context?

Hence, the equal protection of laws aspect of such special regulations is the central problem. Inevitably, there will be accusations of inequality.[79]

If a building owner or businessman is allowed to retain his property in an urban renewal area but is required to rehabilitate it to a special degree, he may protest that he is being subjected to requirements more stringent than those applied to his counterparts in other sections of the city. However, such a property owner or businessman also finds himself in the middle of a favored situation; after the initial travail of the redevelopment process, he may look forward to the future use and appreciation of his property in a renewed area. In all likelihood, his property value will benefit materially. His business is also likely to be improved if it has any local impact whatsoever, because the business use is being retained in accordance with a plan which designates such a business for a specific role in that location.

Therefore, even though the retained property owner incurs extra rehabilitation expense, over and above the expense which would be incurred elsewhere in the city under less stringent requirements, such added expense will be offset entirely or in part by a benefit. The special expense of the retained property owner is thus somewhat analogous to a betterment assessment; extra requirements are imposed upon him because he is in a context of special benefit.

The problem of the special regulation is not likely to be severe, as a practical matter, because the property owner has the ultimate choice of investing in the rehabilitation of his property or surrendering it to the

---

[78] Dornan v. Philadelphia Housing Authority, 331 Pa. 209, 226, 200 Atl. 834 (1938).

[79] Of course the very presence of a redevelopment project in the same city which enforces a housing code presents possibilities of inequality. As Mr. Guandolo has pointed out, *supra* note 76, at 25, the enforcement of housing codes or fire prevention codes may require one building owner to vacate and demolish a substandard building while, in another part of the city, the urban redevelopment agency pays for a like property and bears the cost of demolition.

agency for acquisition and rehabilitation by a new owner. In a very real sense, this choice presents an advantage not enjoyed by those forced to sell.

CONCLUSION

There is increasing narrowness of the line between police power regulation and eminent domain in the attainment of planned land use. In this field, eminent domain and the regulatory power seem to come together centripetally. There is an inescapable impression that the old tests of the line of demarcation between them are no longer dependable.

Particularly in the land-use control field, the goals of regulation and purchase have become indistinguishably similar. The widened concept of the public purpose basis for purchase has overspread much of the police power goals. Distinctions between the two powers on the basis of difference in mode of application, as between uniform application and case to case application, become much less useful as the police power is adapted to a multiplicity of shadings and classifications in application.

Logically, we seem to be less concerned about the intrusion of eminent domain into fields formerly left exclusively to police power regulation. Ultimately we may let government redevelop and perhaps develop any corner of the map by compulsory purchase techniques. Less concern is felt here because "just compensation" is still involved. Then the measure of that just compensation, in a bewildering new variety of situations, becomes the crucial problem. Of more concern is the realization that there is no definite, sure, automatic brake upon the counterintrusion of police power regulation into the field where just compensation should be paid. The test of degree enunciated by Mr. Justice Holmes is an elastic safeguard, at best.

Land-use controls in the United States have never been presented in a neat or compact package, with the various tools laid up alongside one other. Instead, we find the several tools of land-use control employed by different hands in varying manners and in scattered places. A continued overview of their relationships to each other and a continued examination of the strength and sharpness of the various tools, in comparison with each other, are essential to their proper and safe use.

COMPENSATION FOR THE COMPULSORY ACQUISITION OF LAND IN ENGLAND

R. E. MEGARRY, Q.C

READER IN EQUITY IN THE INNS OF COURT

THE FIFTH AMENDMENT to the Constitution of the United States of America ends with the words "nor shall private property be taken for public use, without just compensation." There is nothing in the British constitution which makes any similar provision a part of the law of England; indeed, in the American sense England has no constitution. Parliament is sovereign,[1] and no English statute can ever be declared void as being unconstitutional. So far as they are still effective, Magna Carta itself in its many versions or the Bill of Rights of 1689 could be repealed tomorrow by an act of Parliament passed in the usual way.

English law is thus neither enlivened nor bedeviled by any problems such as those that the simple words but complex ideas of a phrase such as "property be taken" must inevitably set. English problems in this field arise not from any actual or potential conflict between constitutional standards and specific statutes, but from the terms of the statutes themselves. When Parliament gives powers of compulsory acquisition, it may provide for whatever payments of compensation it thinks fit, or, indeed, for none at all. It is, of course, improbable in the extreme that the necessary parliamentary majority would be found for a statute which authorized any substantial degree of expropriation without compensation; but the omnipotence of Parliament means that each statute must be examined separately in order to determine where the line is drawn between interferences with property rights which give rise to compensation and those which do not. In the United States, the Constitution enshrines a dominant principle with compulsive force, whereas in England the only clear principle (if it can be called such) is that of the potency of the phrase *ad hoc*.

[1] But consider the remarkable case of Green v. Mortimer, 3 L.T.R. (n.s.) 642 (1861).

The process of the compulsory acquisition of land in England falls under three main heads: first, whether the acquiring authority has power to acquire the land in question; second, what is the procedure by which the acquisition takes place; and third, what provisions for compensation are provided. Before examining the third head in some detail, it is well to survey the first two heads briefly.

A look at the statute book a little over a century ago shows no general provisions for the compulsory acquisition of land. There were, however, a large number of private and local acts which gave powers of compulsory acquisition over specified land; and these acts both prescribed how those powers should be exercised and what compensation should be paid. This was the era of *ad hoc in excelsis*.

The Industrial Revolution, however, was changing things. Railways were being laid down and extended, docks and harbors built, waterworks set up. All these functions required land, and often some of the land required could not be obtained without powers of compulsory acquisition. Further, statutory provision had to be made for the establishment and operation of the concern. Not surprisingly, a standard set of clauses for incorporation in each private or local act came to be established, leaving as the contentious part of each bill the general nature of the scheme and any specific proposals for acquiring land. Ultimately, in 1845 and afterwards, Parliament enacted a series of "clauses consolidation" acts, which set out all the common form clauses. Thus there were the Railway Clauses Consolidation Acts of 1845,[2] the Gasworks Clauses Act of 1847,[3] the Waterworks Clauses Act of 1847,[4] and the Harbour Docks and Piers Clauses Act of 1847.[5] Most important for the present purposes, there was the Lands Clauses Consolidation Act of 1845,[6] which unlike the others (which had more general functions) was preoccupied with the compulsory acquisition of land; for it is upon this act, with many statutory variations, that the present law of compensation for compulsory acquisition rests.

The act was drafted in the language of the day. The moving spirits under the act were the "promoters of the undertaking," meaning the body of persons who under the "special act" were empowered to execute the "undertaking."[7] Today, it is most often a local authority, such as a

[2] 8 & 9 Vict., c. 20 and c. 35.
[3] 10 & 11 Vict., c. 17.
[4] *Ibid.*
[5] 10 & 11 Vict., c. 27.
[6] Lands Clauses Consolidation Act, 1845, 8 & 9 Vict., c. 19.
[7] Lands Clauses Consolidation Act, 1845, § 2.

county council or borough council, which seeks to acquire land compulsorily under some general act of Parliament; but in those days it was usually a commercial venture such as a railway or canal company which sought to exercise the power of compulsion which Parliament had given to it in a special act. The act survives, however, and so throughout one must adapt the statutory language to the present-day realities of the case.

In the latter part of the nineteenth century there was a vast improvement in the local government of England. Thus the most important of local government bodies, the county council, was not established until the Local Government Act of 1888 [8] came into force. The next fifty years witnessed the conferment on most local authorities of wide powers in many spheres, not least in the field of compulsory acquisition for matters such as the provision of houses. The balance shifted radically from special acts giving specific powers over specific areas of land to specific commercial concerns, on the one hand, to general acts giving general powers over all the land in a district to the local authority for that district, on the other hand.

This, of course, raised the question of the protection of the landowner who wished to resist compulsory acquisition. Under the system of specific acts, he had the expensive but efficacious prospect of being able to oppose the passage of the bill in Parliament. Private and local bill procedure provides for prior notification to those likely to be affected, and for an opportunity for them to object to the bill. Such objections are heard by a committee of the House of Commons or Lords (according to the house into which the bill is introduced), or sometimes a joint committee. The procedure resembles proceedings in a court of law, with the case for and against the bill conducted by counsel, and with evidence for and against the bill being heard by the committee. Such a procedure is quite inappropriate to general authorizations to acquire land contained in general acts, and so the general acts set up their own procedure.

This procedure was broadly set up on the lines that when an acquiring authority had decided what land it required for its housing, education, public health, or other purposes, it could make an order for the acquisition of the land, though such an order would not be effective until confirmed by the appropriate Minister, such as the Minister of Health (for public health matters), the Minister of Transport (for highway matters), and so on. Before the Minister can confirm such an order, advertisements must be issued and notices served on those whose land is affected, and if there

[8] 51 & 52 Vict., c. 41.

are any valid objections to the proposal, the Minister concerned must consider them, usually by holding a public inquiry into the objections. Such an inquiry is conducted much as proceedings in a court of law, save that it is heard by an inspector appointed by the Minister. After the report and recommendations of the inspector have been considered, the Minister either confirms or refuses to confirm the order. If it is confirmed, then subject to compliance with certain formalities as to publication, and to an opportunity of applying to the High Court to have the order quashed on the ground that the proper formalities have not been observed, the local authority has power to acquire the land compulsorily.

This procedure varied to some extent from one general act to another. The Acquisition of Land (Authorization Procedure) Act of 1946 [9] laid down a general code on these lines which today applies to most (though not all) cases of compulsory acquisition. The procedure is generally regarded as being more satisfactory than might appear. In theory, it is unsatisfactory for the only avenue of challenge (defective formalities apart) to be an inquiry conducted by an organ of the central government into objections to an order made by a local government authority. In theory, it is unsatisfactory for the case to be argued before A (the inspector) but for it to be decided by B (the Minister), especially when it is known that in most cases the real decision is made not by B, but by X, Y, and Z, who are unidentified officers in the ministry. In theory, bias might sometimes be suspected, one way or another, when the Minister belongs to one political party, and the local authority is controlled by the same party, or by an opposing party. Yet in practice the cases in which there are real grounds of complaint are relatively few.

This is due in the main to the English tendency (itself a real obstacle to reform) to make machines that are defective in design and objectionable in principle work well in practice. Improvements have been made. One result of the report of the Committee on Administrative Tribunals and Enquiries in 1957 [10] was the enactment of the Tribunals and Inquiries Act of 1958;[11] another result was the decision of the government that in the future any persons concerned should be able to obtain copies of the inspector's report, and that the formal letters sent by the Minister should summarize the inspector's findings and recommendations, and then, in giving the Minister's decision, with reasons, state whether or not he is

[9] 9 & 10 Geo. 6, c. 49.
[10] CMD. No. 218.
[11] 6 & 7 Eliz. 2, c. 66.

accepting the inspector's recommendations.[12] After more than two years of this system, it has become apparent that only in a small minority of cases does the Minister refuse to accept the inspector's recommendation. In the great majority of cases, though the inspector is appointed only to hear and report, he in substance also decides. There is nothing to prevent powers of acquisition still being conferred by a specific act, and local acts sometimes do this. But in the great majority of cases, the process of obtaining authorization is on the basis set out above.

Once powers of acquisition have been conferred upon the authority, it is for the authority to decide when, if ever, to exercise them. A proposal for which powers were obtained shortly before the war may have become quite impracticable since the war, and may be abandoned. But if the authority decides to proceed with the proposal, as it usually will do, normally it does so by serving on the landowner, and any persons who have a tenancy for not less than a year, a "notice to treat."

A notice to treat need not be in any particular form. It is primarily a notice that the power of acquisition is being exercised in relation to the land; but it also demands particulars of the landowner's interest in the land and the claims that he is making in respect of it, and it states that the "promoters of the undertaking are willing to treat for the purchase thereof, and as to the compensation to be made to all parties for the damage that may be sustained by them by reason of the execution of the works." [13] It is at this stage that the compulsory acquisition actually begins. It will be observed that what is being acquired is the individual interests in the land, rather than the land itself. Short tenancies may be left to expire, but longer tenancies and the fee simple are subject to notices to treat.

Often the parties will in fact "treat." The valuers on each side will meet and discuss; they will make offer and counteroffer; and in the end, by compromise, commonsense and perhaps a bit of horse trading ("If you will drop your claim on this, I will meet you on that"), they will agree to terms. But often they will not; and in any case their negotiations will be conducted against a background of what their rights will be if negotiations break down. And so one must turn to the provisions governing compensation.

There are three main heads of compensation: (1) compensation for the interest acquired; (2) compensation for disturbance; and (3) compensa-

[12] See Circular 9/58 of the Ministry of Housing and Local Government.
[13] Lands Clauses Consolidation Act, 1845, § 18.

tion for damage by severance or injurious affection. In addition, interest on compensation is payable. These three heads will be examined in turn.

The general basis of compensation is laid down in the Acquisition of Land (Assessment of Compensation) Act of 1919. Rule 2 provides that, with certain qualifications, "the value of the land shall . . . be taken to be the amount which the land if sold in the open market by a willing seller might be expected to realise." The section further provides that no allowance is to be made on account of the acquisition being compulsory,[14] nor is any special suitability or adaptability of the land for any purpose to be taken into account if it is a purpose for which it can be used only under statutory powers, or for which there is no market apart from the special needs of a particular purchaser or the requirements of any government department or any local or public authority.[15]

The general rule of "open-market value," however, does not apply where there is no general market for the land and but for the acquisition it would continue to be devoted to its existing purposes, say, where it is a school. In such cases, if reinstatement in some other place is intended, compensation will be based on "the reasonable cost of equivalent reinstatement."[16] In all cases, however, compensation must be based on the facts as they exist at the date on which the notice to treat was served,[17] so that, for example, the subsequent destruction of the premises by fire will be immaterial.[18]

Before there was any statutory control of town and country planning, the evaluation of the open market price was based on actualities rather than hypothesis. True, the valuers on either side, in their attempts to find the amount which the interest in the land "might be expected to realise," conjured up a "hypothetical purchaser," and indulged in a degree of peering into his hypothetical mind. But these ventures were founded on fact. Each valuer would give evidence on a series of transactions with which he had been associated in which interests in land more or less physically comparable with the land in question had been sold on terms and at dates more or less comparable with the land in question; from this it would be deduced that the land in question was worth x pounds per acre, or y pounds a square foot, and then this figure would be adapted

---

[14] Acquisition of Land (Assessment of Compensation) Act, 1919, 9 & 10 Geo. 5, c. 57, § 2, rule 2.

[15] Acquisition of Land Act, 1919, § 2, rule 3.

[16] Acquisition of Land Act, 1919, § 2, rule 5.

[17] Penny v. Penny, L.R. 5 Eq. 227 at 236 (1868).

[18] Phoenix Assurance Co. v. Spooner, [1905] 2 K.B. 753.

to the case in hand, with any necessary adjustments. In producing these "comparables," much would depend on how truly comparable the comparable was. Land on the edge of a town might be physically comparable with land ten miles away; but the contrast between the potentialities of development of the two plots might be vast.

In England, the impact of town and country planning legislation on compulsory acquisition was small until after the war of 1939–1945. The first timid and relatively ineffective act of 1909,[19] and its successors, had little effect on land valuers. They depended upon the making and enforcement of a town planning scheme for the area, and few authorities ever succeeded in complying with all the requirements for bringing such a scheme into effect. Indeed, by 1939 barely 4 per cent of England and Wales was subject to such a scheme. Many authorities had, indeed, resolved to prepare a scheme, but had never succeeded in finally settling a scheme and bringing it into force. By 1939, some 70 per cent of England and Wales fell into this category. Such land was subject to what was known as "interim development control"; and this was virtually a system of "You develop at your own risk." In other words, if a town planning scheme was ultimately made, any development during the interim development period that complied with the scheme could not be removed or suppressed without the payment of compensation; but any noncomplying development could be demolished or prohibited without compensation, unless it had been carried out under an interim development permission granted by the planning authority. Finally, there was the remaining 26 per cent of England and Wales, which was innocent of any planning control whatsoever.

The Town and Country Planning (Interim Development) Act of 1943[20] made two important changes in this position. First, all land in England and Wales that was not already subject to a scheme was made subject to interim development control;[21] the 26 per cent thus joined the 70 per cent. Second, power was given to take enforcement proceedings against all those who subsequently developed their land in an interim development area (which then covered 96 per cent of the country) without obtaining interim development permission.[22] The planning authority was thus no longer powerless during the period before a scheme was

---

[19] The Housing, Town Planning, &c. Act, 1909, 9 Edw. 7, c. 44.
[20] 6 & 7 Geo. 6, c. 29.
[21] Section 1.
[22] Section 5.

brought into force. For the first time some degree of planning control was made both effective and nationwide.

The act of 1947 [23] carried planning control many steps further. It defined "development" in wide terms.[24] The old, somewhat rigid concept of a planning scheme was replaced by a new, more flexible concept of the "development plan"; and all planning authorities were required to prepare such plans. The plans must be reviewed every five years, but can be reviewed more often.[25] Further, the development plan (unlike the old planning scheme) gives no permission for anything at all; it merely provides an informed prophecy of the types of development which are likely to be permitted and those which are likely to be refused. The basic rule is that planning permission must be obtained for all development,[26] even if it is development in exact accord with the development plan.

These changes in planning were, however, small in comparison with the hotly debated provisions for "development charges." Broadly, the idea of the 1947 act was that, subject to a number of qualifications, any person carrying out development must first pay to the state a "development charge" representing the increase in the value of the land brought about by the grant of permission.[27] This liability produced a corresponding depreciation in the value of all land with potentialities of development; and so landowners were given the right to make a claim against a fund of £300 million for the depreciation which the act caused to their land.[28]

The many and complex details of this system are not directly in point here; but the fundamental idea naturally affected the compensation payable on a compulsory acquisition. This had to be brought into line with the basic thesis that a landowner had the right to continue the existing use of his land, but if he wanted to develop it, he must obtain permission and pay a development charge. A compulsory acquisition accordingly took from him both the land and his existing-use rights, but it did not take the "development value" of the land (that is, its value for development purposes), for the act of 1947 had already done that. Accordingly, it was enacted [29] that the value of an interest in land was to be ascertained

[23] Town and Country Planning Act, 1947, 10 & 11 Geo. 6, c. 51.
[24] Section 12(2).
[25] Section 5.
[26] Section 12(1).
[27] Section 69.
[28] Section 58.
[29] Town and Country Planning Act, 1947, § 51(2). See Sampson's Executors v. Nottinghamshire County Council, [1949] 2 K.B. 439.

on the assumption that planning permission would not be granted for any development other than a strictly limited range of development which was regarded as being comprehended within the existing use of the land,[30] such as rebuilding an existing building, or using a single dwelling house as two or more separate dwelling houses. In a phrase, compensation was based on the "existing use value" of the land: the hypothetical purchaser's mind was made more hypothetical by expelling from it virtually all prospect of using the land for anything save its existing use. Even if an actual planning permission had been granted before the notice to treat was served, that had to be ignored, unless indeed a development charge had been paid for the development permitted, or the development fell within the very limited range of development exempt from development charge.[31]

The financial side of the act of 1947 did not work well. Whatever the theoretical justification, the artificialities of development charges rapidly became apparent. In theory, he who owned land worth £1,000 for its existing use and £10,000 for building purposes should be willing to sell it to a builder for £1,000 in the knowledge that the builder would have to pay a development charge of £9,000; and on this assumption it was right that on a compulsory acquisition he should be paid only £1,000. Yet in practice, on a voluntary sale the landowner would demand (and get) not £1,000, but £5,000 or £7,000; and as the builder still had to pay a development charge of £9,000, this had an inflationary tendency. This emphasized the artificiality and hardship of compensation on compulsory acquisition, for this remained at £1,000. For these and other reasons, the Town and Country Planning Act of 1953[32] halted the system of development charges as a standstill measure, and the act of 1954[33] made detailed provisions for a new system.

The act of 1954 is as complex an act as ever graced the English statute book. One of its main features was that it transformed the claims against the £300 million fund. These claims (none of which had been paid) were used first for making certain payments to those who had suffered certain financial detriments under the previous law; thus there was a re-payment of development charges that had been paid. What was left was annexed to the land whence it had sprung in the guise of an "unexpended balance of established development value." This was available for the future payment of compensation (for example, for certain adverse plan-

[30] Town and Country Planning Act, 1947, 3d schedule.
[31] Town & Country Planning Act, 1947, § 51(4).
[32] 1 & 2 Eliz. 2, c. 16.
[33] Town and Country Planning Act, 1954, 2 & 3 Eliz. 2, c. 72.

ning decisions) and also for compensation on a compulsory acquisition. In broad terms, such compensation was still paid on the same basis as under the act of 1947, save that the unexpended balance was added. In a simple case, this might approximate to the open-market value: for in the example above, £1,000 existing-use value plus £9,000 unexpended balance equals £10,000 market value. To that extent, there was a marked return to reality. But the system contained the seeds of a new artificiality. The £10,000, and so the £9,000, was based on values as they stood on July 1, 1948.[34] By 1958, the open-market value of the land on a voluntary sale might have become £15,000; yet on a compulsory acquisition the land-owner would receive only the existing-use value (which might have increased a little over the £1,000 of 1948) plus £9,000. The existing-use figure had to be ascertained as at the date of the notice to treat, but the unexpended balance was a figure fixed once and for all on a 1948 footing. As the years passed artificiality would become increasingly artificial.

The act of 1959[35] has brought compensation back to reality. The "existing use" basis of compensation has been swept away, and the old "open market" value restored.[36] However, the progress of planning law in general has made necessary what may be described as a process of statutory psychoanalysis. Left to himself, the hypothetical purchaser's thoughts as interpreted by the landowner's valuer might well be wildly different from his thoughts as interpreted by the acquiring authority's valuer. The purchaser might robustly envisage a wide range of development as likely to be permitted, whereas the landowner's valuer would gloomily assume the probability of an almost complete refusal of permission. And so the act proceeds to lay down some assumptions that are to be made.

Valuation is, in general, to be made not only on a basis of any planning permissions which at the date of the notice to treat have actually been granted, but also on a basis of any planning permissions likely to be granted.[37] Thus if the land is being acquired for some specified purpose, it is to be assumed that planning permission would be given for that purpose; and it is to be assumed that permission would be given to develop the land in accordance with the development plan. Further, the local planning authority is required to give a certificate of what development might reasonably have been expected to be granted (with an appeal

[34] Town & Country Planning Act, 1947, § 61(1).
[35] Town and Country Planning Act, 1959, 7 & 8 Eliz. 2, c. 53.
[36] Section 1.
[37] See Town and Country Planning Act, 1959, §§ 2–9.

to the Minister), and this must be taken into account. Broadly, compensation on a compulsory acquisition is once again on a basis which is in line with the true (and not artificial) expectations of the hypothetical purchaser.

There is no statutory provision which in terms confers any right to compensation for disturbance, though the statute recognizes such a right as existing.[38] It covers such matters as legal and other professional costs incurred in making the claim or acquiring alternative premises, any business good will destroyed by the acquisition, and even abortive expenditure incurred in seeking alternative premises.[39] In the gradual development of the principles of compensation for compulsory acquisition, the courts have come nearer and nearer to an analogue of damages at common law in that they allow, in addition to the capital value of the interest acquired, compensation for any loss directly resulting from the acquisition.

This, however, is subject to an important qualification. A landowner cannot eat his cake and have it too. If he values his interest in the land on a footing that necessarily involves a measure of disturbance, he cannot also claim for that disturbance. Thus if he values his farm on the basis that it is building land, he cannot also claim for disturbance of his farming activities.[40]

The landowner is given an express right to claim compensation for damages sustained "by reason of the severing of the lands taken from the other lands of such owner, or otherwise injuriously affecting such other lands" by the exercise of the statutory powers.[41] Thus if by the compulsory acquisition a farmhouse is severed from some of its fields, or if part of an estate is acquired for the construction of some works which will injure the remainder, compensation is payable. In one case, some land was acquired for a school, and the landowner, who had erected houses on another part of the land, was held entitled to compensation for the depreciation in the value of these houses caused by the noise from the school.[42] But there is no compensation under this head if the works are constructed on land other than that compulsorily acquired. Further, if the works cause an increase in value to other contiguous or adjacent

[38] Acquisition of Land Act, 1919, § 2(6); Horn v. Sunderland Corporation, [1941] 2 K.B. 26 at 34.

[39] See Harvey v. Crawley Development Corporation, [1957] 1 Q.B. 485; London County Council v. Tobin, [1959] 1 Weekly L.R. 354.

[40] Horn v. Sunderland Corporation, [1941] 2 K.B. 26; but see 58 L.Q. Rev. 29 (1942).

[41] Lands Clauses Consolidation Act, 1845, 8 & 9 Vict. c. 18, § 63.

[42] R. v. Pearce, *ex parte* The Schools Board of London, 78 L.T.R. (n.s.) 681 (1898).

land of the landowner, this increase is now set off against any compensation payable for the compulsory acquisition.[43]

The foregoing very general survey of compensation for the compulsory acquisition of land shows that in England no question of what is or is not a "taking" can arise. In Northern Ireland, where the Parliament has its competence limited by the Government of Ireland Act of 1920,[44] the question will no doubt one day arise for decision. Quite recently, section 5(1) of that act, which prohibits the Parliament of Northern Ireland from making "a law so as either directly or indirectly to . . . take any property without compensation," came before the House of Lords.[45] But it was unnecessary to explore the meaning and limits of the phrase (though American authority was cited), for, on the facts, pretty plainly what had occurred was not a taking. In England, one merely examines the statute in question to see what provisions for compensation (if any) are contained in it.

Apart from the compulsory acquisition of interests in land, many statutes regulate and restrict the use of land; some provide for compensation, and some do not. As a broad generalization it may be said that such acts tend to follow the policy indicated by Mr. Justice Holmes: "The general rule at least is, that while property may be regulated to a certain extent, if regulation goes too far, it will be recognized as a taking." [46] Take, and you must compensate; regulate, and you need not.

One illustration is the power under the Public Health Act of 1925[47] to prescribe an "improvement line" in a street. Such a line does not affect existing buildings, but it prevents any new building, erection, or excavation from being made nearer to the center of the street than the improvement line. This makes it possible to widen the street as rebuilding becomes necessary; and the landowner is deprived of the effective use of part of his site. The act accordingly provides that "any person whose property is injuriously affected by the prescribing of an improvement line" is entitled to compensation from the local authority; and this is quite distinct from the compensation payable to the landowner if any of his land in front of the improvement line is compulsorily acquired for the purpose of widening the street.

---

[43] Town & Country Planning Act, 1959, § 9.
[44] 10 & 11 Geo. 5, c. 67.
[45] Belfast Corporation v. O.D. Cars Ltd., [1960] 2 Weekly L.R. 148; and see 76 L.Q. Rev. 198 (1960).
[46] Pennsylvania Coal Company v. Mahon, 260 U.S. 393 at 415 (1922).
[47] 15 & 16 Geo. 5, c. 71, § 33.

Another illustration is the Public Health Act of 1936.[48] This gives a wide range of powers to local authorities, some of which relate to land, such as the power to make by-laws regulating the construction and alteration of buildings.[49] Many of these powers are exercised in ways which do not damage a landowner; a landowner can scarcely complain if he is required to construct his buildings of proper materials and in a proper way. But sometimes damage does result; and the act provides that the local authority "shall make full compensation to any person who has sustained damage by reason of the exercise by the authority of any of their powers under this Act in relation to a matter as to which he has not himself been in default." [50] Thus a local authority which constructs a sewer under the act must compensate a landowner if a manhole is made in a public footpath running over his land.[51]

Finally, there is the ubiquitous town planning legislation. Under the scheme of the act of 1947, the refusal of planning permission in general gave rise to no claim for compensation. The landowner (so the theory ran) had his general claim against the £300 million fund, and thereafter his only rights were in the existing use of the land. The refusal of planning permission accordingly did him no harm, especially as he would have to pay a development charge if permission were granted to him.

With the disappearance of the old scheme, the pattern changed. The act of 1954[52] gave a right to compensation out of the unexpended balance for any depreciation in the value of land if planning permission was refused or onerous conditions imposed. This, however, was subject to important restrictions excluding compensation when the application for permission was premature, or was merely for a change of use, or permission was available for some different but comparable development, or the conditions imposed related merely to design or layout. Further, even where compensation is payable, the fact that it is payable only out of the unexpended balance is an important limiting factor. For this means "no unexpended balance, no compensation"; and even if compensation is payable, there is a "ceiling" assessed on 1948 values, which sometimes differ strikingly from present-day values.

The terms of reference for this essay call for "an analysis of the line drawn between regulation of land that requires no compensation, and

[48] 26 Geo. 5 & 1 Edw. 8, c. 49.
[49] Sections 61, 62.
[50] Section 278.
[51] Swanston v. Twickenham Local Board, 11 Ch.D. 838 (1879).
[52] Part II.

that which constitutes a 'taking' for which compensation is required."
The English lawyer would observe that before one can analyze a line
(assuming such a process to be possible), one must have a line to analyze;
and in this sphere English law has no line. The basis upon which compensation for the refusal of planning permission may be claimed is no
logical and coherent policy, but the outcome of changes in a wider policy,
and can be explained only as a matter of legislative history. Indeed, this
is true of the subject of compensation as a whole. It will surprise none
who know what English law is like.

ASPECTS OF

EMINENT DOMAIN PROCEEDINGS

IN THE UNITED STATES

DAVID R. LEVIN

DEPUTY DIRECTOR, OFFICE OF RIGHT-OF-WAY AND LOCATION,
BUREAU OF PUBLIC ROADS, U.S. DEPARTMENT OF COMMERCE

THE GROUP of federal, state, and local government agencies concerned with the provision of public highway facilities is one of the largest public consumers of land and property in the United States. Approximately 22 million acres of land now comprise the rights-of-way for a highway system of three and a half million miles. Recent efforts to improve that system involve the acquisition and control of additional lands. It is estimated that approximately one and a half million acres will be needed for the rights of way of the 41,000-mile national system of interstate and defense highways, involving perhaps as many as 750,000 individual parcels of land. A considerable additional amount of land will be required for the so-called ABC program for federally aided primary, secondary, and urban highways during the next decade or so. Some additional amounts of land will also be required for state and local highways that are not associated with federal aid.

Highway officials are seeking to acquire this substantial amount of land and property under the laws and procedures which prevail in the fifty states and the federal government. It is estimated that approximately 90 per cent of the lands needed for highway rights of way can be purchased by amicable negotiation leading to sales consummated through agreements, deeds, and conveyances. The remaining 10 per cent will have to be condemned, largely under state laws; federal acquisition machinery is used only in exceptional circumstances, and then only after it is activated by state request.

Some states now possess the legal and administrative machinery with which to acquire the needed lands fairly and efficiently from both the standpoint of the public and the property owner involved. But other states do not. Time of possession of the necessary land, determination of just compensation, type of legal interest that may be acquired, payment of awards, condemnation procedures, right of way financing practices, and appraisal procedures are but a few of the special areas where improvements can be achieved in a number of jurisdictions. This paper will seek to explore a few of these areas.

Additionally, it will explore several emerging land-use problems that require early solution in the public interest. These largely involve control of access and land uses at highway interchanges.

COMPENSABLE AND NONCOMPENSABLE ITEMS OF DAMAGE

Through the years, the judiciary in the United States has designated particular elements of damage to property resulting from a public acquisition as compensable, and at the same time has pointed to other elements as noncompensable. When an entire parcel of property is acquired for public or quasi-public purposes, the current fair market value of the entirety has generally constituted the magnitude of the compensation allowed by the courts. It is in connection with partial takings of private property for public uses, and with the remainders the landowners retain, that the problem of compensable and noncompensable items has largely arisen. Most of the property needed for highway purposes comprises such partial takings.

Without determining the equity of including or excluding such items, the nature of the compensable and noncompensable elements of damage should be examined. To be compensable, damages to remainders must be sufficiently definite to be of practical significance, not remote and speculative, and must depreciate the market value of the remainders. Severance damages which have generally been held to be compensable by the courts include the following: (1) cutting up remainders into parcels of such size or shape as to decrease their utility and value and impair their plottage value; (2) leaving deep cuts or high fills, so that remainders are substantially impaired with respect to accessibility and economic utility; (3) substantial impairment of access, air, light, and view; (4) injury to water supply; (5) pollution of waters flowing upon remainders; (6) impairment of irrigation or drainage; (7) diminution in value resulting from a change in the highest and best use of remainders; (8) damage to necessary fencing; and (9) decrease in value because of the proximity of the public improvement to the private installations of the remainders.

Other types of injury, though perhaps involving losses suffered by the owner, but not reflected necessarily in the depreciation of the value of the remainders, have been held generally to be noncompensable by the courts. These injuries may include the following: (1) loss of good will; (2) loss of business profits; (3) diversion of traffic from the remainders or increase or decrease in amount of traffic on the highway; (4) circuity of travel; (5) costs of moving personal property; (6) personal inconveniences, fumes, noise, and other nuisances resulting from a public improvement; (7) frustration of plans to develop, improve, or utilize remainders; (8) change of use of street or highway, within pre-existing widths (as for example, construction of telephone lines within highway right of way); (9) loss of abutters' rights of access to highways on new location; (10) loss of improvements provided by lessee; (11) fear of remote and contingent injury which may possibly occur to remainders (as, for example, explosion of gas lines); (12) anticipated future negligent acts associated with condemner's facilities (as, for example, killing of livestock by motorists); (13) interruption of business during highway construction; (14) establishment of one-way streets; and (15) construction of traffic separators or median strips. While these types of injury are generally not compensable in the United States if the "before and after" value standard is used, elements of some of these injuries are prone to be reflected in the compensation awarded the property owner.

Although the great weight of authority does not recognize the cost of moving personal property as a compensable damage in eminent domain, several states have enacted laws authorizing such payments, and the federal government recognizes this as a legitimate item of damage in its housing program. Moreover, one state has even construed its constitutional requirement for the payment of "full" and "just" compensation to include moving costs.[1] Furthermore, the matter of subjective fears of property owners is being reexamined. Two recent decisions have held that a well-grounded fear of the presence of a gas pipeline might be introduced in testimony as an element of damage to be considered in fixing the market value of the condemnee's property.[2]

Through the years, there seems to have been a trend toward increasing

---

[1] Jacksonville Expressway Authority v. Henry G. DuPree Company, 108 So.2d 289 (Fla. 1958.)

[2] In Northeastern Gas Transmission Co. v. Tersana Acres, 144 Conn. 509, 134 A.2d 253 (1957), the Supreme Court of Errors of Connecticut accepted testimony that there was a well-defined public fear of danger. In Tennessee Gas Transmission Co. v. Maze, 45 N.J. Super. 496, 133 A.2d 28 (App. Div. 1957), the New Jersey Superior Court ruled that testimony involving the probability of a leak in a pipeline would be admissible only if there were evidence that such a possibility was of sufficient strength to depress the market.

recognition by the courts and the legislatures of the elements of damage that are compensable. As is characteristic of many other important issues of the law, there is involved a delicate balancing between the public interest, which dictates that public funds which are becoming increasingly inadequate in terms of the needs for public improvements and accordingly should be safeguarded, and the private interest, which pleads for ever increasing recognition of the elements of damage, some of which is real and much of which is fancied.

SEVERANCE DAMAGES — ON AN EQUITABLE BASIS?

Where an entire parcel of property is taken by eminent domain for public use, the fair market value of the property taken is the measure of compensation. Usually no particular difficulties are involved. But public improvements, especially highways, more often than not do not require that entireties be taken. They require only partial takings, and these necessarily involve severance damages — that is, the measure of the compensation is the value of the land and improvements taken, plus damages, if any, to the remainder properties. Incidentally, the severance damage item today constitutes a substantial portion of the total land acquisition bill for highway purposes.

It is in this realm of severance damage that a grave situation confronts the American courts and public officials as well. At the present time, the usual rules of "fair market value," "before and after value," and "highest and best use" are applied to the remainders, as well as to the part taken, in order to ascertain just compensation. There is nothing wrong with the concepts here involved. But there are no adequate measures of determining severance damage with any degree of accuracy, to guide both the legal and the appraisal professions. While highway departments are paying today for severance damages as they must under present laws, they are noting, with increasing frequency, that allegations of damages to remainders by property owners have not always materialized in fact, after the highway improvement was completed and opened to traffic. Quite to the contrary, the states have been aware that, in some instances, substantial benefits to the owners of remainders have resulted, instead of fancied damages.

Suspicion of benefit, however, is an insufficient basis upon which to mount an appraisal that will stand up under the scrutiny of either the appraisal experts for the property owner, or the courts that seek to arbitrate disputes between public officials and property owners. Moreover, highway officials themselves want to be fair to both the public that must foot the bill and to the property owner.

The best answer to this vexing problem is scientifically derived data, in the form of case histories of comparable properties that have been subjected to partial takings, over a sequence of time. Studies of this kind are now being undertaken in sixteen states,[3] with the cooperation of the Bureau of Public Roads. There is every hope that eventually the data derived from these studies will result in a far more equitable determination of severance damages, from the standpoint of both the property owner and the public.

This comment is offered by way of backdrop for the existing situation with respect to appraisal techniques. If one wanted to seek a further area for improvement, one could refer to the situation existing, at times, where two presumably competent private expert appraisers of unquestioned integrity will testify as to value and damages: one will come up with a finding of $5,000, and the other of $95,000. Perhaps it is appropriate for those who are sincerely seeking to improve the existing situation to devise the ways and means that would either substantially reduce the differences that obtain in cases of this kind or eliminate them entirely, by an appropriate procedure.

PRACTICE IN STATE CONDEMNATION CASES

It is becoming increasingly apparent that the pretrial conference[4] may substantially expedite judicial administration of condemnation proceedings. Pretrial procedure was a direct result of overburdened court calendars. One of the first successful procedures in the United States was established in 1929 by the Wayne County (Detroit), Michigan, Circuit Court on its own initiative, even without the aid of legislation.[5] The court's success in clearing its calendar as a result of this device has now become legendary. The procedure was incorporated in 1938 into the *Federal Rules of Civil Procedure*[6] as rule 16, making its use discretionary with the court. The procedure was made applicable in 1951 to federal

---

[3] California, Illinois, Iowa, Kansas, Michigan, Minnesota, Mississippi, New Jersey, New Mexico, Ohio, Oregon, Texas, Vermont, Virginia, Washington, and Wisconsin.

[4] The pretrial conference, as used in this paper, is a strictly judicial proceeding, held before a judge after the initial pleadings have been served, but in advance of trial.

[5] E. R. Sunderland, *The Theory and Practice of Pre-Trial Procedure,* 36 MICH. L. REV. 215, 224–25 (1937).

[6] 28 U.S.C. 5144 (1959).

condemnation cases.[7] Today, the device is or can be employed in the courts of at least 39 jurisdictions,[8] (discretionary in 37 and mandatory in two).[9] At least 22 jurisdictions make use of pretrial procedures in connection with condemnation cases, though the extent of its application even in these states varies widely.

Proponents of the pretrial conferences point to such benefits as (1) the increased efficiency of the courts by eliminating expense and delay; (2) better pleadings resulting from implementing discovery procedures; (3) reduction of issues at the trial; (4) less likelihood of reversals; (5) less likelihood of admission of extraneous and prejudicial evidence; (6) the greater likelihood of settlements in advance of trial; and (7) elimination of procedural and evidentiary stumbling blocks. A recent seminar for United States judges recommended the use of pretrial procedures in condemnation cases.[10]

Opponents of the pretrial procedure point to the fact that it is employed to a lesser extent in condemnation than in civil cases generally. Individual reactions have been that pretrials led to a few settlements, constituted additional hearings for which they must prepare, and generally were a waste of time and money.

Because the overwhelming consensus of opinion seems to favor pretrial practice, its use in connection with condemnation cases should be further explored and encouraged. It could probably make eminent domain proceedings more efficient.

THE LAND-USE PROBLEM AT THE HIGHWAY INTERCHANGE

The 41,000-mile interstate system will have a large number of interchanges, when it is completed, in order to render the service for which it is designed. Estimates range as high as 14,000 such interchanges, though it is impossible to predict at this time the exact number. These accommodations may be quite costly. The price tags thus far have ranged from as low as $50,000 to as much as $2,000,000.

[7] FED. R. CIV. P. 71 (a).
[8] Arizona, Arkansas, California, Colorado, Delaware, Florida, Hawaii, Illinois, Indiana, Iowa, Kansas, Kentucky, Louisiana, Maine, Maryland, Massachusetts, Michigan, Minnesota, Missouri, Nebraska, Nevada, New Jersey, New Mexico, New York, North Carolina, North Dakota, Oklahoma, Pennsylvania, Rhode Island, Texas, Utah, Vermont, Virginia, Washington, West Virginia, Wisconsin, Wyoming, District of Columbia, and Puerto Rico.
[9] California and Michigan.
[10] Proceedings of the Seminar on Protracted Cases for United States Judges, 23 F.R.D. 319, 408 et seq. (1959), resolution 9(b), at 615.

Each interchange is designed in accordance with established engineering and design criteria, and each interchange ramp has a given design capacity. The criteria and design capacity used are based upon traffic and needs that could reasonably be expected to accumulate as of 1975, and other factors. Highway officials have been directed to anticipate the future at least to this extent by the Congress of the United States.[11]

In meeting this responsibility, highway officials are doing the best that modern highway technology makes possible. But they are technicians, not magicians. It is in this connection that the land-use problem at the interchange arises. In terms of a given interchange, the highway official will assume that certain land-use developments will reasonably occur. He designs the interchange on that basis. In a number of instances, at least, particularly where other location factors are the most favorable, almost before the pavement is dry on the interchange ramps, several industrial plants, a regional shopping center, housing developments, a complex of motels and restaurants, or other large traffic generators will set themselves down right next to the entrance or exit terminal of the interchange, literally at the end of the ramp. After a while, the unanticipated, additional traffic load which these generators create frequently will cause the ramp to break down functionally, but not physically, because the design capacity of the ramp has been exceeded.

How should this emerging situation be handled? There may be some design solutions that will work, under limited circumstances. Control of highway access might be extended beyond the entrance or exit terminals of the ramps. Substantial areas around the interchanges might be purchased outright by public authority, or only development or interchange easements might be acquired in such areas. Entrance or exit control might be expanded. Zoning, subdivision control, setback regulation, and the comprehensive planning device itself might be used to assist the situation appropriately. In any event, here is an opportunity for a new application of the prevailing land-use legal authority to cope with an existing need.

The existing devices now known to us, police power or eminent domain oriented, are not adequate to do the job. The same concepts perhaps need to be applied, but the mix or synthesis may need to be different. As a result, one state has recently introduced legislation that is radically different from most existing devices to cope with the problem.[12]

---

[11] 23 U.S.C. § 158(j) (Supp. V, 1958).

[12] Kentucky. A special state interchange commission was proposed to take full jurisdiction over the private development of all interstate interchanges in the state, within a mile and a half of the interchanges.

CONTROL OF HIGHWAY ACCESS — EMINENT DOMAIN OR POLICE POWER?

For the past decade, highway officials have been seeking to build expressways or controlled-access highways because these facilities have demonstrated their superiority over accommodations of ordinary design in terms of safety, economy, and general convenience. The entire 41,000-mile national system of interstate and defense highways will be of the controlled-access design. In addition, segments of other types of highways, carrying relatively large volumes of traffic, will also be so designed.

This substantial activity presumes that the legal machinery necessary to accomplish the control of highway access is adequate and efficient. While much progress has been made, there is ample opportunity for improvement in the field of access control. A sophisticated legal concept of control of access has not yet been developed. For example, does the authority to control access more properly come under eminent domain or police power? In practice, both powers are being used, sometimes independently, sometimes to supplement each other. With respect to expressways built on new locations, the courts in the United States have almost uniformly held that there can be no compensation for access rights under eminent domain. The legal rationale is merely this: Where an expressway is constructed on a location where no public highway has previously existed, no rights of access have vested, and so nothing has been taken away from the abutter; he is not entitled to compensation for a right he never had.[13] This result presumably is authorized under the state police power.

The situation with respect to controlling access on existing highway rights of way is quite different. Here the prevailing general rule is that an abutter may not be deprived of all access to the existing highway system without compensation; but he is entitled to compensation only where his access has been "substantially impaired." Here, again, there seems to be an obscure fusion between the police and eminent domain powers. Some 26 states regulate private entrances and exits to and from the primary state highway system by promulgating standards of design and location, involving number of entrances, their width, angle of entry

[13] See Carazalla v. State of Wisconsin, 269 Wis. 593, 71 N.W.2d 276 (1955); Robinson v. State, 207 Misc. 325, 137 N.Y.S.2d 673 (1955); Smick v. Commonwealth, 268 S.W.2d 424 (Ky. 1954); State Highway Commission v. Burk, 200 Ore. 211, 265 P.2d 783 (1954); Schnider v. State, 38 Cal. 2d 439, 241 P.2d 1 (1952). NATIONAL RESEARCH COUNCIL, EXPRESSWAY LAW: AN ANALYSIS, Highway Research Bd. Special Rep. 26 (Washington, D.C., 1957).

or emergence, and so on.[14] Generally, the determinations of the state highway departments are accepted by the courts and this conclusion is justified under the police power, unless they result in the total prohibition of access, in which case compensation must be paid under the rules of eminent domain.

Some important legal queries still remain unanswered. For example, does control of access as such legally impinge on the highway right of way at its boundary lines? If so, public authority may be deemed to have continued its activities to its own property and not to have encroached on abutting property. Or, legally, does control of access constitute an encumbrance on the land adjacent to the right of way, so that the abutter can claim damages for a deprivation of a right? Obviously, a multitude of legal consequences flow from the answers.

Again, what is meant by "substantial impairment of access"? If frontage roads are provided, so that adequate access is assured, though different in design from the former situation, is the abutter entitled to damages for impairment of access? Generally not. Suppose that access is preserved, but the abutter must now travel four blocks farther than formerly; is such circuity of travel compensable? Most courts have said no.

Actually, the expressway is a composite of a number of engineering and design elements that have been evolved individually over a long period of time. Some of these elements are the median strip, the one-way pavement, the grade separation, and control of access. Now taken individually, these elements each have enjoyed their own peculiar legal evolution. For example, most jurisdictions today hold that the designation of one-way streets or pavements is a police power function, and refuse to grant abutters or anyone else any compensation for any resulting damages. The same obtains for the divided highway or the median strips. Opinion on the effect of change of grade has had an erratic and irregular development, with the various jurisdictions in the United States divided on many of the principal issues involved. Control of access has met with equally varying fates. Since, in reality, the expressway is an aggregation of design elements known to our transportation system for many years, the legal status of each of these elements has continued to be associated with each

[14] California, Colorado, Delaware, Georgia, Illinois, Indiana, Louisiana, Maine, Maryland, Mississippi, Nebraska, New Hampshire, New Mexico, North Carolina, Oklahoma, Oregon, Pennsylvania, South Carolina, South Dakota, Tennessee, Texas, Utah, Virginia, Washington, West Virginia, Wisconsin. This authority stems either from specific statutes on the subject or from the general state authority to build and maintain highways that are safe and convenient to use.

equivalent characteristic of the expressway. In short, when the one-way character of the expressway design is attacked legally by an abutter, or the inability to cross over because of the median strip, the courts, almost uniformly, do not allow recovery, but talk about police power. On the other hand, with respect to a conversion of a pre-existing highway to expressway design, if a change of grade is involved or access is substantially impaired, the courts will continue to use the "before and after" current market value test as a measure of the damages to the remainders.

Here again, inflexible legal doctrine, originally evolved in a different context, is sought to be used on a new kind of legal creature — the expressway and control of access. Why not recognize this new development in terms of its essential characteristics and then seek to justify it legally on bases that are as realistic as the physical facilities themselves?

MARGINAL LAND ACQUISITIONS

There are several devices, known to the American experience to some extent, that fuse betterment and compensation activities into a single approach. One such mechanism is "excess condemnation," perhaps more appropriately identified as "marginal land acquisition."

Marginal land is territory contiguous to a highway (or other public improvement) in addition to that needed for the immediate physical improvement contemplated. The purposes or objectives of marginal land acquisition are multiple:

1. To protect the public improvement to which it is adjacent.
2. To prevent the creation of small, uneconomic remnants of private land.
3. To promote economy in public land acquisition, by acquiring an entire tract of land, instead of just a portion of it and paying heavy severance damage to the remainder lands.
4. To prevent or remove unsightly structures or noxious uses.
5. To assist the appropriate development of trees and shrubs and landscaping generally.
6. To stimulate appropriate uses of adjacent lands for aesthetic, safety, or general welfare purposes.
7. To provide land for future public improvements at reasonable cost.
8. To diminish the cost of public improvements through the sale of acquired marginal land with appropriate restrictions protecting the public improvements.

Marginal land acquisition is authorized legally in a variety of ways. The constitutions of eleven states[15] contain authorizations for the use of the device. Additionally, statutes in eleven states permit its use under designated circumstances.[16] Its application is authorized in connection with the provision of expressways in 22 states.[17]

Of all the constitutional provisions on marginal land acquisition, the Missouri and New Jersey provisions — both of relatively recent vintage — are perhaps the broadest in scope. The Missouri constitution provides that

the State, or any county or city may acquire . . . such property . . . in excess of that actually to be occupied by the public improvement or used in connection therewith, as may be reasonably necessary to effectuate the purposes intended.[18]

The New Jersey constitution authorizes the state or any political sub-division thereof to acquire a fee simple absolute or any lesser interest; and it may be authorized by law to take or otherwise acquire a fee simple absolute or easements upon, or the benefits of restrictions upon, abutting property to preserve and protect the public highway.[19]

Marginal land acquisition has been used but sparingly in the United States. It has been used somewhat by American cities in connection with public improvements generally and by state governments largely in con-nection with the improvement of public highways. The validity of this device has not been litigated extensively in the United States. Judicial

---

[15] California, art. I, § 14½; Massachusetts, art. X, § 11; Michigan, art. XIII, § 5; Missouri, art. I, § 27; New York, art. I, § 7(e); New Jersey, art. IV, § 6(3); Ohio, art. XVIII, § 10; Pennsylvania, art. 15, § 5; Rhode Island, art. XVII, § 1; Utah, art. XI, § 5(c); Wisconsin, art. XI, § 3(a).

[16] ARK. ACTS 1953, No. 419, § 4; DEERING's CAL. CODES, Gov't. § 192 (1951, Supp. 1957); COLO. REV. STAT. § 120-3-10 (1953); FLA. LAWS 1955, ch. 11413; SMITH-HURD ILL. ANN. STAT. ch. 24, §185(a) (1961); BURNS' IND. STAT. ANN. §48-2107 (1951); ANN. CODE MD. art. 89b, § 8 (1957); NEB. LAWS 1955, legislative bill 187, § 21; NEV. REV. STAT. 408.975 (1960); CODE VA. §15-771 (1950); WASH. LAWS 1953, ch. 131.

[17] ALA. LAWS 1956, H.B. 148; ARK. STAT. 1947 ANN. § 76-2205 (1957 replacement); DEL. CODE. ANN. tit. 17, ch. 3, § 175 (1953); FLA. STAT. § 348.121 (1961); GA. LAWS 1955, No. 333, § 5; BURNS' IND. STAT. ANN. § 36-3105 (1949); IOWA LAWS 1955, ch. 148, § 5; KY. REV. STAT. § 177.250 (1962); LA. LAWS 1955, § 303; MICH. STAT. ANN. § 9.1094(4) (1958); N.H. LAWS 1945, ch. 188, § 7(2); N.J.S.A. § 27:7a-4 (1940); N.D. REV. CODE § 24-0132 (Supp. 1957); O.R.S. § 374.040 (1953; 1957 replacement part.); R.I. LAWS 1949, ch. 2239, § 6 (only applicable to Providence); S.D. LAWS 1953, H.B. 656, § 5; TENN. LAWS 1955, ch. 147, § 4; UTAH CODE ANN. § 27-9-4 (1953); VT. LAWS 1955, H.B. 414; REV. CODE WASH. § 47.52.050 (1962); W. VA. CODE 1949 ANN. § 1474(24) 1961); WIS. STAT. 1955, § 59.965(5)(d)

[18] Article I, § 27.

[19] Article IV, § 6(3).

decisions to date have been based on collateral issues rather than on the broad principles involved.[20] Based upon judicial pronouncements to date, it would seem that recoupment, as a principal objective in marginal land acquisition, would be frowned upon; that the protection and preservation objectives would be entirely appropriate; and that if recoupment should incidentally result from marginal land acquisition, this would not invalidate the acquisition if the protection objective is paramount. At least, in terms of the needs and circumstances known today, such an approach seems entirely in order, and would probably be judicially approved.

OFFSET OF BENEFITS

Another technique which has been employed in a substantial number of states in the compensation-betterment process may be identified as the offset of benefits. Property abutting a public improvement may benefit from that improvement in a variety of ways. Such benefits may include the following:

1. Improved accessibility to a public highway.
2. Conversion from an inside to a corner lot.
3. Improved drainage.
4. Adaptability for a higher and better use, as a result of the public improvement.
5. Provision of fencing, cattle passes, sidewalks, lighting, and the like.
6. Elimination of slide or flood conditions.

Benefit offsets are not permitted indiscriminately in all states. In eight states, both general and special benefits are permitted to be offset; special benefits only can be offset in 27 jurisdictions; in 16 jurisdictions, the law is not clear as to what type of benefit can be recognized. And in two states, there is specific prohibition against the allowance of benefit offsets of any kind.[21]

Another complication that is operative in the area of benefit offsets concerns the circumstances under which benefits will be recognized. For example, only in twelve states and in federal takings, either by statutes, judicial decisions, or a combination of both, is the offset of benefits per-

---

[20] See Cincinnati v. Vester, 281 U.S. 439 (1930).

[21] Iowa CONST., art. I, § 18; Stoner v. Iowa State Highway Commission, 227 Iowa 115, 287 N.W. 269 (1939); Welton v. Iowa State Highway Commission, 211 Iowa 625, 233 N.W. 876 (1930). OKLA. CONST., art. II, § 24; 69 O.S. 1961 § 46(3); Finley v. Board of County Commissioners of Oklahoma County (Okla., 291 P.2d 333 1955); City of Tulsa v. Horwitz, 151 Okla. 201, 3 P.2d 841 (1931).

mitted (of whatever type is recognized) against the value of the land taken and damages to the remainder property. To the extent that other jurisdictions do permit offsets of benefits, they do so only against damages to the remainder properties, but not against land taken.

In connection with benefits, certain additional legal concepts are pertinent. For example, there must be a unity of title before the benefit offset principle can be recognized; that is, the parcel taken and the residue remaining must be in a common ownership at the time of the taking, for the rules to operate at all. Another test might be identified as the unity of use concept. This principle requires that the parcel taken must be devoted to the same kind of use as that of the remainder parcel. There are other rules relating to the permanency and character of the benefits, too.[22]

It is quite obvious from the foregoing that there is already substantial recognition in the United States of the existence of benefits of varying kinds arising out of public improvements. There is, apparently, a willingness, under some circumstances at least, to offset such benefits against the acquisition costs that otherwise would be involved. It may well be that this benefit device could be expanded substantially, giving a much wider recognition to benefits that in fact exist.

ACQUISITIONS OF PROTECTIVE EASEMENTS AND DEVELOPMENT RIGHTS

The acquisition of protective easements and development rights is rationalized, of course, under the power of eminent domain, rather than under the police power. The taking of such easements constitutes another device under which the compensation and betterment elements involving public improvements and private adjacent lands may be brought more nearly in balance with each other.

Property may be looked upon as a bundle of rights — the rights of the owner to sell his property, to encumber it, to have the property pass on to his wife or children, to build upon it, to develop it. It is a portion of this bundle which public authority acquires when protective easements or development rights are taken. We have channel change easements, slope and drainage easements, scenic easements for highway and parkway purposes, highway development rights, reservation easements, air rights, sight-distance easements, easements of view, building protective easements,

---

[22] For a comprehensive discussion of benefits in relation to public improvements, see Enfield and Mansfield, *Special Benefits and Right-of-way Acquisition,* in 1956 ACTIVITIES OF THE AMERICAN ASSOCIATION OF STATE HIGHWAY OFFICIALS.

and many others. Whatever their variation, they essentially involve the acquisition from a landowner of one or more of his building or development rights in his land so that the public interest may be served without having to purchase the entire bundle of property rights in fee simple.

Easements have been used successfully to achieve protection of public improvements or the public control of designated areas. The California Department of Natural Resources, since 1933, has acquired scenic easements from landowners immediately adjacent to state parks. In like manner, the New York State Division of Parks has in a few cases acquired easements to prevent the construction of private commercial facilities opposite the entrances to state parks. The New York State Department of Public Works has also acquired easements — extending to a width of 750 feet from the edge of the roadway — restricting the erection of billboards on its expressways. The New York Thruway Authority has purchased 1,000 feet of easements along its expressway for the same purpose.

The Ohio Department of Highways has made considerable use of "reservation agreements" for designated areas to protect highway rights of way. Texas uses a similar device under the label of "highway development rights." Avigation easements have been used to assure an unobstructed approach to airports. Wisconsin has made extensive use of development restriction easements in connection with its Mississippi River Parkway projects.

The actual costs of such acquisition are not exorbitant. For example, for nine projects, involving 33½ miles of Mississippi River Parkway, Wisconsin authorities paid little more than $19,000 for control over 1,272 acres of land; the average cost per acre was approximately $15. Compensation for reservations over 100 to 200 feet in area adjacent to highway rights of way in Ohio averaged $5 per acre or portion thereof, or approximately $109 per running mile. Flight safety easements on agricultural lands adjacent to the Lemoore Naval Air Station in California averaged $15 per acre.

An evaluation of the existing experience with these protective and development easements indicates that these types of devices offer much promise. They are low-cost, at least in the rural areas. If adequately contrived, they can be quite effective for their intended purposes. Since they are justified legally under eminent domain rather than under police power, they enjoy a large measure of legal stability and endure over time. Their weaknesses, if any, stem from the lack of their widespread application in many areas; from the fact that they are not popularly understood very easily; from the difficulties of setting a price tag on their value in the open market; and from the opportunities they afford for partisan interests to misrepresent their impact on grantors or donors.

OTHER COMPENSATION-BETTERMENT MECHANISMS

There are other devices, in addition to those already mentioned, that may offer some promise, under designated circumstances, of easing the compensation-betterment difficulties.

One that is currently attracting some attention in the provision of transportation accommodations is the control of the use of access openings. It may be rationalized under both the power of eminent domain or the police power. Control of "use" of access involves restricting the *kind* or *purpose* of use that can be made of a private driveway to a public highway. Such control would generally be confined to agricultural or residential uses, rather than industrial or commercial pursuits, because the latter would constitute the substantial traffic generators. There is already some statutory and favorable judicial thinking on the matter.

The designation, by state or local governments, of ultimate right of way widths and official map procedures are means currently available in the United States. These are generally sanctioned under the state police power. Examples of their current applications, though not extensive, may be found in California, Pennsylvania, Washington and several other states.[23] Zoning, subdivision controls, urban renewal procedures, and the planned district concept offer other possibilities for effective action.

CONCLUSION

The emerging needs of what are the largest public improvement programs in history almost demand either new legal tools that can be used to control land use or drastic new versions of some existing devices. These developments seem necessary from the standpoint of both the public agencies responsible for the public improvements and the private individuals that are or want to be in geographic association with the improvements. Both have much to gain from an orderly approach to the provision of public facilities and the development of private structures that characterizes an expanding economy. The needs for new legal mechanisms chal-

[23] CAL. STAT. § 1451 (1947); 36 P.S. § 670-208 (1961); WASH. LAWS 1955, ch. 161, H.B. 246.

lenge the resourceful legal scholar and practitioner alike with an urgency that has not been obvious since the decades preceding and following World War I, when many of the land-use and planning tools, as we know them today, were first contrived.

In Appraisal . . .

COMPARISONS AND CONTRASTS

CHARLES M. HAAR [1]

I. THEORY AND JUSTIFICATION OF PLANNING

NOT VERY long ago, as historians view time, advocates of planning controls both in England and in the United States were fighting the good fight for legal recognition of their views. Little had been done in the way of comprehensive land-use planning — certainly not by either country's government. Hence the claims for planning were largely a priori. The battle over principle now is won: every state in the Union has enacted land-use control laws, many of them lengthy and complex; England has adopted the most thoroughgoing national act yet seen in a common-law country.

The general prevalence and acceptance of planning laws make it easy for even a comprehensive analysis tacitly to assume that controls are justified. Planners are by profession conservators of a scarce resource, however, and it would be anomalous for them to squander the scarcer reservoir of mental energies in comparing the merits of different control systems, if central direction of any kind is doomed to failure. The practical possibility of land-use control through planning laws therefore is the logical basing point for a comparative discussion of English and American land-use law. An incidental advantage to starting at this point is that it is likely to reveal whether self-interest is beclouding objectivity; the implications of a negative conclusion are too far-reaching to be overlooked.

The views expressed in the papers indicate that there is neither an international nor national "planners' point of view," but only the points of view of planners. This is not to say that national influences are absent from the papers or even that they are unconscious. On the contrary, their relevance must be recognized as one of the factors in a comparative analysis. For example, one may explore the possibility that planning might be a necessity in England, but not in the United States. Without excep-

---

[1] This appraisal began as a transcript of a symposium discussing the various written papers, running through some 350 pages of typescript, which subsequently were condensed to the present form. The views expressed are my own responsibility, but they are based primarily on the discussions. The participants, it should be noted, have been given neither opportunity nor jurisdiction to review the errors committed in this summary.

tion, the English participants are of the view that whatever the theoretical considerations, planning controls in England are justified pragmatically — even dictated. But that might not hold true in the United States, where, to English eyes, plenty of land is still available. Further consideration would disclose that although land shortage is not endemic here, it is an acute problem in some areas. Even where it is not, the need for planning techniques might be created by such undesirable land-use conditions as the squalid and unsightly development which disfigures the approaches to many American cities.

As to the feasibility of attaining purported objectives, it is clear that full planning powers are not the open-sesame to physical utopia; this proposition is supported by experience of other societies in the area of population density. Relatively recently, the Soviet Union has adopted a policy of decentralization. Despite intensive efforts, the population of greater Moscow — the particular object of concern — has continued to increase, rising by several million since the repressive steps were initiated. This failure of the rigid and ruthless controls available to a dictatorship is a bad augury for the practical effect of the fairly modest controls of a democratic society.

Undeterred, England in the tradition of the earlier decree of Queen Elizabeth I has attempted to limit migration to its southeastern region. Although London continues to attract people to its larger metropolitan area, the population of the core city is decreasing by about 20,000 persons per year. Whatever encouragement this partial success otherwise might bring is weakened by two circumstances: factors other than planning controls undeniably contributed to it; and more significantly, similar population patterns have emerged in the United States without any deliberate government effort.

The proper attitude toward these experiences depends on what goals are predicated for planning. A possible one is the imposition of an ideal form upon development. But, even if attainable, the goal of utopia by fiat generally is rejected as inappropriate in a democratic society. Moreover, on the presently available evidence, it would be unsound to assume total controllability of the land market. A less utopian goal for planning is that it can make a significant contribution, which, paraphrasing Lord Silkin, is to give the public what it wants, and to give it in the best way. To the possibility of achieving this goal, experience at hand lends some support. But some of those for whom planning is only lubrication for private choice interpret the evidence to mean that the attempt at central planning is a mistake and should be abandoned.

A. *Planning and Certainty.* The opponents of central planning generally stress two not entirely disparate themes. One is that the goals which planning can achieve can better be reached by other means — that central planning at best is unnecessary to their attainment and, at worst, can impede or prevent it. The second theme is that a central planning agency's arrogation of functions interferes with crucial values of a democratic society, particularly liberty and property.

The burden of the first argument is that the "best" is not susceptible of objective determination, and, as for "wants," the price mechanism of a free market remains the superior method both of measurement and distribution. Substantiation for this latter claim is sought in the housing experience of the United States. In New York City rent control shackles the free operation of the market; the result is a housing shortage in which consumers concededly do not have freedom of choice. Eliminate the controls, so the argument goes, and free choice would be reintroduced, as witness developments in other cities following the termination of rent control. However, one may remain skeptical of whether consumers really ever had effective qualitative or quantitative control over any housing market.

The proponents of laissez faire and its blessings and of price as the barometer of choice echo the teachings of Adam Smith. Nor does the similarity end there. It inheres also in the second branch of the antiplanning view, in the stress on "liberty," "security," and "property." But although these are the words of Smith, a significant divergence has taken place. To Smith, freedom meant in large part freedom to own property; ownership meant the extent of rights in property. Liberty was greatest when property rights were most secure, that is, when they were best protected from wrongful interference. The mercantilists' "just price" was a menace to the wealth of a nation because it was a "regulated" price, and it was not made less objectionable to Smith because it was definite. But now, according to Professor Dunham, liberty is to be equated with certainty, with the right to take or to refrain from taking a particular action without obtaining consent — which may be refused in an official's discretion. Property is defined as the aggregate of rights in an object. There may be many such rights or only a few, but so long as even one remains, the object is "property" and the person holding the right is its "owner."

The equation of liberty with predictability produces strange logical consequences. One is that Englishmen are, by reason of England's planning laws, less free than the wretched driver of an automobile faced with imminent death and only one choice to make, a wry illustration culled from Professor Dunham's paper. More importantly, the equation legitimizes planning techniques put beyond the pale in classical economic theory. The traditional objection to central planning is cast in terms of limiting the scope of individual decisions. If, however, the be-all and end-all is certainty or predictability, the bête noire is not planning, but only certain planning techniques. For example, planning officials may project the precise future development of an area down to the most minute detail; the law may prohibit any development deviating from the plan. But as long as each owner can learn precisely what he may and may not do with his property by consulting the plan, there is no undue interference, in Professor Dunham's view, with private property or with liberty. In terms of the two systems being compared, the opponents of central planning would sanction conventional zoning techniques which minutely spell out restrictions in law, leaving nothing to the vagaries of administrative decision. By the same token, they would damn the English approach, with its emphasis on administrative discretion.

B. *Property and Judicial Review.* The invidious element of this comparison can be eliminated if the differences in the two systems are viewed as reflecting different national characteristics. The philosophic cleavage between the two systems can be described on the American side as an insistence on judicial control both of legislation and of whatever flows from it: the need to feel that a certainty, capable of being established, can set legal norms which courts can apply. It means — in terms of planning laws — that the slow and difficult emergence of discretionary powers limits the scope of land-use control in the United States.

The roots of this intellectual strain can be traced to Jeremy Bentham. It may be objected that Bentham wrote not as a lawyer but as a propagandist, and, further, that the political theories he wished to see embodied in legislation led to laissez faire, which has, in turn, proven defective. A graver objection is that the test of predictability and objectivity deducible from Bentham's definition of property is, in reality, an implicit judgment in favor of enforcement through a court, for it can never be satisfied by the exercise of discretionary administrative powers.

But judicial review is not the only means of safeguarding liberty or property. Lawyers may be too used to looking only through their legal spectacles, for situations which satisfy all the legal tests may, in reality, cause loss of liberty. Conversely, political controls may protect liberty and property as courts can not. If, instead of starting with a priori definitions and then seeing how far the facts fit them, the analysis would begin with the facts and build up from them, it would show that private property in land exists in the United Kingdom despite the existence of arbitrary powers to control land use. This would be more apparent but for the tendency of the law to view property as a matter of title or conveyancing and to overlook the content of a right of ownership. From the latter perspective, it is clear that ownership never was an absolute or unrestricted right and, moreover, that many of the restrictions in England today conform to a test of predictability and objectivity.

C. *Limited Review*. Somewhere between unbridled administrative discretion and rigid judicial control lies still another, middle of the road possibility, one which would provide review not of legislation but under legislation. An example is administrative control, which applies a generalized standard set in a document having legal effect. The review could be judicial, but this is not essential. Another approach is exemplified by Canada's use of separate tribunals which both review administrative law and decide policy questions; zoning laws may be rejected either on legal or policy grounds, and an aggrieved citizen may apply to a tribunal for an order directing a local council to amend its by-laws.

Proponents of the middle road often claim that if England is not already traveling on it, she is headed toward it. The 1932 Town and Country Planning Act created a surfeit of certainty and predictability. In attempting to remedy the resulting dearth of flexibility, the 1947 act may have gone too far in the other direction. But insofar as that act aimed at economic factors — and this was its primary focus — the excess could and should be corrected. Subsequent experience with the 1947 act has shown that with a little effort the governing principles — and to some extent the rules — could be articulated to provide a yardstick for the exercise of discretionary powers. Both countries, then, are moving toward a central position, the United States tending to become a little less rigid, and Great Britain tending to insist less upon flexibility.

Moreover, the two systems are closer together than appears from any sharp distinction drawn between rules and policies. The dichotomy wrongly implies that rules are comparatively rigid and that policies are highly flexible and incapable of definition or evolution in the context of the rules. Such a notion overlooks the fact that rules in American law permit substantial leeway as to what administrative agencies may do and that judicial review may not be nearly as close and as tight as presupposed. On the other hand, despite administration in terms of policy, the British system may resemble a system of planning through rules, if the policies' content is made specific enough.

D. *The Special Case of the "Area."* The thesis and antithesis developed thus far tend to regard American planning controls as little more than zoning regulations. But latter-day Smith-Benthamites also give their approval to urban development laws. This is not by way of exception, but on the theory that such laws do not conflict with the rights of private property even when their authority is invoked to force sales by unwilling property owners at prices determined by third parties. The justification for this position stresses the relevance of "area." A proposal involving an entire area is distinguishable from single-lot development by two characteristics. One is a heightened sensitivity to incompatible uses. The other is that an individual, by "holding out," by refusing to sell his one parcel, can block the entire project, or, alternatively, siphon off a disproportionate amount of the profit.

These distinctions are the basis of the rationalization for compelling the minority to sell: redevelopment, which by stimulating development in one area can enhance the welfare of the entire city, should not be stopped by one recalcitrant. Historical precedent has been sought in the improvement districts of the nineteenth century and the enclosure laws of an even earlier period. In both cases, whether to force the building of a sidewalk or the rearrangement of ownership, the majority was permitted to interfere with the minority's free choice. The apologia of both actions was that the individual's decision affected large numbers of people besides himself. A further consideration, operative today, is that a planning scheme calling for large residential developments will prove ineffective if developers can more easily buy and develop single lots. This last is urged not as a justification for planning controls, but as proof that as long as an economy is geared to individual action, even within an over-all planning system, predictability and certainty are essential for its functioning. However, the evidence on this point is equivocal. On the one hand, the English experience suggests that private developers there prefer to undertake projects approved in advance rather than to seek approval of a project from an official. They too may be reluctant to invest in development schemes which can be frustrated by a change in official attitudes. On the other hand, when a change in planning direction is indicated, the private sector of the economy benefits from the greater speed of administrative action and avoids the delay of invoking the legislative process to amend a rigid structure.

A historical view discloses further paradoxes. The emphasis in the English Law of Property Act of 1925 on transferability of land suggests a contemporary view of land as fungible. This contrasts with the feudal perspective, in which land represented family solidarity, status, and strength, with particular attachment to specific parcels of land. Today, money is a fair exchange for the land an individual holds as an investment. When easy alienation of land is fostered so that it can enter commerce in the aid of economic development, the uniqueness of any particular land is de-emphasized. But, as was suggested earlier, land planning assumes that land is tied to land. When dealing with the reconciliation of conflicting values, the unique location of particular plots creates values not easily measurable in terms of money.

The definition of liberty to mean certainty or predictability renders reliance on the market mechanism and freedom of consumers' choice consistent with approval of urban redevelopment programs allowing for the forced acquisition of property held by those who choose not to come into the program. This reconciliation is possible although in every — or almost every — local election regarding a slum clearance program, the dwellers of the slum have voted against the program. For one of the causes of slum conditions is government activity which distorts the operation of the market mechanism. For example, tax laws are so devised that the dweller in the slum does not pay the full cost of the slum's upkeep. He wants to live there because it is cheaper for him, and it is cheaper for him because the city is paying part of his cost. Eliminate this saving, and he may well choose not to live there. Whatever the rationalization, however, the net effect of the compulsory acquisition is a diminished area of consumer choice.

Once the principle of sacrificing consumer choice — regardless of justification — is accepted, the distinction between the central planning of England and the more or less private schemes exemplified by American urban redevelopment programs becomes blurred. This blurring is accentuated by the variety of methods employed in the United States. Slum clearance programs, for example, often combine private choice with government coercion. In one instance in New York City, the public authority purchased some plots at prices lower than would have been paid in condemnation proceedings; those prices were then used as evidence of the value of the property acquired by condemnation. In Pittsburgh, the people on one selected block were permitted to retain their land by carrying out their own redevelopment program. Elsewhere, redevelopment authorities have induced property owners to improve their land by threatening to take the property if they do not.

The differences also lessen upon closer scrutiny of the English system. The difficulties which English developers encounter in executing an area project plan resemble those of their American counterparts. For example, one group bought all of its large land requirements except for one corner, whose owner refused to sell to them. The group had no compulsory powers; but the Corporation of London did. The developers opened negotiations with the Corporation to obtain public condemnation to be followed by resale to the private group. The plan did not need to be carried out because the possibility that it would be, succeeded where chaffering in the free market had failed. The probable reasons for the reluctance of both the English buyer and the English seller to have the powers of government intervene can easily be imagined, and are much the same as would have moved their American counterparts. The more interesting attitude of the government could as easily have been that of an American authority. Despite its determination to act, the English council was still troubled by questions inherent in condemnations of this type. Public moneys are used to buy land without any expectation of return; here land would be purchased only to make possible its subsequent acquisition by private persons who would then reap the return attributable both to it and to the much larger area which they had already acquired privately.

This analysis of liberty thus leads to the somewhat curious result that "a little" government control may do as much violence to principles of laissez faire, and even more to principles of equality, than would "a lot." The holdout is, after all, perfectly consistent with laissez-faire theory. The first parcels are bought up cheaply because the supply exceeds the demand. As the supply diminishes relatively, the price goes up. Equilibrium is reached when the man seeking to buy can do so at a price which leaves him some profit — otherwise he is not going to buy — and the man seeking to sell is getting what he conceives is the maximum price. Forcing the sale at some lower price violates laissez faire because it is an interference with the free operation of the market. And if — as in the London case — the private developer acquires all but one of the interests in the block, how can a public authority then fairly use its compulsory power to take the holdout property at a price determined by a standard different from that used in the voluntary sales?

This then becomes the grave issue: on what terms the acquiring authority should make the condemned land available to the private developer. The issue is avoided, of course, when government consumes the entire pie: if authorities start by declaring an area to be a comprehensive development area, they will buy all the interests, they will buy them all compulsorily, and they will buy them all on the same basis of valuation. Whether they then redevelop themselves or let or sell the property to a private developer, the net result satisfies the equitable criterion of comparable misery on the part of all the old owners, and comparable profit or not on the other side. This problem of equalizing the burdens and benefits of planning is among the most vexatious still to be resolved.

Notwithstanding the growing similarity between the two systems resulting in part from increased activity under United States urban renewal laws, it can be argued that the price mechanism is one safeguard against the danger that the redevelopment process in the United States will engulf the rest of the free-enterprise system with results indistinguishable from the British system of over-all planning. The cost to the public authority would be prohibitive. *Quaere,* however, whether cost may not be an accelerator rather than a brake because of our two-level government. Localities compete to a certain extent for the federal money which compensates for urban redevelopment. Thus, instead of encouraging prudence and concern, high costs may motivate the state or local government to hasty use of eminent domain lest the pot be exhausted by others before it has acted.

While it seems clear that the two systems are growing more alike, a distinction does remain between them. That the distinction is one of degree does not lessen its significance. In this area, if anywhere, there is truth in the view that differences of degree at some point become indistinguishable from differences in kind. And even if that point is not reached by a comparison of English and American planning systems, the differences are at least too great to be dismissed as *de minimis.*

II. LAND-USE CONTROLS — LAW AND PRACTICE

An inquiry focused on the law and practice of land-use controls almost inevitably must consider the philosophical basis of the subject. The goals or values which are or should be sought by planning provide a useful standard for evaluating the detailed legislation, administrative regulations and practice, and judicial decisions. Upon such an examination interesting similarities and contrasts can be seen to emerge and, sometimes, on closer scrutiny, to converge.

A. *Legislative Structure.* The English system, in force everywhere within reach of the national law, relies largely on two control techniques: the development plan and planning controls. An important characteristic of the development plan is that it confers power on the local planning authority to acquire land by compulsory purchase for a variety of public purposes. It ranges from the exercise of statutory powers by local authorities, government departments, and public utilities, through phasing of planning projects, including comprehensive development areas, to the climactic building of new towns. The essence of the planning control is that all development — broadly defined as any material change of use — requires official permission.

The American system of land-use controls differs in that it is largely voluntary and, with its maze of statutes, structurally far more complex. Formally, the law is fragmented into zoning, subdivision, planning, and condemnation acts, often supplemented by various special acts such as those providing for historic districts or park and recreation areas. The American law also is less centralized as to its sources: in some situations the enactments of as many as four legislative bodies must be consulted in order to determine the answer to a legal question. This need to consider the interaction at least of state and local law, and possibly of other law, seems the most striking difference to Englishmen used to the unity of thought inherent in an act of Parliament. Also, the British often distinguish their own system of over-all planning from American planning on the ground that American planning consists largely of districting into zones. But this distinction becomes less important upon comparing the similarity in content and role of the English development plan and the American master (or "comprehensive" or "general") plan.

1. *The master plan.* A plan may fulfill several useful functions. It may enable the planners to obtain a democratic consensus by awakening private individuals to the need for planning and by giving them the opportunity, in public hearings, to participate in its formulation. Because town planning restricts private action, for good psychological reception and, more fundamentally, as a basic in a democratic society, it is important that the individuals affected take part in the process rather than having a plan imposed on them. The formal requirement of a plan also ensures that a

survey, a stocktaking of actual and potential land uses, will be made. Further, the plan is available to local authorities as a guide in reaching specific decisions, such as whether or not to grant planning permissions, and it is useful in deciding appeals from such decisions.

The English development plan is prepared by the local planning authority and is then submitted to the Ministry of Housing and Local Government for review and approval. The approved plan is kept up to date by local quinquennial review. Any substantial modification in the plan, whether resulting from such review or any other reason, must also be passed upon at the cabinet level. The American plan, like the English, may be legislatively prepared and adopted; or it may be prepared and adopted by the planning commission, an administrative body whose members generally hold office by appointment rather than by election.

An English development plan consists of written statements and maps. It projects future development, indicating where schools and roads should be located, for example, and it specifies permissible uses. Also it contains a wealth of statistical data about population and other factors affecting land development. It does not contain — and here it is open to criticism — explicit statements of the policies which guided the choices between alternative planning decisions. American plans show greater diversity in form, reflecting the differences in enabling legislation and also the absence of a unifying force such as state review. Like its English counterpart, an American plan may contain statements and maps and will project future public construction, but it differs in attempting to locate sites generally rather than precisely. Regulatory laws are part of the plan in some states, but they are not in a majority of jurisdictions.

2. *Basis of the plan — the survey.* The survey (whether American or British) is fundamentally a stocktaking of land uses, both present and potential. Under English law, the survey is mandatory and it is available to the public, although normally it is not considered part of the development plan. Beyond this, English commentators offer widely divergent views. Some hold that the survey is the key to understanding the plan, that is, it gives the principles and reasoning which lead to conclusions stated in the plan. Others, however, describe the survey as an undigested collection of facts, incapable of serving as a rational foundation for the plan. Moreover, this view contends that there is no underpinning of connected assumptions or principles supporting the plan, but only one or two isolated ideas which have become either politically or socially fashionable.

In the United States the relation of the factual survey to the plan generally is closer, due to the intelligence of city attorneys and the omni-presence of judicial review. The Pennsylvania practice, for example, is to view the survey — the study underlying the plan — and the plan itself as virtually synonymous. When the planner talks about "starting to plan," he is referring to his initial survey work. Similarly, when a lawyer in litigation speaks of going to the plan to support a zoning ordinance or to support a subdivision control decision, he too is referring to the survey as well as to the plan itself. Very often the survey material and the plan are combined in one document. This closeness seems so natural, or even inevitable to Americans, that one is led to wonder whether the British tendency to dissociate the two is not simply the result of the separate legal identities created to facilitate ministerial review.

3. *Legal effect.* A plan may serve as a prophecy of the future, or it may function as a legal control; it may be simply a letter to an unheeding world. In practice, it is not entirely any one of these in either country. To a limited extent the English development plan has a direct legal effect. The projection of future development may be accompanied by a designa-tion of proposed sites, carrying in its train certain legal consequences. It is, for example, the first step toward a public taking of the property; or it may become the basis of a notice to purchase — the procedure for initiating the right of reverse eminent domain which the act of 1947 gives the property owner, subject, however, to the local authority's right to "shut up rather than put up." This latter concept is not totally foreign to American law; a somewhat similar technique, for example, is incorporated in the New Jersey enabling law. Most states, however, regard the "bite" of a plan as an evil to be avoided. The common use of "generally" to qualify a direction to locate sites for future public development is an ex-ample of the reluctance to project the plan onto the controls. One expla-nation is that legislators are fearful of individuals' claims that title to their property has been clouded by the announcement of possible future acquisition.

The role of the English plan as a prophecy is also limited. This may be caused by an inadequacy of data, for facts, regardless of the merits of the fact-policy argument, unquestionably are the key to the preparation of a plan. Thus, the erroneous population trends projected in connection with plans prepared in the 1947–1951 period were based on the best source of data then available to planners — the outdated 1931 census. Inaccuracies also may accrue from too infrequent review of plans. The specific provision for periodic, quinquennial review may mean that no thorough intermediate review is made. If so, trends observed during the interim which are contrary to planning predictions are not assessed until the quinquennial review; but a decision to revise existing controls to conform to or discourage the trend may have to be made even before the plan is changed.

At best, the plan can be only a partial prophecy, stating broad general uses. Construction specifications, such as whether dwellings are to be multiple or single-occupancy, and similar determinative details, are left to be worked out at the individual application stage. Thus, even where the proposed development conforms to the plan — as, for example, a proposal to erect a one-family dwelling in a residential area — the owner may be refused permission. The act directs the Minister to pay only some heed to the plan; it does not make it binding on him. At most, the plan is a limiting factor, a check against capricious or unreasonable behavior.

Two cases, both turning on aesthetic considerations, illustrate this area of uncertainty. In one, the planning authority denied permission to erect a dwelling styled after a mosque on a site zoned for residential use. The refusal was appealed. After a lengthy discussion of tastes, the Minister affirmed the denial, concluding that a mosque-like dwelling would be so out of keeping with the area as to constitute a classic instance of bad neighborliness. In the other case, differing only in that the proposed structure was modern, the Minister decided that he ought not to stand in the way of developing architecture, young architects, or the modern approach, and consequently allowed the building to go through.

At worst, a plan may decline to prophesy at all. One plan labels a large area simply as "outstanding landscape value." Numerous plans, particularly for rural areas — which cover quite a large proportion of the country — are nothing but existing land-use maps. Then there are those, such as the Kent Development Plan, which contain quite formidable proposals, but leave by far the larger part of the county "white." In this area the planning authority is uncommitted; it may deny planning permission on any basis, and it is more likely to deny permission here than in a location zoned for specified uses.

These weaknesses inhere in the prophecy, regardless of the reason for consulting the plan. However, when the aim is to glimpse the future of an entire city rather than to anticipate the result on an immediate application for development permission, more profound elements of uncertainty appear. A plan may reflect the thinking of the planning authorities accurately enough and still run counter to the intentions of one of the myriad executive departments of government. Conflicts of this kind have resulted in industrial development in areas designated on the plan as "greenbelt," or in superhighways cutting through areas slated to remain quietly residential.

Most of these difficulties arise in other planning systems as well. The white area of the British plans, for example, has its counterpart in both Canada and the United States, even though planning in the United States is often identified with zoning, and, particularly by British observers, zoning with vested rights. This identification of zoning and vested rights is one of the intellectual vestiges of the English planning experience from 1932 to 1947. During that interval, the adoption by a town of a planning scheme, as with some provisions of United States zoning ordinances, conferred an absolute right on property owners to proceed in accordance with the plan's proposals. Most localities (in fact, 96 per cent of the country) regarded this as an overly rigid commitment. Their technique of avoidance was simply not to adopt a scheme — which left them free to make *ad hoc* decisions.

The English apparently did not experiment with the techniques used in the United States for increasing flexibility. One much used device of this kind is to zone an area as unrestricted; the uncoordinated decisions of private enterprise thereafter rough out the future of the area. Once trends become discernible, the zoning ordinance is amended to establish a legal pattern based on the trends which appear to the lawmakers to hold the most promise for the optimum development of the area. This has now, by and large, been superseded by other techniques. Again, an ordinance may zone every square inch, putting in the most restricted category areas too undeveloped to disclose trends and hence to admit of proper classification. The lawmakers retain control over future development because would-be developers must obtain their permission to exploit the land for any other use. One locality using this method has amended its "agricultural zone" provision 142 times. Another technique, of relatively recent vintage, is to create a zoning use classification without precisely designating a district for the use. Zoners using this device might, for example, provide for a shopping center district within a larger zoning area, but without locating the district in advance. The district "floats" until brought down to earth by the developer who successfully competes for the opportunity to put the shopping center on his land. This method, however, is more cumbersome than necessary because it is accomplished through legislative action and amendment instead of administratively.

Although Canadian plans, binding on local governments, would seem to prophesy more accurately, the Canadians have their own variant of the white area technique, developed in response to their particular political pressures. In Ontario, for example, the provincial Minister, who was strongly in favor of municipal planning, did not have the power to impose it. The municipalities desired just as strongly to establish local zoning boards of appeal, but this power was conditional on the adoption of a plan to be centrally approved. There was thus a strong motivation on the part of municipalities to plan, and on the part of the Minister to approve. The result has been the creation of many plans, but only rarely containing more than a major road layout and some farm land specifically labeled agricultural; the balance, being unplanned, is not bound. The real thinking of these municipal planners is committed to the "top drawer" plan. Being unofficial, this document is flexible; it can be changed at a moment's notice, and for one man and not for another. There is thus considerable similarity between the three countries; yet, important differences of emphasis remain. In the United States and Canada techniques of flexibility are used only occasionally, whereas in England they form the crux of the system.

4. *Comparative evaluation.* The initial step in effective land-use control must be to condition the owner's right to build upon his first obtaining permission. For the English this is also the intermediate and last step since, although plans must be prepared, they maintain that the grant or denial of permissions must not be subordinated to the plan's proposals. The reason is mainly psychological: a sacred significance can, all too easily and quite unconsciously, attach to the plan, giving it a rigidity and a formalism which it ought not have.

The existing procedure in England assures that the plan exists as a flexible guide for those who have legal power over development; effective public hearings on the plan are then the best means to protect democratic values. Whether on an original plan or a major amendment, English hearings explore the issues thoroughly. The extent of the inquiry is suggested by a hearing held on a proposed amendment to the Cambridge development plan to permit construction of a shopping center. As always, the criterion was whether the proposal constituted "good" planning — not merely with regard to the individual lot concerned, or even in the impact on the immediate neighborhood, but in its effect on all the other sectors of the corporate territory. Specifically, the hearing took up the effect on the university, existing stores, roads, and parking facilities. It discussed rival shopping centers, whether this was to be the only shopping center, whether there was already an adequate secondary center somewhere else, and whether it would be better to expand an existing shopping center than to increase the number of shopping centers.

It should be emphasized that the grant or denial of planning permission can be justified only if based upon a plan. To order the private land market to cease operating according to its own lights, without the rational basis of a plan to support the government alternative, seems both absurd and arbitrary. And plans are useless unless there are controls to ensure conformity to them. On the other hand, the land market cannot simply be told to suspend operations without a plan to ensure the rational administration of controls. In a sense, therefore, it is meaningless to ask which is primary. But there may be some importance in the mental attitudes induced by the different ways of talking about a planning program. The relaxed approach to plans and serious attention to controls of the English permit flexible administration attuned to changing circumstances. Putting a program into effect by establishing the plan first and instituting controls only later may lead to an attitude regarding conformity to the plan as an end in itself and thus to rigid administration of controls.

B. *Coordination.* Neither the United States nor England has adopted procedures which fully coordinate development plans over the whole country. Both regard some coordination (though not necessarily total) as a desideratum. But the techniques of achieving it and the degrees of success vary.

In the United States, the enabling legislation of many states authorizes control by municipalities over land beyond their borders, typically a concentric belt of three to ten miles. Underlying this delegation of extraterritorial power is the theory that such power merely anticipates the forces of growth which someday will push the city's perimeter outward. It is, however, doubly qualified: first, although it usually includes control over new subdivisions, with very few exceptions it excludes power over zoning; second, incorporated units within the belt are excluded. In some areas, regional planning is accomplished by the voluntary coordination of plans. Also, there are an increasing number of countywide or intercounty regional planning agencies. Although some of these are privately financed, most are not; but regardless of the source of support, such agencies almost invariably are powerless to do more than advise.

Many states are actively seeking to further coordination, some by lending to localities expert and often free planning assistance in drawing up their plans. The plans are then the subject of public hearing and discussion, and the local units usually accept the state-prepared plan largely as written, although they may reject or modify it. A few others provide for some kind of state review of local planning. A great many states exercise direct control over land adjacent to major highways and the roads which provide access to them. The state's plan may not always accord with the program of an affected municipality, but it prevails; this has a unifying tendency, at least on the strips of land along major arteries. Further steps in the direction of coordination probably will be taken, but only slowly, because of the strong belief in local autonomy on these matters.

The English law has a greater present potential for coordination. It gives to the Minister responsibility for framing a consistent national land policy and the power to effectuate it by withholding approval from locally prepared development plans. There is no expressly prepared "national master plan," and it is at least questionable whether there should be one. A more explicit master plan for all of England and Wales may well be impracticable if not impossible. As a compromise, explicit but less than national (and perhaps advisory) plans might be considered, which would coordinate the plans of all localities within a single region. It should be noted on the theoretical level that local planning has a built-in check not operative in national planning. Planning mistakes which induce industry and private residents to move elsewhere damage the planner's community and will be corrected. The larger the governmental unit making the decision, the less effective is this check.

A fact complicating regional planning in the United States and Canada is that the main source of municipal funds is the property tax. Revenues literally are limited by municipal boundaries, carved out by accidents of history rather than by any rational criterion, such as an adequate tax base. Hence, while they may plan, most suburban communities in Canada and the United States lack the resources to carry out proposals which entail the expenditure of public funds. This problem is avoided to some extent in England by the system of derating industry and by a degree of nationwide planning.

A second problem is to coordinate the various levels and agencies of government so that the actions of one body are not frustrated by those of another. That this frequently happens can be well documented. In one recent instance, the Minister of Fuel and Power prevailed in the location of a power plant over a united opposition that included the Minister of Housing and Local Government. This outcome was reached because the plant could function properly only on that one site; usually the facts permit greater latitude.

Where several alternatives exist, a reasonable effort at communication could prevent difficulties. If the planning agency could not modify the programs of other departments, it could at least incorporate such programs into its plan with the least possible conflict. But in at least one instance in Canada, the institutionalization of this solution proved unsatisfactory: Toronto drew up an official plan and, in accordance with prescribed procedure, sent it to the Minister, who, before approving it, presumably sent it for comment to every provincial department, including the Department of Highways. Nevertheless, within two years the Highway Department announced that two major highways were to be run through the city in such a way as to divide it into five sections, necessitating the relocation of schools and other community facilities. When such conflicts do arise, the executive agencies tend to prevail — because they not only plan, they *do* something as well. This points to a need for some procedure for settling interministry disputes, perhaps by cabinet decision or decision by a cabinet committee.

C. *Planners*. Plainly, qualified personnel at the highest level of responsibility are essential to an effective planning system. In England, planning is vested in the hands of elected council members, who are more responsive than the appointed decision makers in the United States, since the latter are not accountable at the polls. On the other hand, just as war is too important to be left to generals, planning may be too important a matter to be left to politicians. The logic of this analogy would seem to lead to the curious conclusion that politicians may be entrusted with the life and death decisions of war but not the lesser decisions of land use. In any event, availability of trained personnel is, of course, a problem; the scarcity of planners both in the United States and in Canada may preclude compulsory planning in both countries.

III. THE INDIVIDUAL AND PLANNING: HEARINGS AND APPEALS

A particular concern of the lawyer is the impact of development plans and various planning concepts on individual property owners. Especially interesting is a comparison of the opportunities the English and American systems each afford for action by individuals, both as community members participating in the planning process and as property owners seeking or aggrieved by a particular exercise of governmental powers. Both provide such opportunities early in the planning process.

A. *Hearings on Plans and Amendments.* Both in England and in the United States, private persons may participate in the planning process at least as early as the stage of community adoption of a plan. The English Town and Country Planning Act and the enabling legislation of most states require that public hearings precede the adoption or major amendment of a plan. A planning proposal or its rejection may touch off a public inquiry. In England, prior to the Minister's report on a proposed amendment, anyone with sufficient standing may request that the entire plan be reconsidered with full-dress adversary proceedings. Standing in this context is two-dimensional. One is the right to initiate a hearing; the other is the right to participate in a hearing in process. The initiation of a hearing is the more limited right.

Permissions, when granted, usually run with the land. Occasionally, personal permissions are granted, as are permissions limited in time. This might be the case, for example, if permission were requested in an area which is expected to be redeveloped in the foreseeable future; planners might be willing to give only a temporary permission to a particular individual rather than one generally applicable to the land. A limitation particularly pertinent here is that individuals who do not have a material interest in the land, at least to the extent of being a "prospective purchaser" (which covers a multitude of optimisms), may not apply for development permission.

Official practices in the United States are less clear. The nonconforming-use cases generally hold it illegal to grant a permission personal to the applicant. The applicant must have some connection with the land, even though in most states this means nothing more than an option to purchase, which is satisfied by the conditional contract of sale typical in these situations. In form, it is the seller who usually makes the application. In fact, the application almost always will be processed by either the seller or purchaser, whoever has the greater political influence.

In neither country do even these nominal limitations apply to the right to participate in a planning hearing, which, at least in theory, is public in the fullest sense. Anyone and everyone may attend. And in England, they apparently do, if the figures stated are a reliable indication. Thus, hearings on the development plan for the County of London elicited 6,000 objections, and hearings on the plan for Kent frequently were attended by as many as 1,500 or 2,000 persons. Completed plans are published, and some, such as the London County Plan, have become best sellers. American hearings generally do not provoke the same lively interest and participation.

The effectiveness of a liberal standing rule and broad, public inquiry depends on the adequacy of notice given to persons who may be interested in the outcome of a planning proposal. Greater headway has been made in England in this area too, partly because of the wide publicity given the planning process by the Ministry during and after the passage of the 1947 act, and partly because the exigencies of their situation have made landowners conscious of town planning. When a hearing on the plan for a particular area is announced, it becomes a common topic of conversation. Absentee landowners are advised of it by their local agents. The plan itself is on display for an appreciable period, at least four weeks as a rule. Generally, all objections will be entertained at the hearing, even those not interposed within the liberal two-month period allowed by law. These notice requirements apply only to major planning changes, but there is probably adequate publicity even of lesser proposals.

Some American jurisdictions have evolved a superior notice procedure for pending development proposals, one where neighbors have standing to protest. A proposal may be objectionable to the people living adjacent to the development site even if it is only a minor departure from the plan. English law had nothing comparable until 1959. The planning act of that year narrowed the gap by authorizing the Minister to require advertisement of applications. Thus far, he has required it for only a small category of "bad neighbors": refuse dumps, public swimming pools, and dance halls. Disappointment has been professed at the sparing exercise made of this authority, but there also have been complaints by applicants, not without merit, of undue delay caused by too many objections. The Minister's policy may be an attempt to strike a balance between the right to notice and the need to avoid obstructionist tactics by private planning councils made up of little pressure groups of neighbors.

An alternative or supplementary notice procedure would require a sign on the property itself stating the use for which application is pending. This would ensure that notice is given to people close to the property. A political solution — voting out those responsible for bad planning decisions — would be unrealistic. Experience in England indicates that members of a town council seldom are unseated because of objections to the grant or refusal of planning permissions.

B. *Review*. Common to both countries is the developer aggrieved by the partial or total refusal of his application for building clearance: in the United States, for a variance, special exception, or subdivision approval; in England, for the ubiquitous planning permission. This, in turn, raises the problem of review.

1. *Feasibility of judicial review.* The contributors to this volume join issue on the appropriate role of the judiciary in a planning program. The alignment along national lines suggests, as the authors themselves note, that the decisive factor is less the merits than habituation to the institutions of one's own country. Another element may be the extent to which aesthetics enters into planning controls. While a judge may have opinions on aesthetic matters, and particular judges may even be well qualified to make them, such qualification is not a requisite of the office. Their opinions, therefore, are not entitled to any significant weight. Since the aesthetic element looms large in English town planning, the courts there appropriately play a far more limited role in planning procedures than they can in this country, where the aesthetic element generally is nominal.

What really is important, of course, is not the name of the reviewing body, but the limits on the scope of review — that the decision of the planning authorities not be reversed simply because the reviewer would have reached a different outcome. This is the rationale of the American judiciary for allowing administrative decisions to stand if they are at all reasonable. More and more, the English Minister is manifesting a similar attitude in reviewing local decisions, affirming plans which he would not himself have adopted. There is, however, a common possible danger: carried to excess, the policy of restraint could reduce review to a hollow formality in all but the most outrageous cases.

2. *Review in England.* The establishment of a satisfactory review process naturally is vital to the English system, under which, subject to general development order dispensations, planning permissions are needed for everything from putting a gate on the garden fence to constructing a multimillion-pound factory. And two factors operating today make it even more crucial. First, the recent spectacular rise in land values has augmented *pro tanto* the value of permissions, creating a dangerous and difficult situation. The shortage of land also makes for troublesome competition among governmental agencies: the housing authority wants a site to ease the housing shortage; the education authority wants to build a much needed primary school; the highway authority sees the same site as ideal for a bus depot.

As with American law, a basic aim of English law is to provide a "reasonable and fair system" for adjudicating any dispute. The elements essential for satisfactory review of planning appeals are basically the same as for any other category of cases. Those concerned want the relevant facts to be established and understood; they want assurance that opinions will be received and considered; they want a clear explanation of the reasons for a final decision; and they want the policy underlying particular decisions to be made reasonably clear, so that whether or not they approve of the policy, they can understand the issues involved.

The most common criticism of English planning appeals is that the result reached and the facts proved too rarely have any apparent relation. In one case the Minister rejected an appeal on the ground that numerous alternative sites were available, although the unrefuted evidence showed that all the suggested sites actually were developed and unavailable. Another criticism is that although the report to the Minister usually will inform him of all the arguments stressed during the inquiry, there is no process for ensuring their communication. Again, it is complained that the Minister "explains" his appeal decision in a writing, which, if not quite a form letter, often contains little more than routine phraseology or a reference to the arguments deemed persuasive in the appended inspector's report.

The 1959 act created a statutory right to contest the Minister's decisions in court, albeit a closely circumscribed one. The decision still need not articulate the facts and policy which underlie it — what the ordinary man most wants to know. But it may be reviewed for procedural defects, *ultra vires,* or noncompliance with some requirement of the regulations under the act. However, even where the local authority or Minister is found to have been remiss in one or more of these respects, the court, perhaps for practical reasons, is empowered only to quash the erroneous result, not to reverse it. Since the remedy is so unsatisfactory, few people seek judicial review. The rationale of planning appeal decisions may not be any more obscure than the basis of decision in other kinds of appeal. The inability or unwillingness to be honest and articulate in stating reasons — generally the cause of the obscurity — probably is no more prevalent in this area than in others. In the case of planning appeals, however, the openness of the proceedings focuses community attention on the decisions and their defects.

Closely related is the desire for a greater degree of predictability. There are, of course, some appeals even now which obviously are going to succeed, as where local authorities wish to shift to the Minister responsibility for permitting a proper but locally unpopular development. In other cases, the local authority may prefer to have the Minister resolve a dispute between it and its delegate rather than decide the dispute for itself. The creation of a clear, consistent policy, so essential to prediction, has become more difficult recently by reason of a change in the internal structure of the Ministry. The previous appeal structure, which was unitary, had tended naturally toward uniform application of policy; the appellate function of the Ministry now has been divided among eight offices, each having independent jurisdiction over a geographic region. There is nonetheless a tendency toward greater predictability, although it is painfully and unnecessarily slow.

Studies of appeal decisions reveal patterns based on policy grounds. If a proposal can come under the umbrella of existing policy, it can "get away with murder." One general policy seems to be that planning applications are to be given the benefit of the doubt; although a particular use may not be the most desirable one, unless it injures an acknowledged interest, permission will be granted.

The Franks Committee report on the administrative aspects of city planning may be regarded as a "lawyers' counterrevolution," attempting to introduce procedures which would increase the predictability of state action in regard to land use. Thus the Committee recommended that an appellant be permitted to argue that the facts upon which the inspector based his opinion were wrong. This particular proposal failed to win parliamentary support, perhaps because it would have required a substantial recasting of the entire system. The changes actually wrought by the legislation based on the Committee's recommendations are relatively slight. Previously, the planning authority was required by law, and the Minister was moved by policy to explain publicly, albeit imprecisely, the reasons for their respective decisions. Now as a result of the Franks Committee, the inspector's report is also available. This tends to increase the pressure on the Minister to explain more precisely the reasons for any decision contrary to the report. This change is for the better if it does no more than bring home to the Minister the importance of his decision to those affected and their desire to know why he disagreed with the inspector. And, as in some American administrative procedures, the examiner's report, even though not accorded legal weight, can be a useful basis for argument.

The English contributors agree here that predictability is far greater in court proceedings, such as nuisance cases or suits to have covenants declared unenforceable, than in ministerial proceedings. The reasons judicial and ministerial proceedings should so differ are not immediately apparent. True, planning appeals may be broader in scope than the typical nuisance case, since they weigh whether the proposed use is good for the community as a whole. But in nuisance cases, too, the judge must balance the conveniences and equities, and consider the social consequences of enjoining the erection of a factory in a residential area. The same sort of inquiry and value weighing is required of a court as the English Town and Country Planning Act requires of the Minister.

One possible distinction is that the judge's training leads him to inquire into the facts as a first step, while, for whatever reason, the Minister does not always consider the facts before considering what policy should be applied. In addition, the judge has a knowledge of the law; he understands the rules of law, sees their relevance, and hence can apply them in disposing of a case. Planning appeals are heard by inspectors who seldom have legal training. Legal arguments can be impressed on them only with difficulty, and even then might be omitted from the report or, if included, be incoherent; this has made for dissatisfaction with the act of 1960, which injects the inspector into appeals from enforcement notices. Thus far, the best way of coping with this problem has been to prepare a memorandum on points of law in advance.

More generally, simply trying a case before a judge encourages the use of precedent and increases predictability, while the appeal procedure, despite a superficial resemblance, is not assimilable to the judicial process because it is primarily concerned with planning and planning policy rather than with legal rules. The distinctions may simply be those characteristics differentiating the administrative process, which attempts to develop and further a policy, from the judicial process, which emphasizes the dispensation of equity in the particular case.

However, the contrast should not be overstated. Both the Minister and local authorities have been sympathetic to cases of personal hardship. Where an application is "on the razor's edge as a matter of planning policy," permissions sometimes are given to avoid hardship. And the "Brandeis brief," which argues the facts as hard or harder than the law, is a much used weapon in courtroom warfare. Perhaps then, the crucial factor is not personnel, but policy. The transfer of planning appeals to the courts, in that case, would not affect the result greatly because it would not eliminate the policy questions.

3. *Review in America.* Judicial review of planning decisions in the

United States aspires to the same high standard of English review procedures, with the additional requirement, only implicit in the English system, that planning policies should be fair: public gains should not be realized at excessive cost to individual landowners. The problem here, too, is to strike a proper balance between flexibility and the rule of law, between the disciplines of planner and judge. Any program for the control of land use must have flexibility; and this conflicts with the constitutional principle of equal treatment for those similarly situated. But where the English system errs on the side of flexibility, if at all, the American system quite definitely errs on the side of the rule of law. The lack of flexibility derives from the assumption of zoning programs that municipal legislation can describe the land uses appropriate to a specific area definitively — and in advance. In theory, the cumbersome amendment process is the only procedure for gaining consent to a use not permitted by the existing ordinance. This may involve persuading the local planning board that the proposal is justified from a planning point of view. Usually the developer must next persuade the legislature of the political wisdom of the amendment as well. If he passes these two tests, he may still have to submit to a third: amendments to ordinances or by-laws often are attacked in court on constitutional grounds, and have been struck down in a number of cases as "spot zoning," primarily because the area affected was relatively small.

In practice, of course, flexibility enters through the back door. Local enforcement agencies may simply ignore violations of the zoning ordinances in the belief that they are thereby furthering public policy. Despite the increased flexibility, this is a dubious practice. It produces decisions taken without adequate consideration of the issues and without public attention being focused; more generally, it disregards the values inherent in the rule of law. An unhealthy flexibility also has resulted from perversion of the zoning variance. Its original function was to avoid constitutional problems by affording relief to landowners who would be subjected to unique hardship by the application of the ordinance. At least on the local administrative level, however, the variance procedure has been used to satisfy the needs, real or apparent, of individual property owners; at times, for example, variances are granted solely because the applicant is a widow.

This kind of flexibility, of course, is not related to planning considerations. The administering boards are made up of lay members, who have neither an orientation toward planning themselves nor the advice of a professional staff such as is available to a planning agency. Legal considerations are equally scanted, since the board does not possess the attitude of the judiciary toward constitutional values. If it does formulate coherent policies, they may be inconsistent with those applied to zoning exceptions administered by a different body. Thus, from any point of view, the zoning appeals board is an inadequate institution. Some localities are considering the adoption of a unitary administration, whether by a statewide board of zoning review or by a professional administrator acting locally.

Courts have been less sympathetic to the need for flexibility and have counteracted to some extent the effect of administrative deficiencies. A grant of permission by the board of appeals can be contested in the courts, which generally construe the applicable statute more strictly than do the boards. The courts have ruled out the use of variances as devices for making "charitable gifts to the needy" or for injecting planning considerations. Although this is still the judicial attitude toward variances, there is a trend in other areas toward more sophisticated evaluation of planning problems and greater hospitality to techniques for increasing flexibility. Nevertheless, the insistence on strict adherence to the rule of law remains widespread and works to the detriment of flexibility.

Judicial review of planning is carried on largely in the state courts; since the *Euclid* and *Nectow* cases in 1926 and 1928, the United States Supreme Court has not considered any zoning cases. The state courts do not all follow the same approach. Many, like the English courts, will go no further than the question of *ultra vires:* so long as a decision does not violate the terms of the statute, it is upheld. Other courts, however, will make their own analyses of the facts and reach independent planning conclusions.

The impediments to effective reform in most states are not constitutional. Both the state courts and the Supreme Court have sustained legislative programs providing only the vaguest kind of standard to guide the exercise of broad discretionary powers. Although strong constitutional objections could be made to a system like the English one, with no statutory standards at all controlling the authority's right to deny development permissions, a similar result could be reached without such objections under a statute stating only very general objectives or standards. Indeed, available mechanisms probably are sufficiently flexible. The real root of the difficulty is inertia, an unwillingness to make use of them. Badly needed is a legislative body which responds to problems as they emerge and courts which carry out the legislative response consistently with the public interest.

It may be that too many questions in the United States are determined by the adversary process and judicial decision. In particular, it may be that the courts are depended upon too much as the guardians of ultimate values; too little attention is paid to them at the legislative and administrative levels. While English administrators voluntarily concern themselves with the protection of these values, American policy makers tend to assume that they need not be very interested in fairness to the individual because he will be protected adequately by the courts.

C. *The Role of the Expert.* Whether the forum is judicial or administrative, the procedure employed should establish the relevant facts and the appropriate policies. The planner may qualify as an expert on either or both questions, and he may appear as an expert witness or as an advocate for the views of his employer — the town council in England or the local legislative body in the United States. Because his testimony has great potential influence on the outcome, the capacity in which he speaks should be made clear in every instance. Although the problem is the same in both countries, it probably has greater urgency in England because the planning process as a whole is more in the mainstream of national development there. If witnesses produced by local authorities under color of expertise give biased evidence, substance is lent to lingering suspicions of unfairness, and the program is brought into disrepute.

Certain procedures in the English system are designed to prevent confusion as to the capacity in which the planner speaks when he testifies at hearings. One is a prohibition against the appearance as an advocate of any person who might be called as a witness. Whether for this reason or not, the planning authority almost always has present at an inquiry both an advocate — a barrister, solicitor, or officer of the corporation — to present its case, and a planning witness to give evidence. And, since the town council follows its expert's advice in most instances, his opinion usually conforms to the council's position. When they disagree, the council may call an outside expert or one of its own officers, or it may present no evidence at all. If the planning expert is called as a witness, he generally will state his opinion honestly, even if it conflicts with the council's decision. Based on this experience, it would seem most accurate to regard the planner as an ordinary expert witness called to state facts and give an opinion, notwithstanding the fact that he is employed by one side. As a witness he is subject to cross-examination, and in Canadian proceedings, is often asked to speak for the other side.

D. *Enforcement.* The individual is brought into direct — at times, painful — contact with the machinery of planning through its efforts at enforcement. Institutionalized nonenforcement such as exists in the United States has equally important, direct, and immediate consequences, even though he may be completely unaware of them.

In England, the major difficulties of enforcement stem from the attempt to have a single, comprehensive system of control cover everything from the most trivial offense to the most serious, and from the most obvious to the highly debatable. As a consequence, the controls have been surrounded with such safeguards as the right to appeal, which produce endless litigation and frustration for the planning authorities. Nevertheless, enforcement has not created a great problem, largely because the procedure has not had to be used very much; the mere threat of enforcement is sufficient in most cases. Developers usually do not use their own money, and they cannot borrow the necessary funds for projects which do not have planning clearance. In twelve years the London County Council never has had to take enforcement action involving the removal of a building or a substantial part of one. Enforcement measures have been applied largely against lesser infractions, such as changes of use without permission. If the change yields a quick profit greater than the cost of delaying tactics, it can be financially worthwhile to go on with it until the enforcement notice becomes effective.

In general, there is no problem of discovering the violations. Building plans must be submitted for approval, and construction is supervised by inspectors. These controls are so well accepted by the community that planning authorities quickly learn of any substantial building operation without employing hordes of enforcement officials. Here again, the problem arises chiefly with respect to changes of use. As to these, planning authorities rely largely on neighbors, who, if adversely affected by the illegal use, usually will complain in writing either to the planning authority or to a member of Parliament. The planning authorities, subject to ministerial control, have power to eliminate nonconforming uses even where the user has existing-use rights. But this power is strongly limited by budgetary restraints; after four years, a use can be restricted only on payment of compensation.

Some light is shed on successful enforcement by England's two outstanding failures — caravans (trailers) and London drinking clubs. From the beginning both the local authorities and the Minister evinced a distaste for caravans as a supposedly substandard form of living accommodation. Large numbers of people nevertheless were determined to avail themselves of the advantages offered by caravan homes, and caravan camp operators had every incentive to cater to the demand. Since there were no legitimate sites, numerous violations came into existence, with which the enforcement machinery could not, and in some instances would not, cope. The basic error was the refusal to accept the presence of caravans and to provide for them in a positive, practical way. Only after the situation had become aggravated, and under great public pressure, did the Minister initiate an investigation. The report concluded that the available evidence showed that caravans, far from being substandard, were often healthier accommodations than the smaller type of house. Recent legislation, in effect, abandons planning controls as a method of regulating caravans and makes keeping them without a license an independent offense.

The stubborn persistence of drinking clubs has been attributed to the fact that, as with caravan camps, the modest investment required can be recouped with profit during the more than a year needed to obtain sufficient evidence to close a club. The real difficulty simply may be that planning controls are not the proper means for policing illicit drinking. Public houses long have been required to obtain adjustor's licenses and never have had to be regulated by planning controls. Nor are planning controls used to deal with statutorily offensive trades, which have been controlled on public health grounds since 1875.

In contrast, outstanding success has marked the attempt to control advertising. Strong public support backed the program. Planning authorities were empowered to remove advertisements without paying any compensation (except for removal costs in the case of well-established advertisements). Despite the power of the advertising industry, the battle for regulation has been won with little likelihood of future renewal of the struggle. The industry's capitulation was largely a common-sense recognition that it would be foolish to disregard public sentiment against vulgar advertising in attractive places. It saw that widespread disapproval of an advertisement might produce the reverse effect of that intended by the advertiser; unless advertising was self-policed, people using public thoroughfares would feel that advertising was being forced upon them and, out of resentment, might develop a negative reaction. The industry made a virtue of necessity and restricted outdoor advertising to places where it would be acceptable.

In addition, the advertising industry was consulted extensively in the framing of regulations. Consequently, it accepted them more readily and also accepted their actual administration. This cooperation now is so complete that a private code might effectively supersede the regulations. When coupled with the difficulty of obtaining financing for illegal uses, this suggests the possibility of moving from legal sanctions to private enforcement. It raises the conjecture that enforcement of planning controls in the United States could be accomplished through private institutions such as title insurance and mortgage companies, rather than through the less desirable and more costly system of inspectors who are part of the planning establishment.

The success with advertising suggests the potential power of enlightened public opinion, especially when contrasted with the failure to control the popular caravans. Enforcement is easy to the extent that planning corresponds with consumer demand; if there is no correspondence, enforcement is impossible. Of course, this is not the whole story. It is easier to remove an advertisement than a caravan furnishing human shelter. It is also cheaper, if the caravan site has become a nonconforming use, since the owner then is entitled to the difference between the value of the land for agricultural use and its value as a caravan site. Finally, it should be recognized that the machinery for enforcing advertisement controls differs significantly from the machinery of ordinary planning control; it is not simply a case of the same machinery working differently in two areas.

American experience with advertising controls has hardly been marked by signal success. The major obstacle is the power of the advertising industry. Its employment — only about 50,000 persons — is not commensurate with the tremendous political pressure it exerts, largely through an army of lobbyists, especially in the state legislatures. A second obstacle is public indifference despite the American Automobile Association's championing of billboard regulation. As a result, forty years of attempted control have achieved only a feeble licensing mechanism except in some cities, notably in Wisconsin and California, where advertising has been restrained, at least in residential areas.

This failure is even more depressing in the light of the offer of financial incentives by the federal government to states developing control programs. In 1958, federal legislation increased the federal contribution to highway construction in states which prohibited private advertising within

660 feet of interstate highways. Alternatively, if the state itself acquired the advertising rights within that area, this cost would be paid in the regular federal-state ratio of nine to one; the acquisition of such rights, therefore, would cost a state only ten cents out of every dollar. One problem in the acquisition of advertising rights is that no one knows what they are worth; they have been appraised at all kinds of fictitious values. In some cases, a fee interest in the land could almost be bought for the price asked for so-called "rights of view." So far only four or five states have qualified for federal participation.

Some states have attempted to deal with highway advertising by other means. Since billboard advertising must be seen to be effective, it is almost by definition a distraction to the motorist. Safety studies were made in an attempt to prove that the advertising was therefore a hazard, but the advertisers claimed, perhaps correctly, that they were inconclusive. Arguments based on common-law principles such as the excessive use of easements by the billboards detracting from the value of public passage, or that there is no "right" to be seen from the highway, have not been extended by the courts here. The right to privacy remains too esoteric a ground for control. Consequently, when cases do reach the courts, the usual argument for control is based on aesthetic considerations. And although the courts are at last beginning to recognize in connection with urban redevelopment that aesthetics may be a sufficient justification for government control, that rationale has not yet been applied to the billboard problem.

IV. REGULATION AND TAKING OF PROPERTY UNDER PLANNING LAWS

A large part of the problem of compensation arises, paradoxically enough, because planning creates benefits in the form of increases in market value. If these benefits are not redistributed to compensate for the losses inflicted by the same planning controls, inequities result. The need for flexible planning is an aggravating factor, for *ad hoc* treatment on a lot-by-lot basis creates the possibility of special treatment on the basis of favoritism or political corruption. The continued failure to find a means of equating the gains and losses in the market caused by land-use controls could jeopardize the whole planning system.

Compensation for all losses, even were it practicably possible, is not a panacea, as the experience of both countries proves. It does not assure popular acceptance of planning: English advertising controls, although not compensated except by amortization, were enforced without difficulty, while caravan controls aroused much adverse criticism even with compensation. Nonmonetary losses cannot be compensated, as, for example, the quasi-civil right to retain one's home recognized by the lower court in *Berman v. Parker*. Acceptance of compensation in some cases may even generate new problems, such as whether a compensable loss is caused by the mere designation of private property for future public acquisition and development.

Two aspects of the English compensation system of particular interest are, first, the procedures for taking property and fixing compensation; and, second, the basis of compensation. The procedure for taking land is essentially an adversary process closely resembling a planning appeal. Both sides often are represented by counsel, and neighboring landowners may come in to have their say. The "political" element in this adversary proceeding is illustrated by the kinds of considerations which may be introduced at the hearing. In a taking for a new highway, for example, it may be argued that the highway is not needed, or that there is better land for it elsewhere — in short, anything at all except the question of compensation, which must be left until later proceedings before the Lands Tribunal.

In the United States, too, such planning considerations are raised, but the context is legislative, not adversary, as, for instance, in hearings for federal highway takings or urban redevelopment. Where, as in New York, the terminal points of a highway are specified by statute, the only remaining question is how to join them; in such a case, of course, questions of what land is to be taken must be raised largely at the legislative level. Here, also, "politics," but in a quite different sense, often plays a regrettably large role.

Two basic differences between the systems lie in the answers each gives to the questions, first, whether or not there is a clear "better solution" for at least some locational problems; and, second, whether or not most such questions involve too complex a set of factors to admit of satisfactory judicial determination. By and large the American system rejects the assumption of a better solution and treats the questions as too polycentric for judicial determination. The English system is bottomed on the contrary convictions that the "better solution" does exist, that it can be found, albeit with difficulty, upon consideration of technical data and public policy, and that the adversary process is the best means of sifting the pros and cons even of complex and multifaceted questions. Whichever premise may be correct, there is theoretical agreement on one point:

executive agencies should not conduct the hearings held in connection with their own takings. The danger here is that the agency and the landowner will reach ex parte agreements, as sometimes occurs in the United States. One solution is the Scotch-English system, which appoints the hearing examiners from among private architects and appraisers.

In England, the determination of compensation formally begins with service on the landowner of a notice of intent to take by the government. Next, appraisers for each side negotiate, often reaching compromise agreements. If they fail to agree, the question of compensation is submitted to the Lands Tribunal. Before the case is heard, the authority may submit an offer which remains sealed until after the Tribunal makes its award. If the offer is higher than the award, the landowner pays the costs of both sides including, as is the English practice, lawyers' fees; if the offer is not high enough, the authority bears the costs.

The Lands Tribunal, composed both of appraisers and lawyers, conducts its proceedings in adversary fashion. Each side may and often does call expert witnesses, who are subject to cross-examination. The adversaries now must exchange valuations before the hearing, a departure from previous practice, under which valuation was not disclosed because it was considered part of the evidence. The information disclosed includes the appraiser's working figures and comparisons with neighboring land. Consequently, valuations tend to be fairly realistic — often even approximating true value. This combination of flexible procedures and judicial safeguards has earned the Tribunal the high esteem of those who have appeared before it.

The absence of a written constitution allows the English system greater flexibility in deciding when to compensate. Parliament makes the sole and final policy judgment as to what is fair. If it provides for compensation, then there is compensation; if not, then there is none. Once it has been determined that there shall be compensation, the amount is set, since *Harvey v. Crawley Development Corp.*, by a broad version of "common-law damages." Before that decision, awards were based on meticulous analyses of the compensation statutes. Now the courts fix awards at amounts that will compensate not only for loss of the land itself, but also for disruption of business, loss of good will, and removal expenses. The aim is full compensation for the whole change in the landowner's position before and after the taking.

The American system, by contrast, devotes considerable ingenuity to distinguishing between compensable takings and noncompensable regulation. Never easy, the distinction is rendered increasingly difficult because the techniques of purchase and regulation no longer are confined to distinct, traditional areas and methods, but overlap in considerable extent. This has been made possible by the relaxation of judicial restraints. Thus, the "public purpose" limitation on compensable takings used to require a showing that a harmful land use would be eliminated; it now suffices if the purchase will promote future good by promoting development. This opens the way to the public purchase of development rights in land to preserve greenbelts, a technique comparable to the compensation and betterment scheme of the English act of 1947. (It does not, of course, solve the difficulties in assessing changes in value which led the Uthwatt Committee to damn appraisers as fools, incapable of distinguishing one element of value from another.) Also, it offers an alternative to such traditional regulatory techniques used to attain much the same ends as large lot zoning and tax incentives. Conversely, the *ad hoc* treatment of individual parcels, formerly held discriminatory if uncompensated, is now upheld when accomplished through such regulatory techniques as zoning variances, amendments, and special exceptions. This has a dual potential. On the one hand, substitution of plot-by-plot regulation for area-wide districting can by achieving a mixture of different residential uses end the undesirable social stratification inherent in any compartmentalized approach. On the other hand, *ad hoc* treatment, if not governed by firm standards, lends itself to discriminatory ends.

Subdivision controls, too, now substitute police power for compensation, as, for example, in the common requirement that the subdivider install roads, sidewalks, and sewers as a condition of approval. Since the cost of these improvements will be passed on to the new subdivision residents, who will benefit from them most, this approach is essentially fair. But regulation sometimes is used unfairly, as where high use classification zoning is used to prevent all development in an area, perhaps because a city intends to acquire it for a park when it has sufficient funds. This practice, quite similar to the English designation of land for future compulsory purchase, usually has been condemned by the courts as subjecting the individual landowner to unreasonable economic pressure and hardship.

Urban redevelopment and urban renewal present an interesting contrast between compensable and noncompensable controls. The redevelopment technique is to acquire the land in an area, tear down existing improvements, and develop the area anew, often by private interests under contract with the government. The renewal technique leaves the property in the hands of the present owners provided they renovate their homes or businesses to conform to the standard set for the renewal area. Here again relaxation of judicial doctrines is apparent in the courts' sanctioning the extension of powers previously limited to slum clearance cases to commercial and industrial land. Even measures to compel the reuse of open land have been upheld recently on the theory that government action is appropriate whenever land is not being used effectively for the benefit of the community.

But the most dramatic distinction between compensable and noncompensable regulation exists in the treatment of nonconforming uses which antedate the zoning ordinances prohibiting them. Courts have upheld the uncompensated prohibition of such uses when they involve only bare land, prohibited features on otherwise conforming structures, or inexpensive structures such as billboards. However, they have struck down measures to eliminate nonconforming structures of any substance unless either compensation or a period of amortization is provided.

Amortization provisions grant the owner some time in which to recoup his investment. At the end of the fixed period the structure must go, and no compensation is paid. But the length of the amortization period — in some cases as much as forty years — makes this an impractical method; and a recent New York case indicates that short amortization periods probably would not pass scrutiny by the courts. Often the real difficulty is not time, but politics: the owner of a building on which time is running out goes to the city council and receives a five-year extension, and so on ad infinitum. Moreover, during the amortization period it would not be proper under existing law to subtract the right to sell from the nonconforming user's bundle of rights — the courts have held that a property owner may not be deprived totally of the right to sell the rights in his property. Thus, the burden of removal may fall on a new owner who can argue, with some logic, that he has not had time to recoup his investment. For these reasons, amortization is an unsatisfactory solution except in removing billboards and other short-lived uses.

Another possibility is to extend the common-law doctrine of nuisance to eliminate nonconforming uses. This solution is not yet ripe for evaluation because until quite recently, proof even of "nuisance-like" nonconforming uses was deemed insufficient by the courts to establish a legal nuisance.

Legislatures and executive agencies, too, are struggling with the question of what ought to be compensable, not only as a constitutional necessity, but as a moral obligation of government. While more generous compensation may accord with prevailing ethical standards, it raises serious practical problems. Public funds are limited; every expenditure necessarily eats into the fund available for land, sewers, roads, and other facilities. Moreover, acquisition expenses, large to begin with, have an insidious way of multiplying. Today, under California law, the abutter has a compensable right of access to the road in both directions; tomorrow, this doctrine conceivably could be extended to hold that the landowner one street removed also has a compensable loss. Thus it is necessary to draw the line of compensation firmly by balancing private injury against public good.

While these questions have a decided constitutional flavor in the United States, they nevertheless resemble the issues raised by the compensation provisions of the Town and Country Planning Act. Parliament also compensates some losses and not others, and it must draw some line if there is to be any rational basis for differentiating between them. Although the only line ever articulated publicly by the English government is that of "good neighbourliness," the language of section 19 of the Act suggests an analogy to the American constitutional restraints. It confers — or recognizes — the right of an owner to compel an authority which imposes restrictions preventing any reasonable beneficial use of his land to purchase it. This terminology — "reasonable beneficial use" — is also used by American courts in defining the constitutionally created boundary between police power and eminent domain. Moreover, although the right to section 19 compensation is conditioned on the loss of the entire value of the property rather than of its development potential, this is the very standard at which the Supreme Court seemed to be aiming in the *Euclid* case. There, restriction to residential use of land bought for industrial development, causing substantial reduction in value, was held not to require compensation. That decision is clear authority for public "taking" of certain economic potential without compensation.

Despite the use of identical language, certain differences do remain between the two countries. Under *Euclid* the police power cannot validly be used to restrict all possibility of development; under section 19 of the English act, there is no right to compensation if any use can be made of the land in its present state, regardless of its development potential or lack of it. Thus, for a farmer to invoke section 19, it is not enough to show that he has been refused permission to develop; he must show that his land is not useful even as a farm. Moreover, the statute demands that the land "has become" incapable of beneficial use — that development has encircled the farm and, presumably, that small children and large dogs delight in trampling down the crops. In such a case the land has become incapable, in an economic sense, of reasonable beneficial use in its existing state, and the farmer can obtain compensation. This seems comparable to the practice under American official map laws, reserving land for future extension or widening of streets. The compromise worked out there is to give relief to a property owner who, because of a projected street widening, would otherwise be unable to develop the rest of his land beneficially. In that situation, he is given special permission to build according to the dictates of his wishes, but subject to whatever agreement he is able to work out with the adjustment board.

A slowly developing rational pattern does seem to be emerging in both countries, one which distinguishes regulation demanding compensation from that which does not. In the United States the formal process is that of a court interpreting the Constitution, while in England it is more a political one — what Parliament will enact. But even the two decisional processes are growing closer. In the United States the waning of the "public use" doctrine and the wide scope granted to state "police power" make the question of compensability more and more a legislative judgment; in England the question is moving slowly out of the political arena, as decisions are reached through a unanimity which cuts across the spectrum of political views.

Betterment poses an obverse challenge: how to tap the added increments in land value caused by public improvements and planning which otherwise would constitute a windfall to a select group in the community. Examples are the merchant within a renewal area who reaps a larger profit from his business solely because of the renewed potential of the area, or the increase in the value of property located near a new road or similar public improvement. Both countries have tried the attractive method of excess condemnation or marginal land acquisition. This contemplates taking more land than actually is needed for a public improvement, the excess to be used to protect the improvement or for recoupment. During the great railroad-building era of this country, the railroads were given parcels of land along their rights of way to sell off to those who wanted these choice locations. Again, in Boston's Back Bay, the government bought swampland, filled it in, and sold it back to private enterprise at a higher value. Despite these precedents, the legal status of excess condemnation in the United States is not entirely certain. The *Vestor* case suggests that a taking solely for recoupment may be improper, but that need not preclude the recoupment incidental to protection. The theory of this judicial limitation may be a condemnation of taking excess land as sheer profiteering, when the only purpose is to siphon off the increase in value due to public improvement. A more important limitation on this technique is a political one — the traditional fear of allowing federal, state, or local government to enter the real estate business.

Neither legal nor political barriers to the use of excess condemnation exist in England. The only obstacle is financial, since the land must be purchased before it can be resold at the augmented value. In its Notting Hill Gate improvement, for example, the London County Council was able to take a large enough area of land to assure a reasonable measure of recoupment. And it could be confident that taking the excess land to recover for the public some of the expenditure on improvements would meet not with protest, but with approval.

Frequently, the same piece of property may be both benefited and damaged by an improvement, a fact which, if not considered in fixing the award, results in unfairness. The classic case is the taking of part of a farm on the outskirts of the city for a highway. The public pays for the land taken and also for damages to the remaining property because of the severance. Then the road is built, making subdivision or commercial development feasible, so that the value of the remaining land is in fact increased, not diminished. This has led to the rule in some states that benefits accruing to property may be deducted from any award made for damages. One difficulty with this approach lies in determining what is a benefit and what sorts of benefits should be offset. Generally, it is possible to draw a rough line between "general" and "special" benefits; for example, a new road brings a general benefit in that it enables everyone, including the owner whose property was taken, to get into town faster, but it may also bring a special benefit in improving drainage on an adjacent parcel. But fine distinctions are hard to draw: a new transportation system, for example, will have an effect on many aspects of urban life, on industry, agriculture, and residences.

Another means of reaching benefits derived from public improvements is through special assessments, which transfer the cost of an improvement to the property owners benefiting from it. Subdivision controls may be viewed as a special assessment passed through the subdivider to the ultimate property owner. If so, subdivision controls would be a use of the taxing power, and not a noncompensable regulation. Historically, however, certain improvements such as schools or police stations have been financed through general taxes and not through special charges.

Some jurisdictions in the United States currently are experimenting with still another method of recoupment. They take a large area of land and sell it to private developers under an agreement to pay to the government any value added to the land by the development permission. The difficulty here, as with the excess condemnation scheme, is that the capital cost of land may be so great as to forbid large-scale acquisition. This difficulty has already been felt in England, where land values are rising rapidly. An added difficulty there is that the compensation for a planning restriction is much less than the price obtainable for an actual purchase, the difference being so striking, and at the same time so fortuitous, that legislative changes almost surely will be necessary. This kind of inequality poses a danger to the development rights schemes now being proposed in the United States. The cost of rights in land with no present development value will be minimal. But as urbanization increases and the rights to develop become valuable, the landowner who has sold his rights years before for a pittance will feel he has been unfairly treated and demand their return. This difficulty can be side-stepped by purchase of the fee interest instead of the smaller development right, with a view to leasing the land back subject to restrictions.

The greatest problem is financing acquisitions large enough in scale to provide recoupment to the public. California has used a revolving fund to purchase land for highways, replenishing it by the sale of land that has become eligible for improvement. The state expects to receive, during the next twelve years, a dividend of between twelve and fifteen dollars for each dollar invested. A new Ohio law permits the diversion of up to ten per cent of the state's social welfare funds — totaling one billion dollars — for advance acquisition of land; the public will recoup on the acquisition expenditures, and in addition, the welfare agencies will receive interest on the funds released. These same techniques could be used to eliminate nonconforming uses. The state could appraise the monopoly value of the nonconforming use and use the result to calculate the amortization period; if the benefit conferred is substantial, the period will be shorter than that granted by present amortization provisions.

While some new technique of financing acquisition and of enabling the government to benefit from increments in land value clearly is needed in England, the feasibility of adopting the new American methods is questionable. The cost of purchasing vast amounts of land, including enough for recoupment purposes, is just too great for the capital presently available; moreover, there is some question as to the wisdom of suddenly releasing purchasing power in this magnitude upon the economy. Regrettably, it would be politically disastrous for any government to return to the compensation features of the 1947 act, for the solution was a viable one which might have succeeded had it been intelligently administered.

One solution lies in borrowing capital from fiduciary funds administered by private trustees. This would be similar to the financing of toll roads in the United States by corporations which borrow the money on bonds issued to trust funds and other private sources. The public would, as in the United States, pay a charge for the use of the road to pay off the bonds. The bondholders would not be likely to oppose the purchase of excess land on the ground that it would lower the value of the bonds, for the experience of American toll road authorities has shown such practices to be profitable. They have bought excess land and leased it out for roadside concessions, and, in many instances, they receive enough from these concessions to pay for the road's maintenance. Such a scheme for tapping private funds is worthy of consideration, for when English authorities are forced to expend funds for future acquisition, they are seriously hampered in carrying out present plans.

In planning, then, as in so many things, a central issue turns out to be money — money to finance public improvements and to compensate individual landowners for the burdens they must bear. But happily, planning can originate and augment values. And perhaps, in the last analysis, its ability to create values sufficient to pay its way will be the ultimate test of success.

Index

INDEX

This book is one of a series published under the auspices of the Joint Center for Urban Studies, a cooperative venture of the Massachusetts Institute of Technology and Harvard University. The Joint Center was founded in 1959 to do research on urban and regional problems. Participants have included scholars from the fields of architecture, business, engineering, city planning, economics, history, law, philosophy, political science, and sociology. The following books have been jointly published by Harvard University Press and the M.I.T. Press:

The Image of the City, by Kevin Lynch, 1960.

Housing and Economic Progress: A Study of the Housing Experiences of Boston's Middle-Income Families, by Lloyd Rodwin, 1961.

The Intellectual versus the City: From Thomas Jefferson to Frank Lloyd Wright, by Morton and Lucia White, 1962.

Streetcar Suburbs: The Process of Growth in Boston, 1870–1900, by Sam B. Warner, Jr., 1962.

Beyond the Melting Pot: The Negroes, Puerto Ricans, Jews, Italians, and Irish of New York City, by Nathan Glazer and Daniel Patrick Moynihan, 1963.

The Historian and the City, edited by Oscar Handlin and John Burchard, 1963.

City Politics, by Edward C. Banfield and James Q. Wilson, 1963.

Law and Land: Anglo-American Planning Practice, edited by Charles M. Haar, 1964.

The Joint Center also publishes monographs and reports.